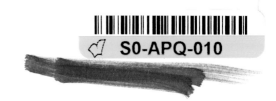

PUBLIC
SPEAKING:
PRINCIPLES INTO PRACTICE

JAMES R. ANDREWS
Indiana University

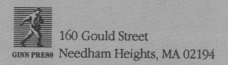

160 Gould Street
GINN PRESS Needham Heights, MA 02194

Printed in the United States of America

This book is printed on recycled, acid-free paper.

10 9 8 7 6 5 4 3 2 1

ISBN 0–536–58372–2
BA 0241

 GINN PRESS

160 Gould Street/Needham Heights, MA 02194
Simon & Schuster Higher Education Publishing Group

CONTENTS

PART I: AN OVERVIEW

1. THE PROCESS OF PUBLIC SPEAKING 3
Understanding Communication   4
Public Speaking as Communication   7
Preparing Yourself to Speak   10
    Know yourself   11
    Know your audience   13
    Know the situation   15
    Aim for a response   16
    Discover relevant material   17
    Present a reasonable argument   18
    Involve your audience   19
    Give your message structure   20
    Speak directly with an audience   21
    Develop confidence through practice   22
Preparing Yourself to Listen   23
    Listen actively   23
    Listen critically   24
    Develop a listening strategy   24
Principles into Practice: A Summary   24

PART II: APPLYING BASIC PRINCIPLES

2. KNOWING YOURSELF: THE SPEAKER AS RESOURCE 29
Finding a Suitable Topic   30
    Intellectual interests   30
    Educational interests   31
    Career goals   31

    Problems and social concerns   32
    Leisure activities and interests   32
  Narrowing the Topic   33
  Yourself and Others: The Speaker's Image   34
  Ethos in Communication   35
  Assessing the Speaker   37
  Ethos and Situation   38
  Creating Your Own Ethos   39
  Principles into Practice: A Summary   41
    HOW TO CHOOSE A TOPIC   41
    HOW TO CREATE YOUR OWN ETHOS   41

3. **KNOWING YOUR AUDIENCE AND THE SETTING: ANALYSIS AND ADAPTATION** **45**
  Understanding Audiences   46
  Who the Listeners Are   47
    The age of audience members   48
    The sex of a listener   49
    Listeners' responses to messages   51
    The educational level of a listener   54
    The occupation of the listener   56
    The income of the listener   57
    The listener's principal roles   58
    Memberships held by the listener   60
  Qualities of Audience Adaptation   63
  Understanding the Setting for the Speech   68
    Circumstances under which listening takes place   68
    Where the listeners stand   71
  Principles into Practice: A Summary   72
    HOW TO ANALYZE AND ADAPT TO AN AUDIENCE   72

4. **AIMING FOR A RESPONSE: SPEECH PURPOSES** **75**
  Making Appropriate Choices   76
  Situation and Strategy   77
    The Military Model   77
    The Educational Model   79
  Rhetorical Strategy   81
  Purposeful Speaking   83

Informative Purposes   84
    Persuasive Purposes   86
        Speeches to stimulate   87
        Speeches to convince   89
        Speeches to actuate   91
    Entertaining Purposes   93
Purposes and Multiresponses   95
Testing Specific Purposes   97
Agreement and Conflict in Speakers' and Listeners' Purposes   99
Principles into Practice: A Summary   100
        HOW TO DESIGN A GOOD SPEECH PURPOSE   100

5. **DISCOVERING RELEVANT MATERIAL: RESEARCH
    PURPOSES AND PROCEDURES** 103
Searching for Relevant Material   104
Gathering Information: An Overview   104
Interviewing: Gathering Information from Others   107
Using Published Sources   109
Preparing Yourself Through Research   111
Relevance and Integration: Putting What You Have
    Learned Together   112
Principles into Practice: A Summary   113
        HOW TO DO RESEARCH ON YOUR SPEECH TOPIC   113

6. **PREPARING A REASONABLE ARGUMENT:
    SUPPORTING IDEAS** 115
Making Ideas Understandable and Believable   116
Communicative Evidence   116
    Example   116
    Statistics   120
    Testimony   122
    Comparison   125
Communicative Methods   127
    Repetition and Restatement   127
    Visual Aids   128
Determining the Quality of Argument   133
The Rhetorically Sound Argument   133
Principles into Practice: A Summary   140
        HOW TO PREPARE GOOD ARGUMENTS FOR A SPEECH   140

7. INVOLVING YOUR AUDIENCE: MAKING IDEAS MEANINGFUL 143

Emotion and Involvement   144

Meeting Listeners' Needs   146

    Satisfying basic physical needs   146

    Assuring their personal safety   147

    Feeling love and a sense of belonging   147

    Feeling confident in themselves and appreciated by others   148

    Striving to realize their own potentials   148

Appealing to Listeners' Beliefs and Values   149

Engaging Listeners' Emotions   152

Attracting Attention   157

Establishing Common Ground   159

Introductions   161

Conclusions   164

Principles into Practice: A Summary   166

    HOW TO INVOLVE YOUR AUDIENCE   166

8. STRUCTURING YOUR SPEECH: ORGANIZATION 169

The Relationship of Ideas to Purpose   170

Determining When an Idea is a Good One   172

    Clarity of ideas   173

    Simplicity of ideas   175

    Situational considerations   177

    Ideas that make sense   178

How Ideas Relate to One Another   179

    Ideas and patterns   179

    Sequencing ideas   183

Transitions and Internal Summaries   187

The Whole Speech and Its Parts   188

    Structure and the clarity of ideas   188

    Form and the persuasiveness of ideas   188

Listener Responses to Patterns of Ideas   189

Principles into Practice: A Summary   190

    HOW TO ORGANIZE YOUR SPEECH   190

9.   **PUTTING IT ALL TOGETHER: OUTLINING** 193
Outlining and Preparation   194
The Process of Outlining   194
Outline I: The Zodiac   198
Analysis of "The Zodiac"   201
Outline II: From Sugar to Honey   203
Analysis of "From Sugar to Honey"   205
Principles into Practice: A Summary   208
      HOW TO CONSTRUCT A GOOD OUTLINE   208
      SAMPLE OUTLINES   208

10.   **SPEAKING CONFIDENTLY WITH YOUR AUDIENCE:**
      STYLE AND DELIVERY 227
Style: Promoting Understanding and Belief   228
Language Should be Clear to Listeners   229
Language Should be Interesting to Listeners   232
Language Should be Appropriate to the Situation   235
Style and the Listener's Response   238
Delivery and Predictability   240
Developing Confidence   241
Speaking from a Manuscript   243
Using the Voice Effectively   244
      Volume   245
      Rate   246
      Clarity   247
      Variety   248
The Basis of Good Delivery   248
"Sounding Good" and Being "Sound"   250
Principles into Practice: A Summary   251
      HOW TO DEVELOP GOOD STYLE AND DELIVERY   251

11.   **LISTENING CRITICALLY: THE INFORMED RESPONSE** 253
Effective Listening   254
Listening as an Active Process   254
A Strategy for Listening   255
      Think about your own identity   255
      Listen with a purpose   255

Understand the setting 257
Try to understand to whom the speaker is talking 257
Examine your assessment of and knowledge about
    the listener 257
Consider the speaker's purpose 258
Listen defensively 258
Principles into Practice: A Summary 260
    HOW TO LISTEN CRITICALLY 260

PART III: BECOMING AN EFFECTIVE SPEAKER AND LISTENER: A PLAN FOR ACTION

12. HOW TO BECOME AN EFFECTIVE SPEAKER 263

13. HOW TO BECOME AN EFFECTIVE LISTENER 269

EPILOGUE 275
    Speaker and Listener as Confederates 275
    The Speaker and Listener as Adversaries 276
    The Last Word 277

APPENDIX: SAMPLE SPEECHES FOR ANALYSIS 279
    Student speeches 281
    Contemporary Public Speeches 292
    Historic Speeches 332
    Suggested Readings 351

INDEX 353

PREFACE

An educated person is not only one who knows, but one who can *communicate* what he or she knows. There is no type of education—education in the liberal arts, professional education, technical education—that can be complete or successful if the person being educated cannot talk clearly and convincingly in public situations. Nor is education successful if the person cannot respond intelligently to messages directed at him or her.

A course in public speaking, then, is one designed to help the student become a more articulate speaker and a more discriminating listener. The aim of this book is to further that purpose by describing and explaining the basic theory of public speaking and directing students toward ways of becoming more effective speakers and listeners by putting that theory into practice.

The underlying assumption of this book is that speaking is a *process*. As such, it is not to be mastered simply by applying standard formulas to stock situations. The dynamic of communication demands that the student be aware of the shifting qualities and emphases of the situation. It also demands that the student be aware that his or her own role in communication changes with the situation, thus creating new pressures and requirements. Recent research and theoretical probes in our field have clearly pointed out the dangers of assuming that prescribed techniques, added together properly, will always lead to a given effect on an audience. Certainly, the best of traditional rhetorical theory and criticism has always urged against this kind of "cookbook" approach to effective communication.

Consistent with the idea of process, this book emphasizes the *choices* to be made by speakers and listeners in public speaking. The book attempts to deal with the *why* of successful communication, so that the student is equipped with generalizations that will be useful in making choices. Of course, *the student has to translate the "why" into what he or she can do in real situations.* So, the book does two important and complimentary things: First, it *provides the student with an essential body of theory;* from those theoretical generalizations the student can make predictions about what should occur in speaking and listening situations. Second, the book offers *practical and concrete directions and explanations that show how theory can be made useful in real situations.* The result is to arm the student with *an informed rationale for practical action.*

The book begins, in Part I, with an overview of the public-speaking process, explaining *the basic nature of communication* and laying out the principles of effective speaking and listening that will be developed. Part II takes up each of the essential principles, explaining and applying them, showing what the principles are and how they work. *Every chapter ends with a specific list of pointers for students to follow that summarizes the principles and suggests how to put them into practice.* Part III, pulling together all that has gone before, lays out a *plan for action* so that the student can follow *specific directions on how to become an effective speaker and listener.*

Following the text is an appendix that includes a sample of speeches by a variety of speakers—college freshmen, professionals in different fields, politicians and reformers past and present—that will afford students an opportunity to try out their own analytical and critical abilities by seeing how the principles of public speaking have been put into effect by others.

The ideas in this book are naturally a distillation of what I learned as a student, what I have learned over the years from the hundreds of public speaking students I have taught, and what I have learned from my colleagues. I appreciate the efforts of all those who have provided so much stimulation and information over the years. I wish to thank especially Professor Edwin Rowley of Indiana State University and Mr. Todd Thomas, director of the public speaking course at Indiana University, for their useful suggestions for revisions of this edition. Observations on the teaching-learning process by my wife, Professor Patricia Hayes Andrews—herself a gifted teacher and scholar of communication—have always enriched and extended my own. My daughter, Ms. Jennifer Bradley, helped me see this text from the student's point of view and made a special contribution to the section on sample outlines.

All those who have contributed to this work, directly or indirectly, have helped produce what strengths it has; for weaknesses the author assumes full responsibility.

James R. Andrews
Bloomington, Indiana

PART I

AN OVERVIEW

CHAPTER 1

THE PROCESS OF PUBLIC SPEAKING

After studying this chapter you should understand:

- What communication is and what factors are always present in a communication situation.

- How the speaker, speech, audience, response, and context affect public speaking.

- What the difference is between preparing yourself to speak and giving a speech.

- What the ten principles of public speaking are and how they influence the speaker's preparation.

- What constitutes good listening.

UNDERSTANDING COMMUNICATION

Communication is something with which we are all familiar. We communicate everyday; we have been communicating all our lives. We all know, for example, that there are different kinds of communication and that we feel differently about communicating when we are in different situations. Certainly there are differences in what we say and how we say things when we talk to a parent, a little brother, a friend, a professor, or a prospective employer. And there are differences between the way we talk and act in these kinds of situations and the way we talk and act when we are part of a group that is trying to think of ways to raise money to increase membership in an organization, to increase productivity in a plant, or to organize to lobby the legislature for more student loan money. Again, there are differences between the way we talk and act when confronted with giving an oral report in class, when making a formal proposal to a group of coworkers or decision makers at work, or when speaking to a group of high school students about what it is like to study at our college or university.

If we think about it, then, we already know from experience about some important factors and underlying principles of the communication process. If we think about the aforementioned examples and others from our own experience, we can discover those factors and principles. What are the factors that are always present in a communication act? That is, what are the ingredients necessary for communication to take place?

1. *For communication to take place someone has to initiate it.* The first ingredient is a person, the *source* of the communication, who sends out the communication.

2. *For communication to take place someone has to be present to get the communication sent by the source.* The second ingredient, then, is the *receiver*.

3. *For communication to take place something has to be communicated.* By a look or gesture, by spoken or written words, a person sends a *message*, the third ingredient.

4. *For communication to take place the sender and the receiver have to interact with each other.* So the message sent calls for the fourth necessary ingredient, a *response*.

5. *Communication always takes place in a specific setting.* Who the sender is and who the receivers are, what the sender is trying to accomplish by communicating, and where and when the communication takes place all make up the final ingredient of the communication act, the *context.*

These, then, are the ingredients of communication:

Source
Receiver
Message
Response
Context

From these ingredients we can develop a working definition of communication: *Communication is an interaction between a source who intends to get a response from a receiver within a specific context.*

The following is a simple model of the communication process:

--- C O N T E X T --------- C O N T E X T --------- C O N T E X T ---

Source --------- Sends *message* to --------- *receiver*

Receiver --------- Sends *response* to --------- *source*

--- C O N T E X T --------- C O N T E X T --------- C O N T E X T ---

The fact that communication is a *Process* adds another dimension to our model. Process suggests something that is continuous; it does not remain the same, but is always changing. "One thing leads to another" is the way we often describe process in everyday terms. Communication is like that; one action leads to another. Look at the model and consider this simple example.

You have something important to do on Wednesday that will make you be two hours late for work. Here's how the communication interaction might go:

YOU (to employer): Would it be all right if I got to work at three o'clock on Wednesday?

EMPLOYER: Sure, Wednesday's a slow day.

YOU: Thanks a lot.

or

YOU: Would it be all right if I got to work at three o'clock on Wednesday?

EMPLOYER: Why?

YOU: My aunt's in the hospital and my little cousin has a half-day of school on Wednesday. I said I'd try to take care of him until his regular baby sitter gets there.

EMPLOYER: Well, I suppose it's all right, but, you'll have to make up the time.

or

YOU: Could I come to work at three o'clock on Wednesday?

EMPLOYER: Well, I don't know.

YOU: It's really important to me, and I'd stay an extra two hours to catch up on the work.

We could go on for a long time with variations of this dialogue, but the point is that when you (the source) say something (the message), your employer (the receiver) reacts to what you say (the response). Whether or not Wednesday is a busy day, whether or not the employer is considerate, or whether or not unspoken past experiences, such as your attendance record, (all of which are matters of context) will influence both you and your employer in this situation. The process is clear when you consider that the message sent is then reacted to in such a way that you may modify your message, by adding more information, for example, in order to solicit another response. So, our model could be modified to suggest process:

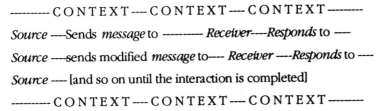

--------- C O N T E X T --- C O N T E X T --- C O N T E X T --------

Source ----Sends *message* to --------- *Receiver*----*Responds* to ---

Source ----sends modified *message* to---- *Receiver* ----*Responds* to ----

Source ---- [and so on until the interaction is completed]

--------- C O N T E X T --- C O N T E X T --- C O N T E X T --------

Our discussion of what communication is and how the process occurs has, to this point, focused on basic, underlying concepts that may appear rather simple. We can derive these concepts from our own experience if we take a few minutes to think about it. Yet, we also know that communciation in practice isn't always so simple. Let's turn now to public speaking as a communication process, translating the basic concepts that we have been considering into principles for public speaking. As we do so, we will explore the complexities that are involved in these "simple" ideas.

PUBLIC SPEAKING AS COMMUNICATION

First, consider the basic model of communication discussed earlier:

---- C O N T E X T --------- C O N T E X T --------- C O N T E X T ---

Source ---------- Sends *message* to --------- *Receiver*

Receiver ---------- Sends *response* to --------- *Source*

---- C O N T E X T --------- C O N T E X T --------- C O N T E X T ---

Making a few adjustments in terminology, we can adapt the model to public speaking:

---- C O N T E X T --------- C O N T E X T --------- C O N T E X T ---

Speaker ---------- Gives *speech* to --------- *Audience*

Audience --------- *Responds* to --------- *Speaker*

---- C O N T E X T --------- C O N T E X T --------- C O N T E X T ---

The basic ingredients in a public-speaking situation are:

Speaker

Speech

Audience

Response

Context

Now, let's take the complexities that we all know exist and see if we can produce a slightly more inclusive model.

Because communication is only a part of our lives, any communication event will not exist all by itself; it will fit into our total experience. When you give or listen to a speech, that speech is only a part of everything else that's happening in your life and the lives of those who are sharing that communication event with you.

Think of it this way. If you've ever looked at the ocean, you know that the water is never still. You cannot identify a single section of water that is unrelated to the body of water in which it exists. You can, however, scoop out water from the ocean with a bucket, thus separating it from the rest, and carry it on the beach. Like the water confined in the bucket, a speech can be separated and distinguished from the "ocean" of events, feelings, knowledge, attitudes, beliefs, and so forth that exist in us and in others.

How you use the water, like the purpose of any single speech, is limited by the nature of its environment For example, you can get a friend's attention by pouring the water on her, but you can't give her a drink of the salt water to relieve her thirst. A speech is a part of the total environment that surrounds us. We can't attend to any message as if we know nothing except what the speaker is telling us. When we listen to a speech we bring our world along with us. We filter what we hear through the screen of our own experience, our own prejudices, and our own knowledge. We are very much a part of a speaking situation and what we do and how we react will influence the communication process.

"Influence" does not describe very well the impact you can have on communication. To carry on our comparison with the ocean, how extensively can anyone "influence" the ocean? There is an old legend about the eleventh century Danish king of Britain, Canute, who was supposed to have attempted to demonstrate his power by setting himself on his throne at the water's edge. He then commanded the tide to retreat. He was no more successful than is a small child who hopes to stem the steadily advancing water with a wall of sand. Nevertheless, we can do something to control the ocean: land can be reclaimed from the sea. Jetties can stop erosion. We can travel over the top of the ocean. We can lay a transcontinental cable on its floor. No one can completely control the ocean; we don't fully understand its complicated nature and operations. Neither can one say that the ocean is totally unfathomable or unmanageable. Similarly, communication is a complex process that cannot be completely controlled; there are no sure-fire, ready-made, formulas for success in public speaking. But it is possible to be effective if you recognize your own and the situation's limitations—and if you know how to use public-speaking principles in the best way possible.

As you learn how to be an effective speaker, you will begin to understand that you play different roles at different times in the public-speaking process. *What is "effective" for you depends on who you are in any particular situation.* Consider, for example, a speaker who hopes to persuade an audience to support a cause he supports. Suppose that the speaker is effective and that each listener gives five dollars. If you were the speaker in that case, you would probably congratulate yourself for having communicated effectively. If you were the listener, you might or might not have found the exchange to have been effective. If the speaker showed you how you could use your money in a way that would help people you want to help and that would make you feel good, then you were part of an effective interaction. On the other hand, if the speaker swindled you out of your five dollars and you later felt that you could kick yourself for being so stupid, then you were part of a situation that was ineffective for you.

Because communication is an effort on the part of someone who initiates a message to get someone else to respond in a way that the communicator predetermines, some might say that if the speaker gets what he or she is after, the speech is effective. In a sense, that's true—at least for the speaker. Much of what follows in this book is designed to help you, the speaker, be effective by getting the response you want. But that's only part of the whole picture. Those who alledge that whether or not the speaker attains his or her goals is the only measure of effectiveness are certainly not the disappointed listeners. *How effectiveness is judged, then, depends on how both parties come out.* That's something you need to keep in mind as we talk about response; and it's something we'll get back to later when we consider what is ethical in public speaking.

Let us concentrate, first, on you as a speaker. When you send a message, you have a reason for acting; you talk to people because you want them to do something. You want them to learn, to buy, to believe, or to feel. You want a reaction from them or you wouldn't have given a speech. Now, it is true that there are speakers who don't seem to want to communicate, who don't care how angry, bored, or uncomfortable they make their audiences. These are people who don't know or don't care that the end of communication is response; they like to hear themselves talk, or they like to get their aggressions or hostilities out regardless of how those to whom they are speaking react. It might be better for such people to take up finger painting, handball, or another means of self-expression, because they seem bent on expressing themselves rather than on communicating. Consider the following example.

If you were to go out to your car one morning and find a flat tire, you might aim a few vituperative remarks at the car. Such self-expression won't bother the car, and it might make you feel less tense and upset. But, no matter how angry you were, you wouldn't go to a neighbor's door, pound on it loudly, and demand that he or she hurry down to help you fix that flat tire. If you have any brains at all, you would realize that asking a friend for help is a time to *communicate* and not a time to vent your frustration. Because you would have a specific response in mind, you would try to ask for help in a communicative way, that is, in a way designed to get the desired response. You communicate effectively when you get the response you hope for.

Giving a speech, of course, is a much more complex matter in many ways than is communicating with a friend you'd like to help you. Nevertheless, many of the same principles apply. Let us return to the above example. If your friend is a late sleeper, you might wait before going to ask for help with the tire. If your friend is inclined to think that more physical exercise would be good for you, you might wish to remind him or her of your bad back. If your neighbor is a rather frail eighty-year-old lady, you might consult her if you needed comforting sympathy, but you would look elsewhere for practical help. When you talk to more than one person, you must be careful to know both something about those persons and something about their relationship to your message. You must know something of their predispositions, tastes, prejudices, and knowledge. And you must know what the audience you speak to can or may be prepared to do about your request. If you hope to get a response from your listeners, you need to consider what characteristics they share as a group and what qualities individual members bring with them to the public-speaking situation.

With this in mind, we shall look at a communication model again, this time as a *model of public* speaking that shows some of the complexities we have been discussing. (See Figure 1-2.)

This book is devoted to helping you fully understand how you can operate in the kind of situation expressed by the model. The various parts will each be taken up, so that you can develop into an effective speaker and listener. But, for now, let's look at an overview of the principles that will direct your steps as you learn to become an effective speaker and listener.

PREPARING YOURSELF TO SPEAK

At the outset, you should think about the communication act in which you are going to participate in the way that will be most helpful to you. Naturally, you will think about preparing a speech for presentation, but, in reality, you will be better off in the long run if you think about preparing yourself to speak rather than preparing a speech. This is not just a trick of words; rather, it is a way of thinking about what you need to do to get ready to give a speech and a way of developing a strategy you can use each time you give a speech. *Preparing yourself to speak, then, involves considering the principles operating any time you get yourself ready to give a speech.* Let us now look at each of those principles briefly. Understanding and applying them will be the major goal of your public-speaking course, and they will receive most of our attention as we go on through this book.

1. *Know yourself.* The speaker's own beliefs, ability, knowledge, and potential is the foundation upon which the speech is built.

It is important to say right away that very few people have speeches in their heads that are just waiting to be delivered. Getting ready to give a speech is hard work. Starting with what you know doesn't mean ending there. But, it is important for the speaker to think about himself or herself first

Speakers first need to canvas their own interests and concerns, asking questions that can lead to a topic to talk about and to potential sources for enlarging knowledge about the topic: What are the things that matter to me? What are the things that I know most about? What do I like to do in my spare time? What are my career goals? What gives me most pleasure? What do I worry most about? What things are going on in the world around me—the smaller

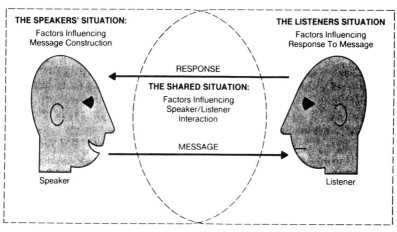

FIGURE 1-1

world of my clubs or organizations, my school, my family, and my hometown, and the larger world of my state or region, my country or other countries—that affects me in some way? What are things that I do well or that I would like to do better? What are things that I know most about? Answers to questions like these can lead speakers to possible topics and help them to pull together and focus on what they already know.

Knowing yourself also implies knowing what you *don't* know. By beginning with gaining an understanding of where you are right now, you also give yourself directions about where you want to be. Identifying your own attitudes and beliefs is the first step to examining those attitudes and beliefs: Why do I believe what I do? Are there good reasons for the attitudes I hold? Do I know enough to make sensible decisions about how I should react to all those things in the worlds that affect me? What do I need to find out to do what I'd really like to do with my life—right now, tomorrow, and in the future? Answering such questions will help speakers clarify their own thinking and alert them to gaps in their knowledge or understanding.

Speakers need to think of another dimension of themselves aside from what they know or care about. We've all heard the old expression, "If you could only see yourself as others see you." A speaker's task is to do just that; to try to see himself or herself as others do. Scholars who study public speaking use the word ethos to describe the speaker as the audience sees him or her. Very few people know everything about someone else, and most people in our lives know us primarily from a specific perspective; as a student, a friend, a son, a girlfriend, or an employee. We realize that it takes a long time to "get to know" somebody. A speaker has very little time for those in the audience to get to know him or her. Yet in spite of the little time available, listeners will naturally form impressions of the speaker, and as they listen, they will begin to put these impressions together to make a judgment about the speaker's ability, authority, understanding of the audience, and trustworthiness. The pattern of these impressions, the speaker's ethos, may or may not be an accurate reflection of what the speaker is really like, but it will reflect what the audience thinks the speaker is like.

What the speaker does to prepare for the speech and what the speaker does during the speech can affect his or her ethos. Being well prepared, for example, can help to assure the audience that the speaker takes them and the topic seriously and is in command of the facts. Speaking directly and easily with an audience suggests to the listener that the speaker can be trusted. In short, the speaker's ethos, while it may be affected by a variety of factors such as the topic itself, the setting for the speech, and the particular experiences of the audience, is still subject to some extent to the control of the speaker who anticipates how he or she will be perceived.

Certainly the speakers' own values and behaviors, which make their ethical systems, are under their control. Knowing oneself, then, also means knowing what one believes in and values. The best speakers will make their own ethical systems clear and explicit to themselves and make any choice about what and how to communicate in the light of such systems.

2. *Know your audience*: The audience's needs, interests, beliefs, and knowledge help to determine what will be talked about and how the speech will be put together. Speeches are given for audiences. Speeches have no reason to exist apart from their efforts to get people to respond in some way to ideas. Speakers' knowledge about themselves, then, needs to be supplemented by and compared with knowledge of those who will listen to what they have to say.

A speaker's interest in engineering may lead her to ponder the mystery of Stonehenge or the marvels of the pyramids; here are possible topics that the speaker may want to explore. Before deciding how to go about such a task, however, she should know to whom she will be talking. For example, a typical audience of college freshmen may have little knowledge of either engineering or history; an audience of engineers may not have to be told much about the principles of leverage, but they may never have heard of Stonehenge; and an audience of history majors may know that the pyramids were great feats of engineering, but they may be totally unaware of the technical problems that were overcome in their construction. In other words, the same topic has to be dealt with differently—different details given, different explanations developed, different examples used, and so forth—depending upon what an audience knows about the topic a speaker has selected.

Similarly, modifications will have to be made when an audience's beliefs or attitudes are considered. Some groups will be offended by what other groups take for granted. The speaker must consider his or her audience just as carefully as the speaker considers himself or herself in getting ready to speak. Of course, it is much harder to answer the same questions about an audience that one can answer about oneself Nevertheless, the effort must be made to know as much as possible about the listeners. They are the ones for whom the speech is given; they are the ones that the speaker hopes to influence in a specific way; they are the ones who will ultimately judge the success or failure of the speech. So, they are the ones that the speaker must know something about.

Knowing an audience, of course, implies doing something with that knowledge. If a speaker anticipates that a technical word he will use will be unfamiliar to an audience, he will *adapt* to that audience by defining the word. If a speaker believes that an audience will reject a value that she holds, she will seek for other common values upon which to base her argument. If a speaker plans to present a proposal first to the Engineering Department and then to Sales, he or she will *adapt* the content in these two presentations (even though they deal with the same proposal) to mesh with the technical interests and concerns of one group and the marketing priorities of the other.

Knowing an audience, then, means that a speaker must consider carefully the characteristics of the audience that are relevant to the speech to be given and

Effective speakers must adapt to specific audiences.

take this understanding into account as he or she prepares himself or herself to speak.

3. *Know the situation:* The speaker must understand the setting in which the speech will take place and the factors outside of the speech itself that could influence the outcome.

You have probably been in a situation in which you suddenly realize that you have not heard what someone else has been saying. We have all been the target of the complaint, "You haven't heard a word I've said!" at some time or another. Or we may have found ourselves worrying about a personal problem, suddenly "coming to" in a classroom where we haven't taken a note for twenty minutes. It is not uncommon for factors unrelated to the speech event itself to intrude on a listener, and it is even more likely that relevant thoughts, ideas, events, or information will break into a speech situation to distract your audience or to work for or against you as you try to influence your listeners.

The actual setting can exert an influence on how an audience responds. You can be speaking in a comfortable or uncomfortable setting. You can be close to your audience or separated from them by an orchestra pit. You can speak directly to them or indirectly by means of a microphone. You may be talking to them first thing in the morning or right after lunch. They may be there because they are interested in what you have to say or because they have to be there. You can surely imagine how all these different possibilities could influence the way listeners would respond to you. It should be obvious that you would be a lot better off by knowing in advance something about the setting in which you will speak. To take an extreme example, if you brought with you a book containing two contrasting pictures that it was important for your audience to see, and if you arrived at the place to speak only to discover that it was an auditorium with a formal stage, your plans would have to change drastically at the last moment; this is always an unpleasant and unnerving task for a speaker.

Besides the setting of the speech, there is the whole context to consider. Imagine, for example, that you are giving a speech on the role of government in student aid. A news story that details pending cuts in aid programs has just been published in the student newspaper. It is likely that your audience will be aware of this turn of events and will seek to find some reaction to it in your speech. What is happening in your audience's world that is relevant to your topic is something about which you need to be aware so that you can prepare yourself to speak as the context requires.

There are occasions where what might be happening in the listeners' world has nothing to do with your speech or is beyond your control. But, what *you* do is not beyond your control. You, the speaker, always need to be prepared to compete with the forces exerted on the listeners from outside your speech. The situation may be working against you in ways that you can't always predict, but you need to ensure that the speech is as interesting and relevant and compelling for the audience as you can make it.

4. *Aim for a response*: The speaker must always keep in mind that the purpose of the speech is to get listeners to react in a specific way.

Speakers naturally tend to think of what *they* will say and what *they* will do rather than what their *listeners* will do after they hear the speech. The purpose of speaking is not to *give* something—giving is, rather, the *means* by which the speaker *gets* something. In other words, the speaker does not come before a group to "give a speech," the speaker is there to get a *response.*

It is simply human nature to see a situation in terms of its impact on ourselves. So, when facing a speaking situation, we tend to think of what we will say, what we will look like, how nervous we will be, and so forth. But the process of preparing yourself to speak should involve learning to see situations from the point of view of others who are involved in them. Perhaps the most important perspective that a beginning speaker should develop is an *audience-centered perspective.* That is, an understanding that what you do as a speaker is done because you hope to influence an audience; this is fundamental to everything else you will learn in public speaking. If you want to speak to "get something off your chest," to show them what you know, or to talk about something that really interests you, you certainly can do so—sometimes doing so is a means to getting results—but if this kind of self-satisfaction is all you care about, then the chances are that you will miss the opportunity to communicate with an audience, to get a response from them that is consistent with the response you hoped for.

This principle can influence everything you do as you prepare yourself. Knowing what you want the audience to do will help you determine what ideas will be helpful in doing it; if, for example, you want them to understand how Stonehenge works as an astrological calendar, you won't spend a lot of time describing how these rather primitive people got huge stones transported, standing, and arranged in a circle. If your purpose were to get them to understand how the engineering feat was accomplished, you wouldn't want to spend too much time explaining how the great stone circle might function to predict the changes in the seasons. Knowing what you want of an audience will help you select the right material for the speech. As you might suppose, knowing that you want an audience to take a specific action rather than simply to understand a specific concept would cause you to make different selections. The history of the American Red Cross might prove interesting to us, for example, but we would probably want good reasons provided for our giving to the Red Cross if we were asked for donations. A speaker who wants listeners to understand the history of rock music might choose to play selections from different periods in the development of that kind of music; if the same speaker wanted us to agree that Culture Club is the ultimate or perfect rock group, surely he or she would pick different musical selections for listeners to hear.

In short, since the goal of public speaking is to get a response from an audience, determining precisely and specifically what that response is in advance will profoundly affect everything that you do as you prepare yourself to speak.

5. *Discover relevant material:* The speaker must explore the potential sources of information in order to discover information, opinion, and the like, that contributes to the purpose of the speech.

There is likely to be a vast quantity of information available on any topic; indeed, there will probably be much more than a speaker can use. Some information will already be in the speaker's head, but most will have to come from other sources. The speaker first must know the purpose of the speech if he or she is to know what to look for. Once the topic and the purpose have been established, the speaker may tap several sources to gather pertinent information.

People who have positions in which their work may relate to aspects of the topic may prove helpful, so the speaker will want to conduct *interviews.* If, for example, you are giving a speech on grading policy, you may want to interview an appropriate dean or the registrar. If your speech concerns the crime rate, local law enforcement officers or an expert on crime in your school's Sociology Department might be interviewed.

Any topic of importance will be better developed if the speaker carries out research. *Library resources* will be most helpful to this task. Catalogs and indexes will lead the speaker to past and current work on the topic. Computer searches can be done to uncover recent materials written on the subject. Certainly it would be necessary to study periodicals, both general and specialized, to find useful information.

When material is gathered, it must be assembled by the speaker in a way that will prove useful to him or her. The fundamental rule is to put together material with a workable scheme, using the speech purpose as a guide and keeping the constraints of audience and setting clearly in mind.

6. *Present a reasonable argument:* The ideas chosen by the speaker are those that further his or her purpose; they must be supported with data that make those ideas understandable and believable.

Ideas grow from the purpose of a speech. When a speaker knows what he or she wants to accomplish in a speech, then he or she must set about framing ideas and finding material that supports those ideas. To take an example, suppose you believe that a pass/fail grading system rather than a normal grading system is not a good idea. You want your audience to agree with you that it would not be in a student's best interests to elect to take courses pass/fail as allowed by your school. Your problem is, first, to discover ideas that will be convincing, that is, those that will encourage the audience to agree with you. After thinking, reading, and talking with others, you come up with an idea: *Employers are suspicious of transcripts with pass/fail recorded in place of normal letter grades.* Undoubtedly, your initial explorations into the topic turned up specific data or relevant information that would help you make this idea more believable for your audience. For example, you might have read a report that indicated that a large percentage of employers surveyed said that they look carefully at transcripts to see how well students have done in courses that would be helpful to them on the job. Or you might have had an interview with a personnel director who said that in her opinion a recording of pass/fail instead of grades suggested that the student was trying to get around requirements in an easy way. Or you might have talked with the director of the placement service at your school who said that employers tend to ask him a lot of questions about the pass/fail policy and why students would elect to take courses that way.

As in the example, you begin to find material that is relevant. This material will help you formulate ideas to further your purpose and provide data that will make those ideas more likely to convince an audience.

7. *Involve your audience.* The speaker prepares and uses available material in ways that the audience finds appealing.

Audiences that are asked to understand something, believe something, or do something will quite naturally ask why they should respond in the way the speaker wants them to. A very normal reaction for us to make when presented with a message of any kind is to wonder what we will get out of listening to the message. In order for a speaker to get the response he or she wants the audience must feel involved in the topic, and the audience must want the speaker to succeed because they see the speech as contributing to their own welfare.

The speaker, then, will let the listeners know how her or his topic can *meet their needs.* The topic might involve meeting physical needs, needs to be safe and secure, needs to be loved and wanted, needs to feel confident and appreciated, or needs to be the best that we can be. People have different needs in different circumstances and in relation to different topics. It is part of the speaker's task to assess these needs to determine in what ways and to what extent the response he or she wants will satisfy them.

Audiences and speakers share beliefs and values, but they may have beliefs and values that conflict. The speaker must make an attempt to distinguish between the two in order to stress what is shared and challenge what is not in a way best calculated to get a fair hearing.

All of us have emotions. We sometimes make ourselves believe that this is bad; everything ought to be logical, we think, and we make "emotional" the opposite of "logical." If we stop to think about it, however, emotions are good and useful things; they are what make us, along with our ability to reason, human. The character from the Star Trek television series and movies, Mr. Spock, is known for his purely logical character; without emotion, he makes judgments that are exclusively rational. Many times, however, love, sacrifice, and hope make such judgments irrelevant to the situations in which people find themselves. Decisions we make can be good or bad, but they are rarely made without some reference to how we feel about them. We would not think it wrong, for example, to risk our own lives-in the hope of saving the lives of people we love; we would not think it wrong to feel anger if we saw a helpless old woman knocked to the ground by someone who then steals her purse. What kinds of acts would we engage in if we did not feel emotion? Would we give our money to a cause that we didn't care about? Would we spend hours working for a political candidate if we didn't care whether or not the candidate got elected? In short, action is usually based on how we feel. *To be emotional is to be involved.* Speakers who neglect the feelings of an audience are not likely to achieve their purposes.

Audiences are not likely to respond to a speaker if they are not at all interested in what he or she has to say. They might realize that the speaker is addressing an issue important to their well-being, and they might feel strongly that action should be taken. But they might also, because of many factors outside of the speech influencing them, be bored, restless, or preoccupied. The speaker, then, needs to concern himself or herself with getting and keeping the listeners' attention. By appealing to what is vital, by using novel material, by employing constraints, by showing how what he or she is saying may resolve conflicts for listeners, by choosing materials carefully to enhance the listeners' enjoyment of the speech, a speaker maximizes the potential for audience involvement.

8. *Give your message structure.* The speaker will arrange material in such a way that it is easy for the audience to follow, to remember what has been said, and to understand the reasons for responding as the speaker wishes.

The ideas in a speech and the material used to make those ideas understandable and believable are all geared toward achieving the speaker's purpose. This means that once the desired response is known, the speaker will carefully work out *good ideas.* These are ideas that are clear and simple without being simplistic; that take into account the situation in which the speech is being given; and that makes good sense.

Ideas are related to the purpose of a speech and to one another. If an audience is going to follow them, they have to be arranged in a way that will help the speaker achieve the purpose and will help the audience know what's going on and what the speaker is driving at. There are many ways that a speaker can go about imposing order on his or her speech, depending on the topic and the audience. The speech can be arranged so that ideas follow one another in a chronological way. It can be arranged so that ideas make sense because they relate to one another spatially. Ideas can be arranged so that they lead the audience to a climax, or they can be arranged so that they show listeners how to solve a vexing problem. A speaker may find it best to discuss a topic so that each idea contrasts with another idea or so that a problem is traced from its cause to its effects. In short, ideas have to be seen in relation to one another and, taken together, they must present the kind of coherent picture necessary to accomplish the purpose.

A speaker can move the audience smoothly from one idea to the next by planning carefully just how this movement can best take place. This will lead him or her to build sensible transitions into the speech and to select places where it makes sense to summarize for the audience what has been said before moving on.

The speech, then, must form a clear pattern for the audience. Such a pattern helps audience members take "mental notes" so that they will remember what has been said. The pattern also makes clear to them how everything in the speech fits together and points to the desired response.

9. *Speak directly with an audience*. By choosing language suitable to the audience and the occasion and by developing an unaffected and direct delivery, the speaker seeks to promote understanding and belief on the part of the audience.

Having analyzed one's audience and the setting in which the speech takes place, having developed a clear purpose, and having gathered suitable material, the speaker concerns himself or herself with what the audience will see and hear as the speech is given. The language a speaker uses and the way he or she uses it can have a great impact on an audience and the way that audience responds to a speaker. With the audience and purpose in mind, the speaker chooses language that is clear and interesting, and that is appropriate to the context in which the speech takes place.

There is a great difference between giving a "speech"—a document that is set and inflexible—and being prepared to speak. Choosing the right language does not mean writing the speech out or committing it to memory. It means thinking, planning, and trying out ways to best address an audience. Most situations in which we find ourselves will be those in which we need to speak *extemporaneously*. Speaking extemporaneously means that the speaker is well prepared and has thought carefully about how best to say what he or she has to say. It suggests a less formal, more direct, audience-centered delivery.

The best delivery is that which does not call attention to itself; the audience is less aware of *how* something is said than *what* is said. Good delivery is conversational and relaxed. The audience can hear and understand what is said and does not find itself distracted by mannerisms, inappropriate movements, or a too-dramatic presentation. Despite all the preparation and hard work that the speaker puts into preparing himself or herself, it is the audience and what it finally sees or hears that will shape the final response. The speaker needs to make sure that all the effort to be prepared is not lost by poor delivery and inappropriate language choice.

10. *Develop confidence through practice.* The speaker can assure a better response and help to overcome stagefright by repeated oral practice.

It is very important for the beginning speaker to realize that being nervous before and during a speech is normal. Everyone, no matter how experienced or accomplished he or she is, will feel some anxiety about giving a speech and will be uncomfortable just before and even during the actual presentation of the speech. If the speaker has not prepared, then the anxiety is well founded; there is little anyone who is not ready to give a speech can do to bolster confidence. Such a speaker deserves to squirm. But if you have taken the pains to prepare yourself, you can help reduce the discomfort and serve your purpose better if you recognize that effectively expressing ideas orally doesn't happen automatically. Knowing what you want to say is not always the same as saying it

Oral practice is an essential part of preparing yourself to speak. Surely we know that practice is an integral part of doing anything well. Imagine a basketball coach who, the day before an important game, throws his team a ball and asks them to run through some plays a couple of times as preparation for the contest. Or think of someone entering a chess tournament who has learned how the pieces move and played a game or two for practice. What would happen to a band if each member were given a set of directions on how to move during the half-time show but never given the opportunity to try it on the field? How successful would someone be who learned all the grammatical rules of a language and amassed a large vocabulary but never practiced speaking it when he or she tried to talk with a native speaker? Good speaking requires that the well-prepared speaker practice out loud and frequently enough so that he or she recognizes the problems to be faced in putting ideas into oral language, and so that he or she develops a feeling of confidence in his or her ability to deal with these problems.

These, then, are the basic principles that should guide you as you prepare yourself to speak:

1. Know yourself
2. Know your audience
3. Know the situation _ factor that are involved in situation
4. Aim for a response
5. Discover relevant material
6. Present a reasonable argument
7. Involve your audience
8. Give your message structure
9. Speak directly with an audience
10. Develop confidence through practice

Through the advice, help, and criticism provided by your instructor, through reading the chapters that follow, and through preparing and delivering speeches, you will learn more about these principles and how they work in practice. When you have mastered them—that is, when you understand them and know how to apply them—you will be on your way to becoming a confident and effective public speaker.

PREPARING YOURSELF TO LISTEN

The focus of this book is on helping you to become an effective public speaker. Nevertheless, you must not forget that you will spend much of your time in the public-speaking process as the listener. You will make up a part of an audience that the speaker wishes to influence. Knowing the principles of public speaking will make you a more discerning and intelligent listener. There are, however, a few principles of effective listening that you should understand and apply when you are the receiver of messages. These principles will be developed more fully in a later chapter, but let us consider them briefly here.

1. **Listen actively.** It doesn't always occur to us that listening takes effort. We sometimes think that all we have to do to listen is to sit there and let the speaker do the work. But listening is a creative activity that takes concentration. We can help both the speaker and ourselves if we focus our minds on what is

being said, making the effort to understand and to see the relevance of the speech to our own lives and our own goals.

2. **Listen critically.** Concentrating on what a speaker says, of course, doesn't mean accepting everything the speaker says. As you learn the principles of public speaking, you will also be learning what to look for in a speech and how to evaluate what you hear. How well the speaker has prepared, what he or she wants you to do or to believe, and the extent and nature of the material that he or she has presented should affect the way that you respond. It is right to give a speaker your attention and concentration, but it is also proper for you to view what he or she has to say with some skepticism. After all, if you are going to do something after listening to the speech, you have the obligation to yourself to be sure that what you do is reasonable, is consistent with your values, and will lead to a result that you think is desirable.

3. **Develop a listening strategy.** The listener who is active and critical will get the most out of a public-speaking experience if he or she goes about participating in it in a systematic way. This means considering specific questions to raise about yourself, the speaker, and the situation; the answers will help you make sensible choices for your own responsive behavior.

You will want to raise such questions as:

What is my role in the speaking situation?

What is my purpose in listening to the speech?

How am I influenced by the setting in which the speech takes place?

How do I respond to the speaker personally, and how does that affect my judgment? What is the speaker trying to accomplish?

How can I protect my own interests in a public-speaking situation?

As you learn to become an effective public speaker, you will also have ample opportunity to hone your skills as a listener—as you practice listening actively and critically and as you develop and apply a strategy for good listening.

PRINCIPLES INTO PRACTICE: A SUMMARY

This chapter has attempted to present an overview of the process of public speaking as a communication event. *Communication* is defined as an interaction between a source and a receiver in which the intention is to get a response from a receiver within a specific context. With this definition in mind, we determined the basic ingredients in a public-speaking situation to be

Speaker
Speech
Audience
Response
Context

These ingredients work together as the speaker seeks to get a desired response from a listener. The speech is effective for the speaker if he or she gets that response and for the listeners if the response proves to be satisfying or useful to them.

A speaker who wishes to prepare himself or herself to speak well will examine his or her own knowledge, ability, beliefs and potential (know yourself); discover the audience's needs, interests, beliefs, and knowledge (know your audience); understand how the setting and outside factors may influence the speech (know the situation); devise a clear purpose that reflects the desired response (aim for a response); explore potential sources of information (discover relevant material); devise clear, well-supported ideas that further the purpose of the speech (present a reasonable argument); discover and use material that is appealing to an audience (involve your audience); arrange material in the speech in a way best calculated to help an audience follow and understand ideas (give your message structure); use language and deliver the speech in a manner suitable to the audience and the occasion (speak directly with an audience); and practice a well-prepared presentation frequently enough to give himself or herself oral command of the speech (develop confidence through practice).

As well as learning to become effective speakers, students of public speaking will also learn to improve their abilities as listeners if they develop the ability to listen actively and critically. Insuring effective listening entails developing a listening strategy and applying it in public-speaking situations.

PART II

APPLYING BASIC PRINCIPLES

CHAPTER 2

KNOWING YOURSELF: THE SPEAKER AS RESOURCE

After studying this chapter you should understand:

- How to go about canvassing your own resources to find a topic.

- How to narrow a topic so that it is manageable.

- What is meant by a speaker's ethos.

- How ethos is formed and how it affects a speaker.

- How to influence your own ethos.

FINDING A SUITABLE TOPIC

What to talk about is usually one of the first concerns of a speaker. This is particularly true of a student of public speaking whose assignment is to give a speech in class where circumstances, or setting or audience demands do not predetermine a topic. (It would be different, for example, if an employer were to ask you to make a presentation on your ideas on how to market the company's latest product, or if a local service club were to ask you to come to speak about how cuts in student aid would affect you and other students, or if your old high school asked you to come back to talk with interested seniors on what it is like to be a history, mathematics, or communication major at your college or university.) Your problem now, however, is to define for yourself what the best topic would be, given the limitations that might be imposed by such factors as the assigned time, perhaps, or some particular requirement imposed on a specific assignment.

There are a lot of limitations that you will impose on the topic as you proceed to prepare yourself to speak; for example, the nature of the audience of the reasonable chance of accomplishing your purpose will affect how you ultimately expand and transform your topic into a speech. These matters relate to other principles and will be considered as we proceed. For now, start thinking about your topic by thinking about yourself.

The fundamental question to ask is: What things do I already know and care about? Remember, this does not mean, What can I already give a speech about? Don't try to find a speech ready-made in your head; don't try to limit yourself to topics on which you are already an expert. That kind of thinking is probably what leads most students to complain that they "don't have anything to talk about." Keep in mind that one of the real benefits of a course in public speaking is that it will give you the opportunity to learn more about things you *want* to learn more about. Take time to give the matter careful thought. These categories might help you generate suitable topics that will interest you:

Intellectual interests. What are your reading habits? Do you like to read biographies? Perhaps the life of an interesting person will lead to a topic, or perhaps an historical period that compares or contrasts with our own might lead you to think of something to speak on. Do you like to read contemporary novels? What is it about them that interests you? You might want to talk about the work of a particular writer or about what makes a novel appealing. Do you regularly watch *Nova* or *The World of Jacques Cousteau?* Programs dealing with the origins of the planet or discoveries about how the brain works or the behavior of the great white shark might have held your interest and attention and suggested to you a topic about which you would like to know more and about which you would like to talk with others.

Educational interests. When you choose to advance your education, you choose to learn more—more about the world you live in and the world you have inherited. Some of what you study may involve learning how to think about and solve problems, how to cultivate tastes that will enrich your life, and how to appreciate and evaluate the environment in which you live, or how to evaluate critically and intelligently the mass of information with which you are bombarded each day. Much of what you study will provide you with specific or specialized knowledge that will enable you to function more effectively as you pursue a career. Consider courses that you have taken or the major you are pursuing or planning to pursue. If you are majoring in physics, English, or psychology, perhaps you can discover a potential topic in one of these areas. Of course, you can't take a professor's lecture on any particular topic and simply condense it for a speech in class. For one thing, that lecture would have been directed at a different audience and intended to be a part of a series of lectures that made up a whole course. But, you can take an *idea* that may have been discussed as a starting point for uncovering a suitable topic. For example, courses in physics, English, or psychology could lead you to such topics as The Notion of Gravity is Fundamental to Space Exploration; Certain Particular Characteristics Distinguish Poetry from All Other Literary Forms; All of Us Experience Cognitive Dissonance in Our Daily Lives.

Career goals. Many students will have an ultimate career goal in mind. Asking yourself why you might want to become a teacher, a lawyer, an engineer, a research chemist, an accountant, a marketing analyst, or a television producer should lead you to think about interesting aspects of these particular fields. Topics derived from your career goals could address such questions as: What are the characteristics of a good teacher? What ethical problems do lawyers typically face? How safe are the bridges of America? What are generic drugs and how do they affect the consumer? Could a simplified tax law help you? How do consumers make choices among similar products? What role do viewers play in network programming? Your possible career choice, then, could open up a host of possibilities for you to explore as topics.

Problems and social concerns. What bothers or concerns you? Are you frustrated by procedures for registering for classes, or the requirements for a degree, or the quality of reporting in the student newspaper, or the way student athletes are recruited? Are you concerned about what you can do after graduation with the education you have acquired, or how medical schools set admission standards, or whether or not it is advisable to get an advanced degree, or how student evaluations of teachers are used, or whether or not student government plays any meaningful role in student life? There are many things about your immediate world that affect you; you may be interested enough to consider talking about them. There is also the larger world of which you are a part. Do you worry about the effects of unemployment on those who experience it? Do you believe that we are doing all we can to help those who live at the poverty level? What do you think about the relationship between religion and politics? Is America a country that lives up to its own stated values? What are the potential risks or benefits of government policy in Central America? There are issues that may directly involve you or people you know and that also have implications for our society, such as the use and abuse of drugs and alcohol, the suicide rate, and rape and sexual exploitation. You can generate your own catalogue of problems and concerns, and from that list, you can find suitable topics.

Leisure activities and interests. We all have things we do for pleasure or enjoyment, and these activities can provide the source for topics. Travel experiences can be drawn on for topics related to cultural practices that are different from our own. Sports enthusiasts can find topics ranging from how specific games developed throughout history, to scandals in college athletic programs, to the psychology of spectator sports, to the controversy about outlawing boxing. Avid movie-goers could devise interesting topics dealing with the techical problems of special effects, or with the impact of the first sound movies on the industry, or with the history of the horror film. A word of caution needs to be said about choosing topics that deal with one's hobbies or leisure-time interests. Speeches, designed for particular audiences and given in particular settings, may be important in some circumstances and trivial in others. For example, you may be teaching children to play tennis, and, in the course of your

instruction, you may want to show them how to string a racket. That's information that could be important to them and relevant to the setting in which you are
speaking. But if your instructor gives you a short speaking assignment so that
you have the experience of speaking before a group, and if he or she specifically
instructs you to demonstrate to the class how to do something, the topic, How to
String a Tennis Racket might or might not be appropriate. Normally, such a topic
would seem trivial: it would present no challenge either to the speaker or to the
audience; it would demand little preparation for the speaker and it would give
the audience little to take away from the speech. Your roommate may always
compalin about how hard it is to get in a suitcase all the junk he or she needs to
take home over break. In that situation, your expert advice on how to pack
efficiently would be appropriate and useful. Don't take the time of your public-
speaking class to discuss the trivial topic How to Pack a Suitcase.

All of the categories mentioned are offered as *starting points* for you to
think about and discover your own topics. They are not, of course, a list to
choose from; you will need to give serious and concentrated attention to all of
your possibilities. Some people will find several topics coming to mind; others
will have to think about it for some time. It might be useful to you to brainstorm.
Write down anything that comes to your mind under each of the suggested
categories without thinking about whether the topic will be interesting to
anyone else, whether you can get enough material, or anything else; just get a
list of whatever occurs to you. Then go about the process of evaluating each
potential topic before selecting one. Other people might be helpful to you in
working out topics, for example, a friend or your instructor, but you need *first to
examine you own resources yourself.*

NARROWING THE TOPIC

When you have generated a list of possible topics, you will have to refine it so
that the topics are suitable for the audience and the occasion for the speech.

You will know better how to do this after you have studied the next two
chapters dealing with audience analysis and with speech purposes. But here are
some general guidelines to keep in mind when choosing a final topic from all
the possibilities.

0. Pick A Topic That Interests You!

1. The topic you select must be manageable within the time available to you.

2. The topic chosen must meet the expectations imposed by the specific assignment or the nature of the occasion.

3. The topic chosen must be one that is potentially interesting to your audience.

4. The topic chosen must take into account the level of knowledge and experience of your audience.

YOURSELF AND OTHERS: THE SPEAKER'S IMAGE

We have all had the experience of listening to a speaker and responding negatively to him or her without being certain that it was the content of the speech alone that we were reacting to. Sometimes a person's voice may irritate us. Sometimes we may identify a speaker as a member of the political party opposed to our own (or, perhaps, a "politician" of whom we are distrustful simply because we distrust all politicians). Sometimes we may associate the way a person dresses with a lifestyle that we reject. We may be hearing a speaker for the second time and remember that our first impression was that the speaker was boring or confusing. We may question the ability of the speaker to discuss the topic at hand.

On the other hand, we have also had the experience of following someone's advice not so much because we are convinced by the array of facts, or because we see clearly what will happen if we take certain actions, but just because we trust the person who is giving the advice. In other words, it is possible for listeners to react to a message on the basis of what they *think about* the speaker and not on what the speaker *says*.

We all engage in such behavior routinely. For example, if a friend you've been in several classes with, someone you like and whom you think knows and shares your interests, recommends that you take a certain course, you might be likely to take it without finding out too much about the specifics of the course. Your friend's recommendation is enough for you to act. We often do this when we are deciding what movie to go see, what restaurant to eat in, what car to buy, or what store to get clothes from.

It is probable that we will also make very important decisions, some that could affect the course of our lives, on the basis of our reaction to a person sending a particular message. Many people have gone into a career because someone they admired pursued such a career. You may have decided which college to attend on the basis of the advice of a counselor, a brother or sister, or a friend whom you trust. We often find ourselves voting for a political figure because we tend to trust or believe him or her more than the other candidate. We may not understand either candidate's specific proposals for improving the economy, for example, but we'll accept one position because the person advocating it just seems a more likely person to get the job done. The 1984 Presidential race affords an interesting example. Poll data indicated on one hand that many people disagreed with President Reagan's policies as they perceived them. On the other hand, polls showed that voters trusted Ronald Reagan himself and intended to vote for him. Clearly the power of the President's personality seemed to be exerting a great influence on the electorate.

ETHOS IN COMMUNICATION

Students of the communication process have pondered the role of a speaker's personal impact on his or her success for a long time. Over two thousand years ago, the Greek rhetorician and philosopher Aristotle studied the art of public speaking, and his *Rhetoric* has probably had the most significant impact on our thinking about and teaching of public speaking. His observation of public communication in ancient Greece led him to argue that *ethos* is a potent factor in successful communication. By ethos, Aristotle meant the speaker's character, intelligence, and interest in the audience's well-being. The *kind of person* that the speaker is will be evident to the listeners and affect their reactions to the total communication event. Later theorists refined and modified this concept until today we think of ethos as almost synonymous with "image." (Remember, we used ethos in Chapter 1 "to describe the speaker *as the audience sees him or her.*") So we say that the ethos of a speaker is the reflection of that person as seen by the audience.

Who, after all, is the *real* person that addresses an audience? We make judgments about people—who is honest, who is smart, who cares about us, and who is reliable—on the basis of what we know or hear. You have probably had

1. How much we trust.
2. How much we respect the Speaker.

the experience of disagreeing with a friend over a mutual acquaintance. You might think the person is very kind and intelligent, while your friend thinks of him as thoughtless and not very smart. Although people can behave differently at different times and in different places, both of you cannot be right in describing the essential character of the person in question. You are both reacting to what you have seen *reflected,* and on that basis the person has an ethos which depends on your perception.

So when we talk about ethos we are not only talking about a communicator's good character; we are also talking about an audience's belief that the communicator is of good character. A speaker may or not be intelligent, but the audience's *perception* of her intelligence contributes to her ethos. A speaker may or may not have the good of the audience at heart, but if the audience doesn't *think* so, his ethos will be negatively affected. This means, of course, that ethos is both relative (it depends on who the audience is) and fluid (it can change as the audience or the situation changes). A speaker's ethos will not be the same for every listener, and it can change not only over time, but in the course of a single speech.

The speaker's ethos depends on how the audience perceives her/him.

It should be clear by now that *ethos* is *not* the same thing as *ethics*. Ethics might be described as a set of behavioral standards that some might argue are universal and unchanging and others might argue are relative to the culture and situation out of which they grow. In either case, such standards represent a code, and an ethical person would be one who lives by that code. *If* an audience knows (to the extent that an audience can ever know) that a person does, indeed, live by a code of which they approve, then they could consider him or her to be an ethical person. He or she would have a positive ethos. Perhaps the same person, living by the same code, is reported to have said or done something that listeners thought violated the code; then the speaker would have a negative—or, at least, less positive—ethos. His or her "ethics" might not change. The speaker's ethos would change, however, because of the audience's *interpretation* of his or her ethics.

All of this means, then, that what an audience thinks of a speaker will make a difference in how well he or she can communicate with them. Let us examine more carefully the factors that influence those listener perceptions that we have been calling ethos.

ASSESSING THE SPEAKER

Students of the communication process generally agree that there are two aspects of the ethos a speaker brings to a situation that seem to influence an audience most significantly. That is, how we assess a speaker will depend in large measure on: (1) How much we trust the speaker, and (2) the extent to which we consider the speaker an *authority*.

The extent to which these two factors are viewed positively will be reflected in the speaker's ethos. Listeners will tend to listen more attentively and be persuaded more easily by someone who they see as a believable and knowledgeable source. If, for example, a teacher urges you to attend a particular college, factors such as its cost, its distance from home, its kinds and quality of academic programs, its size, and so on, will probably enter into the discussion. How you evaluate the evidence, however, will depend upon how you view the source. If you admire the person and trust his or her judgment, you will tend to believe the assertion that X Community College or Y University is a friendly place without asking for specific proof. Suppose that the teacher is a chemist who tells you that the program in business in which you are interested is a very good one. Your reaction to that assertion will be determined by how you view the authority of the source. If you reason, "What does a chemistry teacher know about the Business School?", then you would either discount the claim or ask for further proof. If you believed that "teachers know about the educational system regardless of the specific field," then you might accept the argument as proven without asking for more evidence. The speaker's past associations, present position, known experience, and reputation in general come with him or her to a communication situation. How it affects that situation will depend on how the audience perceives these factors in deciding if the speaker is trustworthy and authoritative.

ETHOS AND SITUATION

Although ethos is important, it is not important in the same way and to the same degree in every situation. At times the ethos of the speaker will not be an evident factor. For example, suppose you are studying for an exam and go to a review session being conducted by a graduate student or instructor whom you don't know. In this case, you are likely to be highly motivated, and you won't care or perhaps even think about who is sending the message. Underlying this situation is the listener's assumption about ethos (and the assumption is probably unconscious) that the speaker knows what she is talking about and will try to help. In other words, considerations of ethos may not be evident, but for the communication to work, the audience has to start with the belief that the speaker is a trustworthy authority.

At other times, certain aspects of the speaker's ethos may be more important than others. For example, you may know something of a speaker's political views and as a result distrust or dislike him. But if the topic on which he is speaking is How to Buy Real Estate, you may be convinced enough of the speaker's competence in that area to listen for and accept information that you think will help you. In other words, the speaker's ethos changes for you as the topic changes.

Of course, ethos from one area may spill over into another, causing good or bad effects for the speaker. Advertising, for example, often tries to capitalize on the ethos of a popular person, encouraging spillover as it solicits endorsements for products from a popular entertainment or sports figure. It is also possible that a listener can form such a bad image of a particular source that the ethos that results will influence every message from that speaker, regardless of the relevance of the speaker's personal qualities to the subject matter. A popular personality who is involved in a personal scandal is likely to be dropped quickly by a sponsor who is afraid that that person's unacceptable behavior will tarnish the image of the product.

In any case, a speaker's ethos is not carved in stone. It can be changed by a situation, by the speaker's own action, and by the course of a speech itself. That ethos can be influenced by the speaker himself or herself is of particular importance to you as you prepare yourself to speak.

CREATING YOUR OWN ETHOS

We have learned that listeners may be prepared for a communication event partly by their prior knowledge of the speaker and that that knowledge may affect their interpretation of his or her trustworthiness and authority. For example, an audience may gain knowledge about a public figure directly through the news media or indirectly through people who pass on what they have gleaned from news sources. People can also be influenced in their view of a speaker's ethos by the nature of the experience they have had with the speaker, how important that experience was, and how recent it was.

In many communication situations, however, the speaker is almost neutral. The speaker may be unknown and therefore not bring either a positive or a negative ethos with him or her. A listener may not know a speaker's name or may know very little of the speaker; nevertheless, he or she can form an impression from what is known. The extent to which a speaker matches a listener in psychological, social, and cultural characteristics can promote the speaker's ethos. For example, people tend to identify with someone who is their own age and their own sex and who goes to the same church or belongs to the same organizations. One of the purposes of introducing a speaker is to help the audience establish ties with the speaker as well as to establish the authority of the speaker to speak on a given topic. But even with little introduction and in a situation in which the speaker has no established image in the minds of his or her audience, ethos will still be a factor.

What, then, can you do as a beginning public speaker in situations such as in a speech classroom? In a classroom, some students may know one another and may have formed impressions that will give the speaker an ethos. In another classroom, especially one in a larger institution, students may never see one another except the two or three times they meet in class. In such a situation, the listeners most likely will be evaluating the speaker *as he or she communicates*—the ethos of the speaker will actually be formed in the minds of the listeners as they participate in the communication process. This means that *the speaker in the immediate situation must shape listener perceptions of him or her.* The nature of the message itself—what its content is, how the speech is delivered, what the speaker's awareness of the audience is, what kinds of authority the speaker will rely upon, what the structure and clarity of the message is, and how interesting the presentation is—will all contribute to the developing ethos of the speaker.

If, for example, the listener perceives a message to be an attack on social welfare legislation, the speaker's ethos will be enhanced or diminished depending on the liberal or conservative convictions of the listener. Or suppose a listener can't hear a speaker; sitting in the back, straining to catch what is said can be a very irritating experience and can lower the listener's opinion of the speaker. A speaker talking to a student audience about grading would tend to have a more positive ethos if he demonstrated his realization of the pressures to succeed that students have because of parental expectations, the desire to get into a professional or graduate school, and the uncertainties of the job market. A speaker urging that American foreign policy in Africa take a certain direction can enhance her authority by bringing before the audience the testimony of persons who are generally regarded as experts, such as the Secretary of State, the chairman of the Senate Foreign Relations Committee, the President of Kenya, and so forth. A speaker who the audience finds difficult to follow, who keeps jumping back and forth from point to point, and who is dull and uninteresting will not be thought to be competent or prepared by the listeners. His or her ethos will tend to be negative. All of these examples lead to the conclusion that ethos is *not* fixed and unchangeable. Ethos can be created and it can be modified during the course of a speech.

PRINCIPLES INTO PRACTICE: A SUMMARY

HOW TO CHOOSE A TOPIC

This chapter has focused on you as a speaker. We have seen that the speaker must look to his or her own resources in order to find a suitable topic and then narrow the topic to manageable proportions. You should take the following steps when choosing a topic:

1. List your intellectual interests.
2. List your educational interests.
3. List your career goals.
4. Identify problems or social concerns that are important to you.
5. List your favorite leisure activities and interests.
6. Pick a topic from the lists you have made that has high interest for you.
7. Narrow the topic so that it is manageable in the time limit.
8. Make sure the topic meets the expectations of the assignment or occasion.
9. Think of ways the topic can be made interesting for an audience.
10. Think of ways in which the topic will reflect the audience's knowledge and experience.

HOW TO CREATE YOUR OWN ETHOS

All that a speaker can do to improve his or her own ethos can be stated simply: the speaker can give a good speech. If speakers give good speeches, audiences will tend to trust those speakers and to consider them to be authorities. So, you can improve your own ethos if you take the following steps:

1. Make an effort to understand your audience's potential reaction to your topic to avoid antagonizing or offending listeners.

2. Relate to your audience, showing your understanding of their needs, feelings, and concerns.

3. Draw on recognized and respected authorities whose positive ethos reflects positively on you.

4. Be clear and well organized so that your audience can follow and understand you.

5. Practice your delivery so that you can relate to your audience directly and smoothly.

6. Choose material carefully and consider thoughtfully the way you will say things so that your audience will think you are interesting.

Much of what follows in this book will help you do just these things. At this point, you should realize that you, just like any other speaker, will have an ethos and that that ethos will be working for or against you. What you do will make a difference in your own ethos.

Perhaps the best way to summarize the nature of ethos is to consider the various factors that have been discussed in this chapter as a kind of filter through which everything that the speaker says, or does, or stands for passes; what comes out is what the audience thinks the speaker is: his or her image or ethos.

CHAPTER 3

KNOWING YOUR AUDIENCE
AND THE SETTING:
ANALYSIS AND ADAPTATION

After studying this chapter you should understand:

- What factors are important in learning about an audience and how these can influence listeners' responses.

- What general guidelines to follow when developing a strategy for adapting to an audience.

- How the circumstances of the setting for a speech can have an impact on listener's responses.

- How the listeners' relationship to the topic can help to shape audience responses.

UNDERSTANDING AUDIENCES

Experience tells us that we cannot send the same message to different people and always expect the same results. Consider again the example given earlier in this book. You get up early one morning and find you have a flat tire. If you think that your friend next door might help but you know him to be a late sleeper, you might want to wait until later in the day to ask him. If you think that your friend would think that more physical exercise would be good for you, you might want to include in your appeal for help the reminder that you have a bad back that's troubling you. If your neighbor is a frail eighty-year-old woman, you might consult her if you needed comforting sympathy, but you would look elsewhere for practical help. In short, whom you are talking to will determine how your message will be shaped.

When you talk to more than one person you must be careful to know something about each one of those people and his other relationship to your message. It would help you to know what you can about their predispositions, tastes, prejudices, and knowledge. And you should know what the audience you address can or may be prepared to do about your request. The audience that you address is made up of many listeners. Since you hope to get a response from those listeners, you need to consider what characteristics they share as a group and what qualities individuals bring with them to a communication situation.

Audiences are made up of individuals who approach the public speaking situation from a variety of perspectives.

The fact that audiences are different, that is, that their makeup varies and is determined by different factors, affects the nature of our messages. Suppose, for example, that you are majoring in physics and that you have a friend who is trying to decide on a major. If that friend asks you what it is like to study physics, you would tell her something different from what you would tell your five-year old brother who asks the same question. In both cases you might want to define the goals of the study of physics, mention the topics of lectures, or describe what you do in laboratory experiments. However, you would need to use a different vocabulary, make different comparisons, or use different examples with each person, because your two listeners would have such different experiences, different levels of maturation, different amounts of knowledge, and so forth. Your friend might be very motivated to gather and absorb as much information as possible, but your little brother might only need to satisfy his idle curiosity in a matter of a few minutes. Knowing all this, you would choose to talk about the subject in a way that the listener could follow; the same holds true when you prepare yourself to speak to audiences.

You need to think carefully about what you know about potential listeners. The best way to go about considering an audience is *systematically*. Ask three basic questions that will help you to uncover things about the audience that will be useful for you as a speaker to know:

Who are the listeners?

What is the setting in which listening takes place?

Where do the listeners stand?

WHO THE LISTENERS ARE

Many factors go into making people what they are, and many of these factors come into play when a speaker plans a speech for an audience. These factors can influence the way listeners perceive events and how they order the importance of issues. How listeners see things and how important they think those things are can mold the listeners' value structure, can determine how attentive they will be, or can indicate the limits they will be willing to go to to accept or reject change.

Let's examine some specific audience characteristics. After discussing each, we will explore their implications for public speakers.

1. *The age of audience members will influence the way listeners receive messages.* Listeners see the world through the eyes of their own experience. Men, for example, who were college students in the 1960s were subject to the draft during the war in Vietnam. Many such students were in conflict with an older generation who had lived through World War II or the Korean War, when very little significant public protest to those wars was raised. Many older Americans believed that they had responded to the patriotic call to fight for "the American way of life." They found it very hard to understand the reluctance of those who, fifteen to twenty-five years later, would not do the same thing in a different war. The protesters saw those who supported the war as being morally bankrupt. War supporters, the "hawks," seemed all too ready to sacrifice the lives of young people. Protesters, the "doves," taunted the President of the United States, Lyndon B. Johnson, with the chant, "Hey, hey, L.B.J., how many kids did you kill today?"

In contrast, students of today, caught up with a different set of problems, often regard the passionate divisions of the 1960s with mild curiosity or indifference. Thus, the famous "generation gap" occurs because people of different ages, seeing the world from different places, fail to understand how things might look from other people's points of view. But, imagine, for example, if you received in the mail tomorrow a notice that compelled you to leave school, your family, and your friends and begin a process that would lead you to kill other people or to risk being killed yourself. Or suppose that you wondered every time the phone rang whether a voice at the other end would tell you that someone you loved was dead or missing in action. Or think about how you might feel if you returned from a war, thinking that you had served your country well, only to find that some people spit on you when they saw you in uniform and that most people hoped just to forget that what you did ever happened. These are the kinds of experiences that have lasting impact. Being in such situations yourself would influence you, as it did students in the 60s, in the way you thought and acted toward American foreign policy, not only at the time, but for the rest of your life.

People react in different ways, of course, to similar experiences. But, living through certain events, and living in the context in which those events occurred, shapes the way a person sees subsequent events. Being young or old means, in part, living through different times—and all times are changing times. Your level of experience is not only determined by your age. Two people of exactly the same age can have had widely divergent experiences. We will discuss experience later. The point is that passing through a time when events occur makes us see and feel about those events in a unique way.

Because we, as human beings, are always searching for understanding by comparing the unknown with the known, we look for similarities between events that affect us in the present and events that have affected us in the past. *How* events affect us is determined not by age alone. In spite of the generalization, for example, that conservatism increases with age, we all know that there are young conservatives and old liberals. Nevertheless, the shared experience of a generation unquestionably affects an audience's outlook. Of course, this is not the only factor to consider in approaching the question of how age influences the audience.

Matters of immediate concern are different for different age groups. Getting a job, keeping a job, and living comfortably when you have retired from a job, for example, might be the three uppermost concerns for three age groups. What we call "saliency," matters of great personal relevance or importance, can be determined partially by age: older people will usually find questions related to the Social Security program "salient," while college students may be more likely to see the role of the government in providing student loans as more "salient."

Shared experiences and particular kinds of concerns have their impact on *values*. Different age groups may have different values that are reflected in several ways. Anyone who hopes to become an effective speaker should remember that *the worth or importance of values depends very much on whose values they are*. Anyone's inclination automatically to dismiss a way of thinking or a model for living as stupid or irrelevant because it happens to be different from one's own should be resisted. If a speaker fails to make an attempt to understand where audience values come from, he will be less able to adapt to his listeners. This point is not one that relates to age alone, of course. It should be kept in mind as one considers all facets of an audience's composition.

2. *The sex of a listener can influence how a message is received.* As myths of "natural" female roles and relationships with men explode, as the realities of sex roles change, and as men and women in modern society are liberated from the narrow confines of prescribed roles and attitudes, the expectations of how listeners will respond are modified. One can no longer assume that women

want to hear about fashion and men about sports. Jokes that portray women as vain, silly, or nagging are considered in bad taste everywhere except in the staunchest bastions of male chauvinism.

Yet, while expectations about and interactions between sexes are changing, listeners are becoming unsettled and uneasy about certain matters. Both men and women may feel defensive about the roles they play or hope to play. As options are opened up, some people may feel unsure either of exercising them or of continuing to exercise old options. A woman who decides for herself that she wants to and enjoys doing the demanding work of bringing up children and managing a household sometimes wonders if she is inadequate because she doesn't want a "career." A woman who has an aptitude and inclination for engineering can be so influenced by the traditional view of the exclusively male domination of certain professions, particularly those dealing with the technical or scientific, that she may worry that she will be considered "unfeminine." A man who doesn't know and doesn't care to know anything about basketball might get an uncomfortable feeling that such a lack of interest isn't masculine.

A person's sexual identity is crucial to her or his very being. It is inevitable that listeners' understanding of and attitudes toward a speaker and what the speaker has to say can be colored by the listener's sexual identification. It is probably true that, in forming this identification, there is now less influence exerted by artificial and arbitrary expectations about what men and women *should* do, *should* like, *should* work at, and so forth, than there once was. Nevertheless, such influence still does exist, and although the speaker may not want to encourage such attitudes, he or she can't ignore them.

Because men and women have different kinds of experiences in our society, they will have different outlooks on many matters. That is to say, *saliency* will be affected by sex roles. For example, the problems single women and widows face in obtaining credit will be initially more difficult for women than for men. Indeed, some women will find this a more salient problem than will others because of their own immediate circumstances. Furthermore, there are tastes and interests for which our culture tends to program men and women differently. If a speaker wishes to use the testimony of a Green Bay Packer's star lineman, chances are that more men in the audience will know who he is than will women. When such instances occur, the speaker's responsibility is to avoid condescending to women who don't know the player, or making men who don't know him feel like misfits.

Although the point will be discussed again later, it is well to remind ourselves here that *no category—sex, age, or whatever—automatically predetermines a listener's set of responses.* There are women, for example, who were vehemently opposed to, adamantly in favor of, undecided on, and indifferent to the passage of the Equal Rights Amendment. The distinction between generalizing and over generalizing is sometimes hard to make, but if there is one thing that the sexual revolution should have taught everyone it is that, although men and women do have concerns and experiences that are unique to their sex, there are aspirations, attitudes, and aptitudes that are human and cannot be pigeonholed on the basis of sex.

3. *Listeners' responses to messages are affected by the subcultures out of which they come and in which they function.* At one time it was generally believed that Americans were a homogenized people. The myth was that we arrived as immigrants, were melted in the pot for a generation or two, and emerged with a distinctively "American" character. Now, as many students of the American culture have observed, it is true that there are certain characteristics, certain traditions, certain ways of looking at things that seem to be especially "American." In recent years, however, we have come to realize that the melting pot conception is not entirely accurate. Our various subcultures continue to be different and to influence us in many ways. There can be racial subcultures, national subcultures, religious subcultures, or geographic subcultures. Although these groups share characteristics with the general American culture, they may have marked differences that could affect listeners' responses to messages.

Blacks and whites in America for example, have a different history and different cultural experiences through which they filter messages. One hopes that the old suspicions, hostilities, and tensions between the races are easing. Blacks and whites both are coming to accept each other as different but not, as a consequence, evil. Communication between members of different races can be extremely complicated and, too often, fraught with distrust and doomed to failure. Nevertheless, successful communication does occur in an overwhelming number of cases and situations every day. Problems can arise in public speaking, as in any form of communication, partly because of the failure to understand that there can, logically and legitimately, be racial influences operating in listeners' approaches to issues. For example, administration of justice might be viewed in a very special way by urban blacks who have been brutalized or bullied by white police. The problem of how to find more jobs for minorities may cause some white listeners to fear that they are to be sacrificed in order to find jobs for unemployed blacks.

We have come to realize more and more that, as each race has its own integrity, each also has its own perceptions and problems. Recognizing racial influences is not racism. A racist denies the essential humanity of those who are different and thus limits severely his or her potential for communicating successfully. Racists can only talk to other racists. Those who appreciate the distinctions between people of different races are better equipped to talk effectively with a wide and varied audience.

The forebears of most Americans came *from* someplace else. With the exception of the American Indians, people emigrated from other countries to America in the seventeenth century, continued in the eighteenth, reached a "flood" in the nineteenth, and still arrive in the twentieth. Depending partly on when they arrived, partly on what their habits and tastes were, and partly on where they settled, the immigrants had their outlooks colored by their own national history, customs, and experiences. It is understandable that listeners who identify with their heritage will be concerned with both the speaker's perception of their origins as well as how the content of the message affects them as a group here or their erstwhile countrymen far away. That is to say, it should be obvious that Poles will find Polish jokes unfunny or that Italians will deeply resent the association of all Italian names with the Mafia.

Moreover, issues that seem to affect directly the country from which one's ancestors came will be more important to, and shape the reactions of, one who identifies with the particular national group. For example, an Irish-American is likely to be interested in the fate of Northern Ireland and likely to have strong, well-formed opinions of who is right and what the outcome should be. A nation, with its particular network of viewpoints and values, can influence even its transplanted citizens and their descendants, particularly in matters that can be related in some way to that country.

Perhaps it is less accurate to talk of religious subcultures than of religious beliefs that are associated with subcultures. But, in any case, a listener's religion, or his or her lack of religious beliefs, can influence that listener's reception and evaluation of a speech There are issues on which certain religious groups tend to take uniform stands. Catholics, on the whole, for example, tend to oppose abortion; Jews tend to favor strong United States support of Israel.

There are other kinds of influences that religions can have on members of audiences. Some religions stress obedience and conformity, with the result that their adherents may view traditional authority differently from those whose religions emphasize individualistic participation in religious life. Some religions stress personal salvation and hold political or social issues to be beyond any religious concerns. Others insist that all matters relating to the human condition should be of concern to the church and that church members should shape their political and social behavior in accordance with the teachings of the church. What those teachings are can make a difference in the way people respond to a message in a speech; "fundamentalists," for example, may be more open to messages that reflect conservative policies and values than those whose liberal religious views may dispose them favorably to liberal political or social positions.

Conventional wisdom once advised would-be public speakers to avoid talking about religion: "It's too personal and potentially explosive a topic." But, of course, there are lots of possible topics that could be so, given the right place and the right audience. If one chooses to talk about religion, the speech needs to be designed with a specific audience in mind just as any other speech would. The point being made here, however, is that whether or not you choose to talk about religion, religion can well influence the listener as he or she integrates a message that is not on the surface "religious" in nature.

Where listeners live can make a difference in how they process a public speech. Even though people might come from the same part of the country, their outlooks can differ depending on the kind of community with which they identify. Obviously, Newark, New Jersey, is not Franklin, New Jersey; Fort Wayne, Indiana, is not Spencer, Indiana; Dallas, Texas, is not Plainview, Texas; Los Angeles, California, is not Modesto, California.

People who have grown up in the country develop different habits and different life-styles from those who have grown up in the city. The horrors of muggings, commuting on unreliable trains, or moving always at a frantic pace loom large to the rural resident, while the city dweller imagines that the dullness and lack of stimulation in the country would bore him or her to death. Perhaps the reverse is true: the untasted excitement of the city lures one, the longed-for peace and safety of the country the other. We don't always have a very clear or realistic view of other people and what they think, how they live, and why they see things the way they do. As a speaker, you cannot ignore the differences in the people you wish to influence. You must recognize that audience factors, in this case the environment that surrounds your listeners, will make a difference as to how successful you can be.

Let's return to the city versus country example. Each group will have a set of problems that is more important to it. Urbanites will see as vital such questions as: How do we reduce crime? How do we improve mass transit? How do we keep food prices down? The residents of a predominantly farming area, on the other hand, will be more troubled by such questions as: How do we save the family farm? How do we reduce property taxes? How do we keep meat prices at a suitable level?

It's also true that *different sections of the country have, through the course of our history, developed unique ways of looking at things.* The Californians, the Easterners, and the Midwesterners are people who do not all have the same ethnic mix in their population; the same industries do not dominate their economies; the same religious views are not necessarily predominant in their cultures. The South, for example, long proud of its traditions while at the same time defensive over its racial history and practice, is in a state of transition. Its geographic advantages, particularly its year-round warm weather, has created a "sun belt" where many older Americans are living. The political and social impact of such a shift is not yet completely clear. It does suggest, however, that people who live in this region may develop their own particular of looking at social and political problems. All this is to say that *different parts of America exert somewhat different influences on those who grow up and live there.*

4. *The educational level of a listener will influence his or her reactions.* Two audiences might want to hear a lecture on the latest developments in high-energy physics. What they would expect from a speaker and what they would be prepared to deal with would be different if the listeners were, say, a junior high school science class and a college class of physics majors. Of course, other factors in this example—such as age and experience—enter in, but, the same principle of educational level would apply even between a first and second year physics course. Education provides us with specific knowledge, ways to solve problems rationally, an awareness of choices open to us, and ways of evaluating the best choices to make.

How well a listener has been educated will determine in part whether he or she is familiar with the topic under consideration and whether he or she can intelligently evaluate the message. For example, much public speaking takes the form of claims. It is claimed that using a certain product will make us happier or healthier. It is claimed that voting for a particular candidate will improve our economic situation. It is claimed that reading a popular book will enhance our sex life. The educated listener should be in a good position to make judgments about such claims. She should have specific facts at her disposal and should have had many intellectual experiences that can be related to specific aspects of the message being received.

Take, for example, someone studying the subject you are now: public speaking. You will learn in this course that you should be skeptical about generalizations that are made in public messages. Suppose you hear someone argue that force must be used in response to a foreign policy crisis because, the claim goes, we are faced with the same kind of dangerous situation that faced America in the 1940s when we confronted the forces of Nazism. If, as an educated person, you take the time to *think*, you won't be tempted to agree automatically because you know Nazism to be evil. You will ask questions about the quality of the evidence. You will demand that the speaker prove to you that the situation before World War II is really similar to the present situation. You will also bring to bear what knowledge you have—historical knowledge in this case. As you judge the speaker's argument, you will take principles you have learned and knowledge you have acquired and apply them. If you find the speaker unconvincing, and if you cannot fully test the argument by your own knowledge and experience, you will suspend judgment. You'll wait and see—listen to other arguments, read more material, and assemble more facts—before you make a decision you want to act on. You will be acting, then, as an educated person.

Of course, it would be foolish to assume that listeners who are educated will always respond in such a rational way. There are many factors operating that prevent any one characteristic, even education, from dominating a listener's behavior. Furthermore, many people are *trained* in a skill by educational institutions, but are not *educated*. That is to say, they have not acquired much general information or learned to apply it in a variety of situations. One's training may range from relatively simple skills, such as driving a bus, to more sophisticated and complex ones, such as being a doctor. But such mastery of skills does not necessarily produce an educated person.

Education should not be confused with training, nor should it be confused with intelligence. There are some very intelligent people who have not had formal education, just as there are some who have had the advantage of attending good universities who are not very bright. So, keeping in mind the limitations about generalizations concerning what educated listeners will do, you can still expect educated listeners to be more critical and to have more information about certain topics. "Certain topics," of course, can be the key to the part education plays in shaping the listener's response. As with all the characteristics we have been talking about, the precise role education plays in a public speaking situation depends upon the specifics of the situation.

5. *The occupation of the listener will influence the way he or she views the message.* The job you have can make a difference in the attitudes you hold and the way in which you grasp specific information. A cattleman and a city homemaker both will be interested in a news story about beef prices. But they will differ in their responses to the same information. Both will have economic interests in the subject because of their occupations, and both will want to be successful at what they do. It may be, at times, that their goals are just incompatible; nothing one can say about beef prices and how they should be set can completely satisfy them both. It may also be that, while the speaker may propose what seems to be a reasonable compromise, the occupations of the listeners help to form attitudes that make it difficult for compromising messages to succeed.

What occupations we have will make us feel differently about the world around us. Teachers, doctors, construction workers, dancers, postal clerks, and lawyers all spend time in unique ways to deal with problems that are important particularly to them. When people receive public messages, they sometimes ask themselves, "How is this going to affect my job?" Effective communicators need to realize that some people may have jobs that they find boring, tedious, or meaningless. People in such unhappy situations may be affected as listeners; they may want to reject messages that don't help them escape from a reality associated with drudgery and even despair. Or they may be receptive to messages that suggest ways to change one's condition.

An occupation provides people with different kinds of skills. The constant practice of these skills is what establishes people as experts. Such experts, when functioning as listeners, bring a whole set of competencies with them to a speaking situation. An engineer, for example, will respond to technological information as a specialist. In the same way, a teacher will respond to arguments about how to improve our schools, or a lawyer will respond to proposals for no-fault insurance. Yet it is also true that occupations can influence responses in ways that are not so obvious. When discussing the problem of how to improve our schools, for example, a motel owner may be uneasy about the suggestion that schools be kept open all year, since that could mean that people would travel less in the summer and his livelihood would be threatened. All the time that a message is being sent the listener may be asking himself or herself what such a plan or proposal means to a steamfitter, a hairdresser, a dentist, or a sales clerk. In some cases, the answer will be, "Nothing in particular," but chances are that the question will be raised in the mind of the listener. Or take the case of a technical specialist presenting a proposal to improve product design to a group of decision makers in his or her company. If the specialist focuses only on her own occupational concerns, which might be making the product work more efficiently, and if she neglects the occupational concerns of coworkers, her chances of being effective will be lessened. The production manager might be worried about the cost; the sales manager might be concerned about how well his staff can understand the intricacies of the new product; and the advertising manager might be worried about how this change will affect the promotional campaign that is about to be launched. Thus, the occupational interests and concerns and goals of the listeners will be different from those of the speaker, even though all the people all work for the same company. If a speaker fails to anticipate and prepare for responses stemming from different occupational perspectives, then his or her good idea might be impossible to sell.

6. *The income of the listener may influence his or her response.* Again, the extent to which this factor is important and the precise ways in which it functions depends on what the speaker is talking about and what he or she wishes to accomplish. The topic of a message may be one that naturally interests different income groups. How to devise tax shelters, for example, would probably have limited appeal to those of low income. Indeed, some of those hearing such a message might not perceive it as giving helpful practical hints, but, rather as an example of how the rich exploit the law to evade paying their fair share.

The perceptions of groups as to how their income level compares and should compare with others may have deep-seated effects on the communication process. People in the middle-income group, for example, may see themselves as burdened with taxes and yet excluded from the benefits of social welfare extended to the poor. Such people may look on many political and social proposals with the jaundiced eye of those who are going to foot the bill.

Professional persuaders such as advertisers go to great lengths to try to see that their messages get through to the right income group. They carefully choose a mailing list (such as one of American Express Card holders) that will put their material in the hands of those who can afford to buy their product; they choose the kinds of magazines to advertise in, the time slot for their television ads, and the kind of radio station that will most likely reach the target audience. Of course, they are concerned with many factors besides income, but they want people who can afford to buy their products to know about those products.

In any case, the extent of financial resources available to a listener will surely help determine his or her receptiveness to any proposals that involve getting or spending money. The wise speaker will try to anticipate how the listeners' incomes will influence the possible responses to his or her message.

7. *The listener's principal roles will affect his or her reactions to a message.* At different times and in different places we are different people. When you're in a classroom, for example, you will tend to think of yourself as a student. When you're at home, you might think of yourself as a daughter, a son, or a parent. When you're playing baseball or soccer, you're a member of a team. When you're at work, you're an employee or a supervisor. When you're working on voter registration, you're a member of a political party.

We can be many things at the same time. The perceived purpose of the message and the setting in which it occurs will influence the role that a listener will assume. For example, when you listen to a political candidate you might be very aware of your role as a student and be concerned about his or her position on student loans and scholarships. An elderly retired couple may listen to that same political candidate speak and assume the role of taxpayer, concentrating on how the candidate's position will affect their property or income tax.

As roles change, status may change as well. So, how people react in a communication setting can shift as these factors are modified. Take for example a young man who is a basketball player. When he engages in communication with his coach, he both processes the messages he receives and sends messages back with the realization that the coach is in charge. The coach's directions are important, and they are not to be evaluated for their worth as much as they are to be understood and acted on. If the basketball player also becomes captain of his team and discusses possible strategies with other team members, his status will have changed because his role will have been modified. His own messages now become more authoritative. As a listener, he is less apt to accept automatically the suggestions or advice that come from his fellow players, although, if the team is a good one, he will listen carefully and weigh opinions thoughtfully since they come from others whose knowledge and experience he respects. The same player attending an alumni dinner may receive many messages that are purportedly designed to help him improve his game. He will undoubtedly listen differently to these messages. They will seem to him much less relevant or authoritative coming from those who are not actually involved in the activity themselves no matter how avidly they support the team or how closely they follow the game. But, since his role in this situation is partly to promote public relations, he will listen politely, according status to those older—and probably in their own field, successful—persons. Yet he will likely ignore practical suggestions coming from an outside source.

Consider the situation if the same young man is talking with one of the advisors, who happens to be a businessman, about a job. The successful housing developer may be listened to only with toleration on the subject of how to improve the team's shooting average; but he will be listened to very closely if the basketball player wants to get a job in real estate. The basketball player's role, along with his status in relation to the developer, changes. Accordingly, his pattern of listening changes.

Different listeners may view the same speaker differently as the speaker's role changes. A good example is afforded by the graduate student who, at ten o'clock in the morning may lead a discussion in an introductory history class and expect that listeners will accept her remarks on the causes of the American Revolution as coming from an authoritative source. At eleven o'clock she may give a report on the same topic in a graduate class and expect an audience of much more critical listeners.

Note that a person's status in a communication situation can change without role change. This can be a result of actions over time or a consequence of environmental factors. As a student in a speech class, for example, you might achieve high status by giving consistently interesting and informative speeches. Or perhaps your speeches on a particular subject, such as space exploration, will be good enough to establish your expertness in scientific areas and give you status when such questions are discussed in class. Yet you could, while still in your principle role as a student be enrolled in a math class of 150 students and not have your status be especially different from the other students in the course.

So, the lesson to be learned by the effective speaker is that listeners' roles will not always be the same. Thus, the ways in which listeners process the messages they receive will vary and will affect the nature of their responses.

8. *Memberships held by the listener will have an impact on the listener's response to speeches.* Just as we play many different roles, so too do we associate ourselves with different organizations. These associations contribute to the listener's identity, the conception of what he or she is. Being a member of the Sierra Club, for example, marks for a person his or her commitment to preservation of the environment. One who is a staunch supporter of the club is likely to see the environmental aspects of a problem as others in the club would see them. Furthermore, such a listener might identify such aspects as being part of a problem when they are not immediately apparent—a possibility the speaker should be aware of.

As with roles, some memberships may be more important than others at certain times. When you attend a meeting of a particular group (a fraternity, a political club, the American Psychological Association, or the Future Farmers of America) the reasons for being in that organization will hold a prominent place in your life at the moment. You hear and respond to messages as a member of that particular group. Most likely, what you hear at a meeting will be designed to be relevant to your group. At other times, the goals of that group may be quite meaningless because the communication setting or the topic considered seems to you to have nothing to do with that particular membership. It is this phenomenon that religious speakers often work against. Such speakers often try to remind listeners that the principles they hold as they attend a religious service are supposed to be applied in everyday life.

It is difficult, and not really necessary, to keep any one membership foremost in all decisions a person is called upon to make. Whether that person is an active Democrat or Republican, for example, will likely be of no consequence as he or she decides how to respond to a certain manufacturer's plea to buy his brand of toothpaste. Even in the political arena there will be times when party membership will not be a crucial matter in the listener's minds. For example, when there was a threat to the New River in North Carolina, one of the oldest rivers in the world, liberals and conservatives both supported legislation to save it. Most of the listeners in this case (senators and congressmen) did not see their party membership as being an important factor in evaluating the message. So the importance of membership increases and decreases as listeners see the issue at hand as being related to membership.

There is another aspect of membership of which a speaker should be aware. There are times when membership in a particular group or identification with the goals of a group is so important that all messages are evaluated by its standards or all irrelevant messages are virtually screened out. Consider two somewhat different examples.

A young man might be a member (or aspire to be a member) of a fraternity. The membership may be so central to his life that he judges messages about where to eat (or what to wear or who he should vote for) by asking himself whether members of that group would eat that kind of food (or wear those clothes, or vote for that candidate); he would base his perceptions on the tastes and preferences of other group members. None of these things would seem, on the surface, to have any direct relationship to the goals and activities of the organization. Nevertheless, many issues are transformed by the listener into ones that seem to him or her to relate to a particular membership. For example, the National Rifle Association, its members and supporters, is dedicated to the defeat of gun control legislation. So important is this to NRA members that they will often subordinate all other issues to this overriding one. They might well end up voting for or against a political candidate because of his or her position on this single issue. Such a dedicated member may ignore the candidate's stand on the economy, on foreign affairs, or on the environment—issues that might seem crucial to others—because that member's identification with NRA goals is so strong that everything else pales by comparison.

Listeners' memberships will influence the way they see the world and interpret events, but not always to the same degree and in the same way. There will be times when a listener sees his membership as being important to the matter at hand and other times when the same memberships don't even occur to

Messages have to be adapted to the audience and the setting.

the listener as relevant. In other cases, memberships will conflict: you might, for example, be a loyal Republican and a dedicated supporter of the Equal Rights Amendment. Your party's official platform on this subject and on women's rights may create a dilemma for you. In such instances, the listener needs to resolve the conflict; messages aimed at him or her are designed to help the listener reach such a resolution.

Who the listener is, then, depends partly on who the listener thinks he or she is affiliated with, and membership becomes an important factor in shaping the listener's reaction to a public speech.

The whole question of who an audience is is a very complex one. There are so many forces that act upon our lives to shape our identity and to direct the way we will function in a communication setting. *Listeners' ages, sex, subcultures, educational levels, occupations, incomes, roles, and memberships will act together to focus their attention, define the relevance of the message for them, and guide their reactions.* Every listener, of course, lives in a complete environment in which factors other than those discussed can come into play. But the speaker could compile a fairly accurate profile of an audience by asking what is known and what is relevant about the characteristics that have been outlined here.

A word of warning for the beginning speaker is needed. Making such a list as we have just been through can seem overwhelming. It may seem impossible to know all that can be known about an audience. You should realize that a speaker cannot ever do a complete and exhaustive analysis of an audience to whom he or she will speak. But the task of trying to understand listeners and *anticipate* the way they will react to messages is absolutely essential to effective public speaking. Anticipating intelligently depends on knowing as much as you can about who they are and how they see the world and their place in it.

QUALITIES OF AUDIENCE ADAPTATION

It should be clear by now that the speaker's fundamental task is to design a speech specifically for an audience. A speaker must center her thinking on the audience; all that she does should be calculated to elicit a response from an audience. Once a speaker has considered all the factors that make up an audience, he must contemplate the ways in which his message should be adapted to listeners. It is important, therefore, to have a clear understanding of audience adaptation before proceeding to specific strategies for preparing and delivering a speech.

It would be best to say first what adaptation is not. Adaptation is *not* saying what an audience wants to hear. Sometimes beginning speakers feel anything from a slight uneasiness to moral outrage over the notion that they must tailor their remarks for a particular audience. But if one hopes to accomplish something with an audience, one has to adapt. This is not to say that a speaker should only reinforce and never try to change an audience's beliefs or attitudes, nor is this to say that a speaker should always agree with an audience. *It is to say that the speaker should recognize the essential humanity of all listeners and try to focus his or her message on their very real concerns, understanding their necessarily limited knowledge and experience.*

Adapting to an audience, then, involves searching for relationships between the speaker, the message, and the audience, and using the results of such a search to promote identification between the speaker, the message, and the audience. *How* one is to do this is a principal concern of this entire book; but the outlines of a strategy for accomplishing this goal may now be sketched.

1. *Search for and identify audience values.* A speaker devotes considerable energy to discerning values that are shared with his or her audience. The cataloguing of characteristics is partly done to see audience values and to try to understand and perhaps sympathize with those people whose values are contrary to the speaker's. What are the things that are valued by listeners? For certain audiences patriotic values may be extremely important; for others, the need to get ahead; and for others, the value of education. All of us possess a network of interlocking values, some of which conflict with others. For example, Americans tend to admire individualism as a trait while also placing great stress on the need for teamwork. They profess the Golden Rule—do unto others as we would have them do unto us—while also valuing material success that often can be realized only at the cost of outwitting, tricking, or outmaneuvering others. We hear of the "work ethic," the "business ethic," the "Puritan ethic," all of which denote different sets of values at work in our society. The best speaker is one who sees what values are relevant to the communication situation and helps an audience to resolve its value conflicts. Values, of course, are not the only features of listeners that a speaker must study.

2. *Identify and communicate relevant audience dimensions for the audience itself.* From the list of characteristics that were reviewed earlier in this chapter, those that pertain to a specific speaking situation should be known to the speaker. The setting and the topic will suggest the obvious ones to him or her, but successful speaking, based on a knowledge of listeners, will involve using what is beyond the obvious. Because all of us have many roles, memberships, and backgrounds, we may not always be aware of all our own interests at once. When we are thinking of buying a new car, for example, our role as consumer may conflict with our role as parent: we might want to buy a car that is inexpensive with good gas mileage, but that same car may be too cramped to get the children into comfortably for a long trip. Different speakers with different purposes may choose to emphasize different listener roles and to downplay others—ultimately the listener will have to decide for him or herself—but, the speaker who hopes to influence the course of action has every right to make as strong a case as possible for the ascendancy of one aspect of a listener's life over another. The listener who is preoccupied with the immediate considerations

suggested by the setting and the topic may overlook aspects of his or her own life that are, indeed, relevant to the speaking situation; these the speaker can point out

3. *Do not stereotype.* It is important to point out that, as much as we know or seem to know about listeners, we cannot over generalize about people or assume that they all fit into neat little "pigeonholes." We should not assume that *all* older people have the same view of sexual morality, for example. Older people may live together without being married because of the threat of serious loss of income due to Social Security regulations. Many young people are surprised to think of grandmothers and grandfathers doing such a thing, just as many older people may be surprised to learn that all young people do not believe in premarital sexual relations.

Labels often deceive us into stereotyping as well. All women and men who believe in "liberation," for example, do not believe in the same thing. Liberation to one woman may mean the freedom to pursue a career and be married at the same time. To another, it may mean the right to choose *not* to get a job and to remain happily at home without being made to feel guilty about her contribution to society. To another, it may mean the rejection of all traditional male-female relationships. So as we try to construct a profile of listeners and try to adapt to their needs, we should remember that we are talking about trends in behavior among certain groups. Never can we predict with absolute certainty that particular characteristics predetermine responses.

4. *Do not lose your own perspective.* Although you need to see the listeners' perspective, you do need to be warned that your own point of view should not be overwhelmed by your considerations of the audience. Being open-minded does not mean being empty-minded. You don't want to lose your own convictions merely to please an audience. You must try to understand the people you want to influence. But understanding is not the same thing as agreeing; to sell oneself or one's ideas for any price, including audience acceptance, is prostitution—and that is something quite apart from speaking effectively.

5. *Speak with a realistic purpose.* As you investigate audiences, you will see the wide and conflicting variety of interests and needs of listeners. As has been pointed out, the network of values and characteristics is complex and not easily discovered, nor is it easily subjected to drastic change. You cannot assume that one message will cause very marked effects. The web of relationships that make up our lives is tough and not easily reconstructed; a person who has strong

religious beliefs is not likely to shed them because of a ten-minute speech urging agnosticism. A lifelong Democrat will probably not be moved to vote Republican on the basis of a two-minute television spot. Yet we all know that it is possible for people to change their religious convictions or to switch political parties. These actions are usually the result of many experiences, however, that will undoubtedly include a *series* of messages. The teacher, the advertiser, the preacher, and the political candidate as speakers all plan a series of messages in the hopes of getting their audiences to understand, to believe, and to act. A speaker, then, must recognize that there are limitations as to what can be accomplished. These limitations are imposed primarily by the nature of the audience, as well as by the setting and the topic. Yet with limitations are opportunities, too. The speaker needs to keep foremost in his or her mind the challenge to get a response from listeners. A realistic purpose, then, is one that accurately assesses how far listeners are prepared to go and is structured in terms of a *desired response.*

6. *Arrange ideas clearly and intelligently for your listeners.* What a speaker knows about an audience should help her or him to state and choose those ideas best designed to get the desired response. If a speaker, for example, hopes to get an audience to understand how electricity is produced, he will need to know how much the audience is likely to know about certain physical laws and principles of electricity before he can decide how best to frame ideas that will promote understanding. The speaker will also have to decide, based on his reading of the audience, whether it is necessary to arrange ideas in a step-by step way, describing each part of the process from the dam to the light bulb, or whether he should talk about engineering principles and how they affect the process. The way the purpose has been stated will help direct the speaker in being clear and straightforward for the audience.

7. *Demonstrate the sense of ideas.* One of the things that a study of audiences should do for you is to convince you of the diversity of possible responses to messages. Ideas that we find to be perfectly obvious or that we readily accept are discovered to be, sometimes to our great amazement, unclear or controversial to others. We need to understand audiences if we want to select the kinds of material that are needed to make ideas more understandable or believable for them. The speaker, when constructing a speech, needs to know whether a contention calls for elaborate proof or not. Whether, for example, the contention that it is important to get a good education will be accepted by an audience

before a plan for improving education can be suggested and developed. If not, the speaker would have to plan to present evidence to show that education is a good thing in and of itself. Of course, the nature of the proof offered should be tailored to the listeners' needs and experiences. The same speaker, if she were trying to demonstrate the value of education to an audience in a small town in Indiana or Iowa, would be advised to consider examples of how education improved farming or small business practices and forget about how it affected literacy rates in certain areas of New York City. The speaker, then, should substantiate ideas adequately for the audience by identifying those that a listener will need to have supported and by choosing the kind of support to which listeners can relate.

8. *Recognize the relevance of listeners' feelings and motivations.* All of us have feelings about things that we care about. We are only upset, angry, happy, excited, or apprehensive when we care about something. If we hear a message that excites no emotion at all or that arouses no interest on our part then we will probably judge that message to be irrelevant. There are many needs that we all share and emotional states that we experience; these will be discussed in detail later. But you as a speaker should realize that emotion is not an evil force. Quite often we tend to think of logic and emotion as separate things. The former is "good," the product of education and intelligence, and the latter is "bad," the result of primal passions that should be kept under control. But without feelings both learning and persuasion are impeded. If you were asked to take action and if you felt that the action would make you feel good, you would, quite naturally, be more likely to take it than if you thought the action would be a waste of time because it had no relation to you. Sometimes our feelings lead us to do socially undesirable things. Many lives have been ruined because a drug is said to be a way of making people "feel good." Greed may cause a business executive to continue an unsafe or unhealthy way of manufacturing a product because costly changes in the process would cut down on profits. We may even act out of a very positive feeling—love, for example—and still injure the loved one by overprotecting him or her. On the other hand, out of fear we may decide to equip our home with fire safety devices and thus protect ourselves and others from harm. Both good and evil can arise from actions motivated by needs and feelings. What the speaker should be mindful of is that for actions to occur at all the listener must be emotionally engaged at some level and with some intensity.

9. *Talk* WITH *and not* AT *an audience.* Every speaker should try to be articulate. Listeners form impressions of a speaker and his or her ideas partly on the basis of what they see and hear during the delivery of a message. To be articulate is to be direct and clear, to let the language used and the delivery of the speech support the ideas and never intrude on them. Often students of public speaking are advised to be "conversational." Insofar as this means to avoid the stilted, unnatural qualities of a read or memorized address, this is good advice. Being conversational, however, should not mean being sloppy, disjointed, or fragmented as our conversation can sometimes be. The ability to speak directly and unaffectedly with an audience is not one that always comes naturally; it will take work and practice. Remember that in most speaking situations the potential for either engaging or turning off an audience is there. What happens will be partly a result of what the listeners actually experience during the course of the speech.

UNDERSTANDING THE SETTING FOR THE SPEECH

To understand fully how the setting in which the speech takes place influences listeners' responses, the speaker must attempt to answer two basic questions: (1) What are the circumstances under which the listening takes place? and, (2) Where do listeners' stand?

Circumstances under which listening takes place. Audiences come together for a reason or a set of reasons. A protest meeting, for example, has a very specific reason for being. The problem has been sufficiently defined for people to get together to do something or to learn what they might be able to do. They have grievances that they would like to have redressed, or they have in mind particular actions that they would like to see taken or prevented. They would, for example, want television cable service to be better, a rise in tuition to be prevented, safety conditions in a plant to be improved, or they want a street light at a busy corner to be installed. In such cases, what is important to the listener is clear, and the audience factors that may come into play must be seen in the light of the situation. At a public utilities hearing, for example, where the purpose of the meeting is to hear arguments on the need for a rate increase, listeners might define themselves in terms of their income or even of their age, since elderly persons on Social Security will be acutely aware of what a rise in heating costs will do to them. In such an instance, factors such as sex or educational level may not be important audience factors.

Groups also gather when their goals are not specifically related to one particular speech topic. Nevertheless, the circumstances still exert some restraints on communication. Members of the Kiwanis Club, the Student Government Board, or the American Legion will have particular goals for which they associate. These goals will not always determine the topic a particular speaker will address, although they can limit the possibilities. A speaker addressing a group will choose to talk about something that he or she deems pertinent to the group, and listeners will be particularly aware of the group's perspective on the subject. When speakers address labor unions, for example, they will be likely to talk about such matters as unemployment, foreign trade, and the minimum wage. Listeners' will undoubtedly evaluate what they hear with a heightened awareness of the union's position, since the situation will accentuate group membership and other associated characteristics.

The setting for a speech, then, can affect the relative importance of the various audience characteristics that have been discussed in this chapter. On St. Patrick's Day or Columbus Day, audiences gathered in honor of the occasion will be more attuned to ethnic factors. A speech given at a church guild meeting will likely be closely listened to by listeners who are particularly aware of religious standards and practices. And situations exist in which communication can easily occur in such a way that several characteristics are important at one time. Listeners watching a television commercial, for example, may respond well to the message in their roles as parents, may decide if the person in the commercial is like them on the basis of race, may determine if they can afford the product with the income they have, and may judge whether the product is good or bad based on their religious beliefs or the standards of the organization to which they belong. The commercial also offers a further example of what the setting can mean for the speaker. If the message fails to grasp the listeners' attention at once, they may leave the room, turn the volume down, read the newspaper, or do something else.

The opposite of an audience that is almost completely free to attend or not attend to a message, such as the one listening to the television commercial, is a "captive" audience. This audience is made up of listeners who have, or believe themselves to have, no special intrinsic interest in the communication to which they are exposed. Sometimes the listeners may view the communication as a price they have to pay in order to receive another reward. Communication in this case is something to be endured in the pursuit of a different goal, like the thousands of parents who sit each year at graduations listening to tedious speeches in order to catch a glimpse of Peggy in the crowd of graduates or to see Mike walk across the stage to receive a diploma. That event is a happy one, and commencement addresses are endured with fortitude and even good humor. Some audiences, however, are not as tolerant, and sometimes it would be better not to communicate at all rather than arouse the hostility of the listeners.

There are also certain situations in which the audience will perceive itself as being captive, and the speaker's very difficult job in such situations is to demonstrate to listeners that they have a good reason to *want* to listen—they should not need to feel compelled to do so. Such a situation, unfortunately, can occur in the public-speaking classroom. One hopes that by the time you finish reading this book and hearing your instructor discuss public speaking you will realize that you have a lot to gain by improving your listening skills. Listening carefully to other speakers is not only a favor done for them to insure they will pay attention to you, but a positive action that will help you communicate better. Sometimes, however, listeners in a speech class (like listeners in other situations) will not be motivated by the situation alone and will see themselves as being captive. This puts a demand on the speaker to convince listeners that they should pay attention to what he or she has to say.

Factors in the physical setting will help to influence an audience and the way in which it sees itself. The size of an audience, the intimacy of the listeners with one another, the proximity of the listeners to the speaker, the time of day, and the normal functions of the setting in which the speech occurs, can all affect the listeners in what they determine to be important, how they see themselves, and, hence, how they react to a speech. For example, if you attend a speech in a classroom with twenty other students and one or two professors, your student role and the professor's teacher role will most likely be enhanced. Listening to the same speech in a large auditorium with hundreds of other people could blur such role distinctions. Attending a speech in a church building can affect a listener: if you happen to be a member of the congregation of that church, even if the speech topic or speaker is not associated with that church at all, the setting may reinforce perceptions formed by your membership. The listener who sits alone watching a message come to him via radio or television will be less likely

The physical setting influences the nature of the communication interaction.

to make the specific personal identifications and associations that would be made by the same listener hearing the same speech in a hall surrounded by fellow union members.

When, where, and why public speaking takes place, then, will influence listeners and how they interact with other elements of the communication situation. Finding out who the audience is and the circumstances under which the audience gathers will provide clues to answering another important initial question that faces the speaker as he or she prepares him or herself: Where do the listeners stand?

Where the listeners stand. Given the characteristics of the listeners and the circumstances of the communication event, a listener's tendency toward positions on specific issues are, to some extent, predictable. In the previous discussion of audience analysis and adaptation, several examples were given of how listeners with certain characteristics tend to react to issues. Listeners' positions on any controversial issue can range from definitely favorable, to undecided, to definitely *un*favorable. A listener can approach a noncontroversial, informative topic as an expert, or as one who has general knowledge in the area, or as a complete novice.

Not only will *who* the listeners are predispose them in certain ways, *why* they are listening will directly affect their thinking, beliefs, and knowledge in relation to the topic being discussed. Those people attending a meeting to protest the government's policy in Central America, for example, leave little doubt about how they feel on the subject. And those who have come to hear a lecture on the latest research in astrophysics are not likely to be students with little or no knowledge of physics. What the audience may feel or know and what the intensity of those feelings or that knowledge may be will both influence and be influenced by the audience's makeup. A staunch American Legionnaire, for example, is likely to be opposed to unilateral peace initiatives, and his strong feelings about "peace advocates" will reinforce his view of himself as a dedicated member of the American Legion.

Networks of attitudes and beliefs influence one another. It may not be easy to define precisely what a "liberal," or a "conservative," or a "moderate" is, yet it does sometimes seem possible to do so operationally. And "operationally" is the way Americans tend to proceed, seeing things that seem to go together without worrying about any ideological orthodoxy. There can be contradictions and anomalies in a listener's position; often his or her position on one issue can be defined by his or her stand on the other. "Liberals," for example, who favor an activist government might support extension of the Social Security program and the creation of government jobs to combat unemployment. The "conservative," distrustful of government, might wish to restrain the growth of the Social Security program and argue for private initiatives to improve the job situation. Yet, as if to underline the lack of doctrinaire consistency, the liberal might tend to be suspicious of the defense bureaucracy while the conservative might be eager to meet all of it's professed needs. That people have "liberal" and "conservative" positions on many crucial questions is not necessarily because they have a clear philosophy, but is, rather the result of the way a whole network of factors—made up of people's conception of their own identities—develops and functions in a public-speaking setting.

PRINCIPLES INTO PRACTICE: A SUMMARY

HOW TO ANALYZE AND ADAPT TO AN AUDIENCE

In this chapter a comprehensive picture of the factors that contribute to the makeup of the audience has been drawn and how this makeup should be taken into account by the speaker has been discussed. In order to analyze and adapt successfully, a speaker should take the following steps:

1. Know who your audience is by understanding as much as possible about its members':
   - Age
   - Sex
   - Subcultures
   - Education
   - Occupation
   - Income
   - Roles
   - Memberships

2. Develop a strategy for adaptation by:
   - Searching for and identifying audience values
   - Identifying relevant audience dimensions
   - Avoiding stereotypes
   - Keeping your own perspective
   - Speaking with a realistic purpose
   - Arranging ideas clearly
   - Demonstrating the sense of ideas
   - Recognizing the relevance of listeners' feelings and motivations
   - Talking *with* not *at* an audience

3. Determine the circumstances by:
   - Knowing the prescribed purpose
   - Understanding the constraints of the setting
   - Knowing in what ways the audience is a captive one
   - Knowing the physical setting

4. Understand where listeners stand by:
   - Knowing the listeners' purposes
   - Understanding the listeners' networks of belief

CHAPTER 4

AIMING FOR A RESPONSE: SPEECH PURPOSES

After studying this chapter you should understand:

- What a rhetorical strategy is and how it is determined.

- What responses are called for in informative, persuasive, and entertaining purposes.

- How purposes can relate to one another in the same speech or in a series of speeches.

- What a good specific purpose is and how to test it.

- How speaker's and listeners' purposes relate to one another.

MAKING APPROPRIATE CHOICES

Whenever we involve ourselves in a communication situation, we are compelled to make choices. In public-speaking situations, most basically and obviously, we have to decide whether or not to talk or to listen. Once committed to participating, we start selecting what to talk about out of a universe of possible sources of material, or we start selecting what to listen to depending on the factors operating on us during the speech. *Speaking involves a whole series of choices, and the option that is open to us is whether or not we want those choices to be random or reasoned.*

Suppose, for example, that in a class where you have been assigned a 10-minute speech you are going to talk about how a President is elected in the United States. You may have just heard a political science lecture that relates to that subject, so you elect to work up a summary of your notes from the political science class. The network of choices involved in this case are largely random because they are inspired chiefly by ready convenience and not by the demands of the communication setting. The topic, for one thing, is probably much too broad to be dealt with adequately in the time. Then, the source of the material is too limited if the speaker hopes to communicate with *specific* listeners who cannot be expected to have the same background as the members of the political science class who heard the original lecture. That original audience would have heard several other lectures, read the same textbook, prepared the same written assignments, and so forth, thus sharing many common experiences that prepare them in a unique way to receive the communication. The audience for the ten-minute speech would not have those shared experiences. They might not even care about the subject or understand how it relates to them, and they certainly would not have the desire to listen that would come from the need to master the information in order to pass an examination. All the choices that have to be made in organizing the material—how the nature of specific ideas will be laid out and developed, what type of precise reaction is to be expected from the listeners, and so on—are restricted by the original choice of material—a "boiled-down" version of a lecture.

The same sort of objections would apply to a decision to give a speech that is, essentially, a rehash of an article from *Reader's Digest* or another magazine. Any such article is written not for the twenty or so people who will listen to the speech, but for a much broader national audience that can be very different from the one to which the speaker will address. The initial choice, then, will really prevent the speaker from exploring and exercising the options dictated by the need to successfully communicate. The speaker will therefore be unable to plan intelligently a coherent set of choices in dealing with the audience for whom the speech is designed and the setting in which public speaking takes place. *This set of choices form a pattern that we will call strategy;* this will be discussed more fully below.

There is another fundamental objection that should be raised to any action that prevents the speaker from devising appropriate strategy, that is, from making his or her own choices. Not only will the speaker's chances of being successful be reduced, he will shortchange himself. If the speaker makes no choices based on the realities of the communication situation, as she can best understand such realities, then very little learning will take place, because it is through the development of strategy (good choices) that principles can be applied to practical experiences.

So the need of the speaker, then, is to *determine a set of choices that is based on the communication needs of the audience and occasion and is consistent as well with his or her own goals and interests.* In short, if public speaking is to be successful, it must be the result of a careful strategy that grows out of the situation.

SITUATION AND STRATEGY

A strategy, as we have said, is an overall plan that governs the choices to be made. Let us first examine the concept of strategy and then see how it applies specifically to public speaking. Let us consider two examples of strategy—*military strategy* and *educational strategy*—and see how they work. With those examples in mind, we will then turn to *rhetorical strategy,* or the *strategy of public speaking.*

The Military Model. Strategy is a term most often associated with the military, and it is really from the military model that we derive the idea of strategy. Let us assume, for example, that two nations go to war. One of the first considerations of military planners will be war aims, that is, what results will be needed for Country A to say it has "won." The aims will grow out of the immediate and long-range situational factors. To simplify matters, let us consider this from the perspective of Country A only.

Here is a summary of the situation:

1. Country B has infringed on Country A's border.
2. Country B is a serious economic rival of Country A.
3. Country B has encouraged dissident groups to subvert Country A's political system.
4. There is a long history of mutual antagonism between Countries A and B.

These are all situational factors that will shape Country A's aims, as will the condition of both countries' armed forces, the alliance structure of both countries, the public opinion in both countries, and so forth. Depending on the assessment Country A makes of the situation, different war aims could emerge.

Here are some of the aims that Country A might have:

It might hope only to regain the land seized by Country B at the border.

It might hope to extend its territory at the expense of Country B.

It might hope to overthrow Country B's present government.

It might wish to destroy Country B's economic capability.

It might aim to overwhelm Country B totally and dictate the terms of a peace settlement.

The aims will determine the strategy that is implemented.

There are, however, strong forces at work that may prevent a rational consideration of aims and subsequent strategy. That is, events in Country A may make it difficult for its leaders to limit their goals to ones that are reasonably possible. For example, the long historic legacy of bitterness between two countries may cause Country A, in patriotic fervor growing out of inflamed public opinion, to set as its aim the complete destruction of Country B—an aim that is unrealistic in the light of other situational factors. If the aim is not attainable, then no strategy will likely be effective.

Let us say, however, that Country A's major aim finally is to cripple Country B's economy. Then a strategy or series of strategies might be developed along these lines:

A "force" strategy would seek physical destruction.

A "diplomatic" strategy would attempt to isolate Country B from other countries that might buy its goods or supply its economic needs.

A "subversive" strategy would work to undermine the confidence of Country B's citizens in their government's ability to succeed economically.

Each of these strategies will call for a set of *tactics* to make them work. *Tactics, then, are specific actions chosen to accomplish the goals for which the strategy was devised.* For example:

The "force" strategy might call for bombing of industrial targets, commando raids on factories, and a sustained military invasion that drives toward industrial centers. All these specific actions (*tactics*) are designed to further the strategy. And so with other strategies: an attack on Country B at the United Nations, the offer to provide Country C with needed raw materials if it will remain uncommited, and so forth, could serve as tactics to accomplish the "diplomatic" strategy. The "subversive" strategy may be advanced by such tactics as propagandistic radio messages beamed to the people of Country B or the use of agents to sabotage Country B's factories, or to stir up labor unrest. *The situation and the emerging strategy and tactics, then, are intimately related.*

The relationship works in two ways. The strategy and tactics grow out of the aims shaped by the situation, and the execution of the strategy causes reassessment of the aims. If, for example, Country A's bombers never reach their targets, or if their commandos inflict very little damage before being captured, or if the invading army is driven back into its own territory, the "force" strategy will have to be abandoned. Depending on the degree of success of the other strategies, Country A may have to reconsider whether its aims are possible to achieve, and it may have to modify them considerably. Country A may, in the end, hope only to keep the situation the same as it was before the war began. *So aims shape strategy and the success of strategy can reshape aims.*

The Educational Model. Let's consider strategy and its function in another context: a teaching-learning situation. Educational strategy also grows out of a network of situational factors that lead to goals. The ages of students, their known intellectual capacity, the expectations of parents, and the normal requirements imposed on certain grade levels or by particular schools can all form some part of the situation out of which a teacher creates reasonable aims.

The educational strategist, like the military strategist, can miscalculate. Through lack of experience, he or she may demand much more of students than can be reasonably expected, as when a beginning college teacher tries to teach to freshmen what she has just learned in a graduate class. The inexperienced teacher of handicapped children may sentimentally assume that love conquers all and fail to demand that these children reach their full potential through work and discipline. Situational factors can be misread, or they can be correctly interpreted; in any event, they will lead to designated aims.

Educators talk about "behavioral objectives," or specific statements of what they want students to do as a result of being taught. But whether or not one talks about behavioral objectives or simply educational goals, the teacher will devise a series of strategies and attendant tactics to achieve his or her aims.

Assume, for example, that a teacher is designing a unit on colonial life in America. That such a unit must or will be taught already constrains the situation. Other situational factors that might influence a teacher and what he would hope to teach might be the grade level of the students, the amount of time available, or the kinds of physical facilities or instructional equipment in the school.

After carefully considering situational factors, the teachers trying to teach about colonial life in America might aim to have the children understand the quality of life in seventeenth-century New England. (And, of course, this aim could be stated in a series of objectives that could be tested by the children's observable behavior.) To bring about such understanding, a teacher could employ an "involvement" strategy in the hope that children would not only know certain facts about colonial life, but would also share some of the feelings and experiences that children of their age had in colonial times. The teacher might then go on to evolve tactics that would call for the students to make clothes like those worn at the time, to cook foods eaten at the time, to construct models of houses, to reenact town meetings or religious meetings, and the like.

The success of such a strategy in helping children to understand aspects of the colonial environment would depend on the aptitudes and interests of the children. As with other kinds of strategies, the failure of tactics to promote the strategy might call for different tactics (as the same "involvement" strategy certainly would call for different tactics or different specific activities if the students were high school rather than elementary students). Failure might call for the abandonment of the chosen strategy for others, or for the modification of aims.

These two brief examples of strategy in operation—the military model and the educational model—suggest aspects of a strategic model that we can now construct and apply to *the strategy of public speaking: rhetorical strategy.*

RHETORICAL STRATEGY

Rhetorical strategies are the set of choices to be made in the design and execution of a speech; they are based on comprehensive communication principles. *Rhetorical tactics* are those specific methods and procedures designed to further strategic choices. *As you work out the purpose of your speech and devise the ideas that will help you accomplish that purpose, you plan your strategy. When you are developing ways to make those ideas understandable and believable to an audience, you are discovering and using tactics.*

The first element in shaping rhetorical strategy is the *rhetorical situation*. From a total situation certain aspects may be particularly relevant to public speaking. These situational factors may influence the choice of topic, the way the topic is developed by the speaker and responded to by the listener, or both. Let's consider a famous example from recent history that illustrates this point.

In the presidential campaign of 1976, Governor Jimmy Carter of Georgia and President Gerald Ford met in a debate in San Francisco. During that debate the President stated that Eastern European countries were not dominated by the Soviet Union, a comment generally regarded as a political blunder. That statement became a part of the rhetorical situation in the week that followed and led Governor Carter to choose to talk about the conditions of Eastern Europeans in his speeches throughout the week. So that comment by President Ford was a situational factor that influenced Carter's public communication.

In the same week, however, a student in a public-speaking class gave a speech on tax loopholes and how they should be plugged. For him, Ford's remark on Eastern Europe was, from a practical point of view, irrelevant. Although the remark was part of an overall situation and although most of his audience was likely to be aware of the Ford remark, the remark was not a part of the student speaker's rhetorical situation. For him, student concerns about how to finance an education while parents pay higher taxes was a part of the situation with which he had to deal.

As another example, one could imagine a state legislator being invited to speak to a local PTA at a time when a bill was pending that would reduce state aid to local schools; that situational factor would be so important that it would probably dictate the legislator's choice of topic.

For the speaker who must choose a topic, the situation will play an important role. The choice must come from the speaker himself or herself. As was pointed out in Chapter 2, it is foolish to enter into public speaking without some interest in and knowledge of the matter being discussed. Remember that the principal resource that a speaker has initially is himself or herself. Any speaker must realize that what is to be discussed publicly must interest him or her no matter what the situation, or the chances of having successful communication taking place will be practically zero. It is worth repeating, however, that the speaker must not confuse interest with complete preparedness. In order to give a speech, a speaker must first engage in a demanding intellectual process. So the speaker must not assume that a speech must be complete in his or her head before a topic is chosen.

The situational factors, then, working with the interests and tastes of the speaker will produce a topic. The factors could include the many aspects of audience that were discussed in detail in the last chapter; the needs of a particular occasion, such as a sales presentation or a classroom oral report; or the motivations for public speaking that can arise out of the immediate context in which the speaker and listeners live, such as problems that affect the lives of the listeners directly.

A speaker, for example, may assess his or her own interests, which include history and politics, analyze the student audience and identify their concern over job prospects when they finish college, and take into account the election campaign going on at the time. From these situational factors the speaker may decide to speak on the topic Voter Apathy. What the speaker must do next illustrates the next phase in our model of rhetorical strategy.

From situational factors interacting with the speaker and the listener, aims must be developed. Just as Country A had to assess the factors that led to conflict and determine what it had to accomplish to win, so a speaker has to look at the entire speaking situation and determine what he or she hopes to accomplish: *the speaker must create a purpose.* Remember that in the first chapter we discussed purpose and suggested that the purpose of communication was to get a desired response from an audience. So as the speaker refines his or her topic, he or *she will try to translate it into a specific statement of response.* Since all that can be done to insure successful public communication rests ultimately on having a clear conception of purpose, we will consider it in detail here.

PURPOSEFUL SPEAKING

The speaker who has chosen Voter Apathy as a topic now has several decisions to make. The restraints of a situation, such as how many people will be there, how long the speech must be, what time of the day it will be, and so forth, as well as what a speaker can determine about the audience should lead him or her to decide first on the general nature of the speech. The speaker will decide on what kind of general response he or she is aiming for before deciding on the specific response.

In the Voter Apathy example, the speaker could decide that the audience simply is not aware of voter apathy and needs more information about the problem. Or the speaker might have a plan to overcome voter apathy that she would like to have the audience agree to or act upon. The speaker might believe that the audience already looks with disfavor on voter apathy but doesn't feel strongly enough to do anything about it. In such cases, she would first posit a *general purpose*—to gain understanding, for example—and then move to a very *specific statement of the response* sought, such as, "I want my audience to understand the precise ways in which voter apathy has affected the outcome of past elections." Using this example, let us go back and look systematically at the kinds of general and specific purposes that govern public speaking. In order to

PURPOSEFUL COMMUNICATION

Type	General response	Specific response
INFORMATIVE	Understanding	I want my audience to understand . . .
PERSUASIVE: STIMULATE	Eliciting stronger feelings	I want my audience to feel more strongly that . . .
PERSUASIVE: CONVINCE	Gaining agreement	I want my audience to agree with me that . . .
PERSUASIVE: ACTUATE	Inducing overt action	I want my audience to [take action] . . .
ENTERTAINING	Stimulating enjoyment	I want my audience to enjoy [my account of . . .]

FIGURE 4.1

understand "purpose" best, let's consider each general purpose and the specific purposes derived from it

INFORMATIVE PURPOSES

One type of communication is *informative,* and this aims primarily at *gaining understanding.* Often public-service announcements on television and radio, lectures given in class, and reports delivered at meetings of organizations are all aimed at gaining understanding. In this type of communication the initiator or source hopes that the listeners will end the encounter having learned something they did not know before. The concern of the source or speaker is *not that the listeners necessarily do something, think something that they have not thought, or believe something, but, that they know something that they did not know before.* All communication is directed at getting something, and what the speaker hopes to get here is *understanding.* From this general purpose the speaker then moves to create the *specific purpose or the statement of the desired audience response.*

The specific purpose grows out of the topic and the general purpose, shaped by the particular demands of the situation. If, for example, you were going to give a speech in class on the problem of crime, you would, after considering such matters as the factors influencing the audience, the relationship of crime to the audience, and the amount of time available for the speech, decide that the audience should know more about how crime affects them directly. This would suggest to you that you give a speech to gain understanding, and you could devise several goals that could be accomplished in a limited amount of time.

The following are all examples of specific purposes that could be set by the speaker:

I want my audience to understand the economic impact of crime.

I want my audience to understand the kinds of crime committed in the suburbs.

I want my audience to understand the crime pattern at this institution.

I want my audience to understand some of the major causes of crime.

Each of the examples is a statement of how the speaker wants the audience to respond, that is, what he or she hopes to accomplish in the speech. An appropriate strategy can be devised and implemented once the speaker is sure of what he or she hopes to do. When we discuss how communication can be structured and developed in the chapters that follow, we will really be talking about designing and carrying out rhetorical strategies. What is important to remember at this point is that *the fundamental step in devising a specific purpose is deciding on how listeners are expected to respond before doing anything else.*

This step is so fundamental that it deserves additional elaboration. Too often public speaking is less successful than it could be because the speaker is not sure what that communication ought to be doing. A speaker, for example, once addressed a large crowd gathered to protest proposed fee hikes for state colleges. The listeners had come primarily because they wanted to know what to do to stop the increases and to show support for those who were fighting to keep fee costs as they were. The speaker, however, delivered a long, angry attack on student apathy and implied that such stupid, unresponsive creatures deserved whatever they got at the hands of an unsympathetic legislature. The speaker could have talked about the need to become active, he could have attempted to get his audience (already motivated to act) to understand how they could take direct actions that would put pressure on the lawmakers. There were a wide range of appropriate purposes that he could have devised. Instead, he probably decided just to "get up and talk about apathy" with the result that he irritated and alienated an initially friendly audience and injected a depressing note into what should have been an enthusiastic show of unity and determination. If that speaker had thought carefully and systematically about the topic and the situation, it is likely that he would have come up with a more sensible specific purpose.

Often beginning students of public speaking will tend to hurry over the specific purpose without realizing how it determines so much that will happen. A speaker might be tempted, for example, to say that her purpose is "to talk about modern technology." Such a statement, of course, is not a purpose at all. It says something very vague about what a speaker will do, and *purpose in public speaking refers to what the speaker wants to get from the listeners*. Furthermore, "modern technology" is a very broad and nonspecific idea unless it is related directly to what the speaker hopes the audience will understand about modern technology. With the purpose stated as is, the speaker would have a very difficult time making choices about what material to include and what to exclude in such a speech. The result would probably be somewhat random, and the chances of a coherent strategy slim. To get back to our military analogy, it would be like Country A deciding that the aim of the war is "to fight Country B" with the result that no coherent plans would be laid out, since conflict seems to be an end in itself. It is just as foolish to assume that "talking about" something is an end in itself.

The speaker in the modern technology example, after considering her own interests, the listeners, and the situation in which they would all find themselves, might come up with a purpose such as, "I want my audience to understand the ways modern technology makes learning easier." Such a purpose would call for a different strategy and will certainly lead the speaker to different material from that called for by a purpose such as "I want my audience to understand how modern technology creates psychological problems for some factory workers." Both these purposes related to the topic of "modern technology," but both, obviously, will need to be developed differently. The speaker who hopes to be successful, then, will plan the response carefully and never allow herself to be vague or unclear about precisely what her purpose in speaking is.

PERSUASIVE PURPOSES

Students sometimes have difficulty in seeing the differences between informative and persuasive speech purposes. Indeed, there are times when a speaker must be informative before she or he can be persuasive. If, for example, a speaker wishes to support or oppose the North American Free Trade agreement in a public speaking class, that speaker would have to take some time in explaining the provisions of the treaty so that the audience first *understood* precisely what the treaty actually stipulates. If, however, the speaker wants to gain more than simple understanding, if the speaker wants the audience to take a stand for or against the treaty, he or she must *persuade*. What the speaker always keeps in mind is what that speaker hopes to accomplish. In this example, the speaker who opposes the treaty would be disappointed if, after her speech is over, the audience understands the provisions of the treaty but does not see anything wrong with it. The purpose of the speech is to persuade, so the speaker wants to get more than the understanding that is aimed for in an informative speech.

Persuasive speaking aims at influencing the feelings, thought, and behavior of listeners by eliciting stronger feelings, gaining agreement, or inducing action. Traditionally, such persuasive purposes have been grouped under three persuasive categories, and we consider each of these now: (1) speeches designed to *stimulate*, (2) speeches designed to *convince*, and (3) speeches designed to *actuate*.

Speeches to stimulate. In speeches designed to stimulate, the speaker wants to get his or her audience to feel more strongly about something with which they might already be in agreement. This is sometimes described as a speech that reinforces ideas or beliefs that listeners already have. There are times when public speakers hope to overcome apathy or to promote involvement or awareness on the part of listeners. All of us could think of ideas or principles that we would not object to but that don't seem to make much difference in our thought or action. There are political convictions, religious beliefs, or moral values that we might say we subscribed to, but that we do not have uppermost in our minds.

There are many people, for example, who are nominal Democrats or Republicans. Yet they would be unable to tell you who their party's candidates for state or local offices are. They don't seem to care very much which party wins. And they might not even vote themselves. They might agree with Republican principles or agree with what the Republican candidate says in his speeches, but they just don't feel very strongly about it. One might engage such persons in a much more animated discussion of the merits of the local high school football team, or of ways to improve production at the plant, or of the quality of the latest college theater production, or of the pros and cons of staying in school versus taking a year off to get a job. The speaker who would like all the Democrats or all the Republicans to support the party (by working door to door, by giving money, or by voting) knows that people must feel personal motivation before they will be prepared to give such support. Part of the total communication in a political campaign, therefore, is aimed at getting those who already agree with the party's positions and candidates to feel strongly about their political allegiance.

There are many other examples. Religious speakers often try to get audiences to feel more strongly that the principles to which they may pay lip service are important to their lives. Teachers may attempt to get students initially committed to furthering their education to feel more strongly that completing their degree or diploma is a good, positive thing to do. The president of a campus organization may try to create more enthusiasm among members for the group's goals. A student may try to get a roommate to feel more strongly that his or her concentration would improve if a study break were taken. Communication with the aim of reinforcing existing feelings or beliefs, then, is based on the assumption that the listener and the speaker are already in substantial agreement; the coals are glowing, but they need to be fanned if they are to burst into flame.

If one were giving a speech in class to reinforce existing beliefs, and if the topic were Ways to Improve Higher Education, a reasonable specific purpose might be, "I want my audience to feel more strongly that the costs of higher education must be kept as low as possible." Such a purpose states what the speaker hopes the audience will feel when he or she has finished speaking. It is limited in scope, too, and can be handled within the confines of the situation.

Speeches that are sometimes called "ceremonial" usually aim to stimulate existing feelings. Back in 1976, for example, when the United States was celebrating its Bicentennial there were hosts of messages about America and the American heritage that were based on the assumption that the listeners agreed on the essential goodness of the country and its citizens. A student in such circumstances might give a speech with the purpose, "I want my audience to feel more strongly that the American past has favorably influenced the present." If that same student were now traveling in Europe and if he were asked to speak to German students about American history, the same assumption could not be made. In that case, a ceremonial speech would not be appropriate. He would certainly wish to develop a different specific purpose, one more responsive to the situation and audience.

Speeches to stimulate often aim at creating a mood or feeling that might influence the atmosphere in which other forms of persuasion later occur. When President Clinton, for example, gave his inaugural address, he did not outline specific legislative initiatives or make concrete proposals for action. Rather, he attempted to create a hopeful atmosphere in which change would be welcomed—a good, positive mood that would serve as a backdrop for actions that he would later propose. Emphasizing shared values, the new President sought, as most Presidents do in inaugural addresses, to emphasize our common determination to solve tough problems and to cooperate in bringing about necessary change. This kind of speech did not change the minds of members of Congress or of the vast numbers of listeners throughout the country; it was not intended to. Rather it was an attempt to set the stage for later action proposals by establishing a mutually cooperative atmosphere in which policy would be discussed.

Speeches to stimulate, then, are often the forerunners of persuasive efforts to convince or actuate. They must intensify feeling or reinforce existing predispositions so that listeners are made aware of the relevance and importance of beliefs, feelings, and values that they already hold.

Speeches to convince. In speeches designed to convince, the speaker hopes to secure the agreement of his or her listeners. We have all found ourselves in situations in which we want someone to agree with our point of view. The issue might be a political one, such as who should be elected president, or it might be a question of taste, such as whether or not a recent film was as innovative and original as the critics said it was, or it might be a matter of conjecture, such as whether or not Michigan or Ohio State play the toughest football schedule, and so forth. Whatever the case, we have all had experience with this kind of persuasion. This does not mean, of course, that we will all know how to operate successfully in such a situation. We know that sometimes we seem to be able to get people to see things as we do and sometimes we don't. Although the study of persuasion does not assure anyone of success, it does help those who would persuade to increase their chances of effectiveness. Surely one way to give oneself a better chance is to identify the precise persuasive goal that one has in mind. The goal, as are all goals in communication, is shaped by the situation.

In the opening days of the Clinton Administration, the new President proposed to lift the ban on gays serving in the military. Faced with stiff resistance from the Joint Chiefs of Staff, some powerful members of his own party in Congress, and the Republican opposition, the President agreed to some temporary measures and a waiting period during which Congressional hearings would be held. This was a period which both sides—those in favor of removing the ban and those in favor of retaining it—say as one in which the American people could be "educated" on the issue. That is to say, both sides hoped to convince the American people that one or the other course was the right one to pursue. In Congress and throughout the various media forums open to them, advocates sought to gain popular agreement with their position. Gaining agreement, in this case, was seen as fundamental to taking or blocking presidential action. In a country such as ours, where public opinion is constantly polled and where perceptions of public opinion influence the actions of the peoples' representatives, *agreement* with one course or another was what was needed ultimately to effect action. The "American people" were not really called upon to take direct action—the government and the military would have to do that; but the weight of popular agreement with one side or the other would serve as a powerful and pesuasive inducement to act. So, in this situation, messages designed to gain agreement were most appropriate.

It is also important that the speaker understand what is reasonable and possible to accomplish. *In seeking to gain agreement, the speaker has to realize that dramatic shifts of opinion and ideas are very rare. Sometimes, it is better to try a very small step that can be taken than to attempt a large one that is doomed to falter.*

Consider, for example, an exchange student from North Korea who devised as his purpose, "I want my audience to agree that the United States should overthrow its present form of government and adopt a Communist-style one." Because of the average college student audience, such a speaking purpose would be virtually impossible to accomplish. It would be much more reasonable for the exchange student to limit his persuasive goals to such specific purposes as, "I want my audience to agree that the people of North Korea want to be friendly with the American people," or "I want my audience to agree that our system of government is not a bad system for our people." Neither of these purposes could be accomplished without effort, and perhaps the speaker might not be able to realize fully even the more limited goal. It does seem, however, that such purposes are possible, and that is a critically important consideration.

As in all speech purposes, *speeches designed to get agreement should be stated precisely in terms of response.* The speaker who sets out "to persuade my audience about nuclear power," is in serious trouble before he or she begins. It is the "talking about" problem all over again. The speaker has a whole range of options open: he or she has to be absolutely certain of whether the aim is to get the audience to agree that nuclear power should be attempted on a limited basis, or to agree that nuclear power should be rejected as a possibility in the near future, or to agree that the development of nuclear power should be given first priority in our national energy-conservation program, or one of the many other possibilities that exist It is only when such a clear purpose is established that strategy can be formed.

In considering the limitations that by necessity are imposed on the specific purpose, *the speaker should not be so cautious that he or she becomes timid, afraid to take risks with an audience, to challenge listeners, to face difficult issues.* Getting other people to agree with you is not easy. And limiting a purpose to one that can be achieved does not mean that you will always achieve it And it certainly does not mean that a speaker should only tackle the sure thing.

If you were to design purposes that you were convinced would always produce agreement, you would probably end up talking about trivial matters much of the time or, worse, saying not what you think is right but what you believe listeners want to hear. Persuasion is not a knack that one can pick up by learning a few of the tricks of the trade. It is a difficult communication process that takes careful thought and practice; it takes the kind of intelligent planning that grows out of respect for one's own integrity and need to be an articulate human being, coupled with a respect for the listener's needs and feelings. That being so, planning a persuasive specific purpose becomes a thoughtful prerequisite to a well-developed piece of communication and not just a mechanical effort.

Speeches to actuate. In speeches designed to actuate, the speaker hopes to have his or her audience take direct, overt action. Every day we encounter appeals, pleas, suggestions, and demands that we act in certain ways. Politicians ask us to get out and vote. Health experts ask us to get out and exercise. Advertisers ask us to buy their products. Girl Scouts ask us to buy their cookies. A friend asks us to take care of her cats while she's in Florida. Our parents ask us to spend more time at home. Our friends, our television sets, and even total strangers try to influence us in specific ways to do specific things.

One who plans this type of communication has a very definite and concrete goal in mind: a direct action that needs to be taken. Anything short of the action is not sufficient to accomplish the speaker's goal. Suppose, for example, that you are particularly eager to see a certain candidate elected to the state legislature. Your friend, whom you know to be not particularly partisan, is persuadable. After spending considerable time trying to get your friend to commit himself to your candidate, and after sensing that you have finally gained the agreement of your friend, you will be disappointed to hear him say, "Well, I guess you're right. Of course, I can't vote anyway because I never registered." Agreement, while being somewhat satisfying, isn't all that you have had in mind—you want a vote that will count in the election.

In planning a speech to actuate, the speaker needs to determine the precise action that he or she wishes to see the listeners take. If the topic of the speech is Volunteerism, the speaker who hopes to get action will not be happy if the audience only learns something about the role of volunteers in charitable organizations, or if the listeners leave after the speech is over agreeing that volunteers are important, although both these reactions may be favorable. What should satisfy the speaker is the accomplishment of such purposes as:

I want my audience to pledge to spend two hours a week as a volunteer.

I want my audience to refuse to do volunteer work.

I want my audience to join the National Association of Volunteer Workers.

I want my audience to visit the nearest neighborhood recreation center within the next week.

These are all different purposes, and the precise one, of course, would be determined by the interaction of the speaker, the audience, and the situation, but all reflect the speaker's intention to aim for direct action. In many ways, this kind of speech yields the most tangible results; at least if you ask for twenty people to make sizable donations and end up with $1.15, you know that you have not done well. One cannot always tell whether listeners will actually do what is hoped for, but this speech is not one that aims only for mental or emotional response. *The speech to actuate calls for listeners to demonstrate overt, observable behavior.*

Taking action often demands that the listener exert energy, or give up time, or spend money. If listeners are to respond by actually *doing* something, they must feel that the action the speaker recommends is *feasible, important,* and, as much as possible, *convenient.* Students, for example, might consider it feasible to work two or three hours a week as volunteers in a literacy program or at a half-way house, or answering a crisis hotline, but they would likely consider it out of the question to participate in a program to help the homeless that requires them to miss six weeks of school and absorb travel and living costs for that period. The action suggested must be perceived as important to furthering the cause the speaker advocates. Speakers frequently suggest, for example, that listeners "write their congressmen." Many listeners will perceive such advice as a token gesture. The speaker has the responsibility to show that writing such a letter will actually make a difference in the way legislators react. There have been instances to which the speaker can point where contact with representatives made a difference. In Clinton's ill-fated nomination of Zoe Baird to be Attorney General, for example, media reports of the number of negative phone calls that Senators were receiving seemed to suggest that this popular expression of disapproval caused Senators to take the issues involved very seriously and eroded support for the President's nominee. Such an example, developed and explained to an audience, supports the contention that the action taken is important and has the potential to make a difference. As far as the speaker can, she should also make it easy for listeners to take the suggested action. If letters are to be written, the speaker could distribute a sample letter with the mailing addresses of those to whom it should go; if listeners are urged to volunteer with a particular agency, they should be provided with names and telephone numbers of persons at the agency to contact. If they are being urged to vote, they should be provided with information (preferably written out and distributed) about polling places or procedures for obtaining an absentee ballot. No matter what the course of action intended, the speaker should ask himself: "What can I do that will make it as easy as possible for listeners to do this?"

ENTERTAINING PURPOSES

Speeches that are entertaining are those that stimulate enjoyment on the part of the listeners. This type of communication usually occurs in an after-dinner situation, or at a time when the audience does not expect to be asked to think very hard or to take very serious action. In many ways, this is a very difficult speech to give. Humor is hard to plan; professional humorists are likely to employ teams of writers, and even they can and often do flop. Also, what may seem funny to you or to a few of your friends one night may not seem so funny the next morning.

For example, a student was preparing to give a report in class on a famous debate of the eighteenth century given in the British House of Commons. He amused himself and his roommates with the idea that the debate could be reported the way Howard Cosell would have reported it. The next morning at eight-thirty, however, what had seemed so funny sounded strained and overdone in the classroom presentation. Instead of being enjoyable, the experience was embarrassing for everyone. The student in this case made several mistakes. Foremost, of course, was to misread the situation and audience and assume that an entertaining purpose was suitable. It was not, of course; this should have been a speech to gain understanding. But, even if the student wanted to inform and hoped that by increasing interest he could accomplish this, he had obviously not framed his purpose very carefully; the vehicle for presenting material obscured the information itself. It was also fatal to try such a maneuver on the basis of the reaction of a few friends who might share one's sense of humor, and to try such a device without lots of time to refine it and to think about it. Being an intelligent person, the speaker would probably have thought better of his plan if he had given himself time to consider it.

Creating enjoyment, it should be pointed out, does not always mean being funny. In fact, most successful speeches to entertain will probably include a lot of informative material. Enjoyment comes from being interested and relaxed, and not necessarily from being amused. Furthermore, different people enjoy different things: some people like to solve puzzles and play word games. Some people like historical adventure. Some people like to watch television. Some people invariably find a cream pie squashed in a comic's face to be uproariously funny. What people enjoy is not always easy to predict, and often the clues one can get from audience analysis are not helpful.

If you think about it, you can probably guess with some accuracy what kind of music college students find enjoyable, what sorts of television programs most

Speakers aim for responses from their listeners.

people watch, what movies are popular, what the serious interests are of those in particular majors, and so forth. A speaker could give a speech with the specific purpose "I want my audience to enjoy my account of how the pyramids were first discovered," or "I want my audience to enjoy my explanation of how horror movies are made," or "I want my audience to enjoy a description of my motorcycle trip through the Middle East." In all these cases, the listeners may learn something, they may even be actuated in some way—such as going to see a horror movie or taking a trip to Egypt—but that is not what the speaker hopes to accomplish. What he or she really wants is for each listener to have a good time listening to the speech. That means, of course, that the speech will have to be developed differently from a speech with another kind of purpose; to repeat what has been said many times in this chapter, the strategy depends on the purpose. It would be wonderful if every speech were enjoyable, and that is a worthy goal. But the point here is that only those speeches that aim at enjoyment alone can be successful when the sole result is enjoyment.

PURPOSES AND MULTIRESPONSES

As you read this chapter, you may begin to think that some speeches could have more than one purpose. That is not exactly right; each speech will have *one specific purpose*. However, you would be right in discerning that *some speeches will be designed to get more than one of the kinds of responses that have been discussed so far*. There are speeches that promote understanding, that reinforce ideas and feelings, that seek agreement, and that call for action—such responses can all be sought in one speech. What determines the purpose of such a speech is what the speaker hopes to accomplish. This will all be more understandable if we consider some examples.

Were a speaker to talk about the Egyptian pyramids, several purposes would be possible. Let us suppose that the purpose is "I want my audience to sign up for the special Christmas charter tour to Egypt." In such a speech the audience might be given information that would help them understand how the pyramids were built, be reinforced in their feelings that it would be good to get a complete break from the routine of school, be led to agree that a charter tour would be the most economical way they will ever get to make the trip, and, finally, be encouraged to sign up to go on the tour. In other words, a whole range of responses would have to precede the desired one in order for the speech to be successful.

How, to take other examples, could listeners be asked to agree that genetic research is safe and desirable if they do not understand the kinds of problems that are being investigated? How could listeners be expected to agree that nuclear energy is more efficient than electrical energy if they don't understand at least a few fundamental principles that explain how each works? And, to turn the examples around, how can a speaker get an audience to *understand* how energy for our daily lives is produced if the listeners are not *convinced* that such information is important to them? Getting an audience to understand how to conserve energy is very difficult if that audience doesn't agree that energy should be conserved.

Nevertheless, no matter what range of responses is called for, *what determines the purpose of the speech is the communicator's hoped-for end result.* Let's return to the speaker who wanted his audience to sign up for the tour: if the listeners' responses had been positive but had not gone as far as the speaker desired, the speaker would not have accomplished his purpose. If the listeners understood something about the construction of the pyramids but did not sign up for the tour, if they agreed that it would be fun or cheap to go but did not sign up, or if they enjoyed the talk very much but did not sign up, the speaker would not be satisfied. Even though he had promoted understanding, gained agreement, or stimulated enjoyment, if he had not signed up tour members, he had not accomplished his specific purpose. Communication it has been pointed out before, has the best chance of success if the speaker realizes what is possible and aims for the possible goal; that goal is the specific purpose.

It is sometimes more effective to try to accomplish a long-range aim through a whole series of speeches. To get changes in environmental protection laws, for example, many people spent years educating the public—merely trying to get people to understand the nature and gravity of the problem—before they could urge any direct action. In the classroom situation, a speaker may decide to use his or her speaking assignments as a sustained campaign aimed toward an ultimate goal. Perhaps the speaker may want to urge a revision in the school curriculum. The revisions cannot be assumed to be automatically popular. The speaker may want to devote a series of speeches to this general topic with a long-range goal in mind. That could lead to a series of specific purposes such as:

First speech: "I want my audience to understand how curriculum changes are brought about and curriculum decisions are made."

Second speech: "I want my audience to feel more strongly that the curriculum should meet their particular needs."

Third speech: "I want my audience to agree that requirements should include more courses that help them to write and speak more effectively."

Fourth speech: "I want my audience to volunteer to work for the Student Committee for an Improved Curriculum."

Such a sequence of speeches might give the speaker a better chance of bringing student listeners around to his or her position than would only one in which the speaker tries to do everything.

TESTING SPECIFIC PURPOSES

Because specific purposes are the foundations on which all strategy is built, a great deal of space is devoted in this chapter to describing them carefully. Let's consider some quick ways to test the specific purposes you will develop and try to be certain that you can evaluate purposes. Basically, there are three questions you can ask yourself to determine whether or not you have a sound, communicative purpose.

1. *Does the purpose call for a response?* Here are some statements that are *not* specific purposes:

"I want to talk about the need for tax reform."

"Tax reform."

"Ten reasons why taxes should be reformed."

"My views of tax reform."

"What you should know about your taxes."

These might be topics or titles, but, *they do not designate the response that the speaker wants from the audience.* The following indicates that the speaker has planned for a response from his or her listeners, and it thus qualifies as a specific purpose:

> "I want my audience to understand what a tax loophole is and how it
> works."

2. *Does the purpose reflect the realities of the situation?* The audience, the
setting, and the occasion should influence the purpose of a speech.

> "I want my audience to understand the history of Russia," is an ab-
> surdly broad topic to be given in a short period of time and is not a
> good specific purpose. "I want my audience to understand the
> major immediate causes of the Russian Revolution," is a much more
> manageable purpose. "I want my audience to take up skiing as a
> hobby" is *not* appropriate to a Senior Citizens Club, just as "I want
> my audience to plan for retirement" would *not* be appropriate for
> your college speech class.

The skiing speech might be appropriately given to a college speech class.
And, although it would probably be too late to call the attention of senior
citizens to the need for retirement planning, one could give them an appropriate
speech with the purpose: "I want my audience to understand the services and
opportunities that are available to retired persons."

3. *Is the purpose clear?* An audience can often be confused by a strategy that
grows out of a vague purpose. Communication is almost invariably unsuccessful when the speaker is not clear about what he wants to accomplish.

"I want my audience to understand about the Japanese tea ceremony," is
not a good purpose because, although it is couched in the appropriate language
of a purpose, it shows that the speaker does not know precisely what he or she
wants the audience to do. The phrase "understand about" is a clue that the
purpose lacks real clarity, that although the words suggest response (I want my
audience to . . .), the idea is as vague as that suggested by "talk about." The
speaker may want an audience to know how the ceremony is performed, how
persons are trained to do it, or why it is such an important ritual in Japanese life;
the speaker may even want listeners to go see a ceremony performed in a room
on campus. All these would be purposes that reflect a clearer conception on the
part of the communicator regarding the desired audience response.

What we have been concerned with in our discussion of specific purpose
has been the way a communicator lays the groundwork for a successful rhetori-

cal strategy. Audiences are also concerned with the purpose of messages aimed at them. A word needs to be said about listeners' purpose.

AGREEMENT AND CONFLICT IN SPEAKERS' AND LISTENERS' PURPOSES

The purposes of both speaker and listener are often compatible. Advertisers who are trying to persuade people to buy automobiles are listened to by people who, indeed, want to buy automobiles. A lecturer who wants the audience to understand the anatomy of the inner ear rightly expects to find that the medical students or audiology students who are listening want to understand.

Specifically stated, there are learning situations in which the listeners will want to understand what is said. There are persuasive situations in which listeners will feel better about their allegiances or values if they are reinforced; in which listeners will be introduced to and brought to agree with ideas that are consistent with their own beliefs and attitudes; and in which listeners will be urged to take actions that will enhance and fulfill their lives. The listener needs to recognize that it is often in his or her interest, as well as the speaker's, to be informed, persuaded, and entertained. It has already been stated that listening is an active process. *Sometimes that process involves the listener working hard to help the speaker do what he or she has set out to do.* The listener cannot be, and cannot expect to be, acted upon; he or she may sometimes have to overcome boredom, fatigue, initial lack of interest, or any other distracting factors, and interact with the speaker and the message as constructively as possible so that all parties in the public-speaking situation can be satisfied.

On the other hand, *the listener does need to be aware that his or her purpose can be in conflict with a speaker's*. It may be true, for example, that a listener may want to buy a car and that a speaker may want to sell one. But the salesman may want to make the best profit possible from the sale and the listener may wish to spend as little as possible. The listener, for her own defense, needs to define precisely what it is that she wants to accomplish in the communication exchange and judge the message that is directed at her by that goal.

In public speaking, of course, the listener can't always think ahead. When you come into a speech class, you are not sure of what topics will be discussed that day. Faced with a speech on the role of women in intercollegiate athletics, for example, different listeners will have widely different initial responses on which to begin to form any purpose at all. The speaker will, if he or she hopes to be successful, try to relate the speech to the audience. As listeners perceive and evaluate such efforts, they can begin to decide what they ought to be getting out of the speech.

If, for instance, a speech on pollution control legislation is given, such factors as the listener's awareness of national problems or the listener's geographic location will shape his or her initial interest in the question. If the speaker is successful in engaging the listener's attention so that the listener begins to be aware of ways that pollution is directly harming him or her, at that point the listener may begin to form a purpose, such as, "I am listening to this message in order to find out how I can stop pollution in this town." Now the listener's purpose, unlike the speaker's, will be somewhat open-ended and subject to some modification as the speech goes on. Nevertheless, *to try to get the most out of the speech as possible, the listener will attempt to achieve the focus and concentration that a purpose will help to provide.*

Whatever purpose the listener finally evolves, he or she should be cautious in deciding whether or not it has been accomplished. One reason for there being legislation to protect people who sign contracts with salespeople, which gives them a certain period of time to revoke the agreement, is that we often need time to think over our decisions. The speaker may well press for an immediate response to his or her message. The careful listener, however, will try to stave off any irrevocable action on the basis of a speech he or she has just heard until there is adequate time to reflect on whether or not the listener's purpose has, indeed, been achieved.

PRINCIPLES INTO PRACTICE: A SUMMARY

HOW TO DESIGN A GOOD SPEECH PURPOSE

The design and development of speeches is governed by a series of choices— what we call a *strategy*—based on a *communicative purpose that grows out of and reflects the situation.* Rhetorical purposes can generally be described as informative, persuasive, or entertaining, and they are further refined into specific purposes for each communication event. *Specific purposes state the desired audience response and are the foundation upon which a speech is built.* The listener actively and cautiously creates his or her purposes in a public-communication situation and assesses messages in the light of this purpose.

At this point, you should be able, with the help of the analysis of the audience and the total situation, to devise a specific purpose or a series of specific purposes for speeches you will deliver in class. You should also be able to understand more fully the problem that a communicator faces in making public speaking purposeful and be able to evaluate more adequately his or her purposes.

In order to develop a good specific purpose for a speech, then, the speaker should take the following steps:

1. Understand how the situation influences the purpose of your speech.
2. Decide whether the situation and the topic calls for a speech that will try to
   - Gain audience understanding (informative speech)
   - Elicit stronger feelings from an audience (persuasive speech to stimulate)
   - Gain audience agreement (persuasive speech to convince)
   - Lead the audience to take direct action (persuasive speech to actuate)
   - Produce audience enjoyment (entertaining speech).
3. Devise a specific purpose that calls for an audience response.
4. Be certain that the specific purpose reflects the realities of the situation.
5. Make sure that your purpose is clear and straightforward.

We will turn in the following chapters to a consideration of how appropriate material is gathered and how ideas are fashioned and developed so that a reasonable strategy, supported by adequate tactics, can help the speaker to communicate effectively.

CHAPTER 5

DISCOVERING RELEVANT MATERIAL: RESEARCH PURPOSES AND PROCEDURES

After studying this chapter you should understand:

- How material is gathered to support ideas in your speech.

- What the limits and possibilities are of the speaker using himself or herself as a resource.

- What the guidelines are for conducting interviews in order to get relevant information from others.

- How to use published resources effectively in gathering material.

SEARCHING FOR RELEVANT MATERIAL

One of the major problems that faces any speaker is how to sift through the available material on any given topic and choose that which should be used in a speech. In an evening news broadcast, for example, the editor responsible for preparing a story on a speech given by the President of the United States must select from that speech those elements that he considers to be newsworthy. He must characterize an entire speech of perhaps twenty to forty minutes in a space of two to three minutes. If you were to write a letter home describing what you had done over the preceding week you obviously could not give an hour-by-hour, day-by-day description of everything. You would select those events that you think would be most interesting or appropriate for the person you're writing to.

Anyone who wishes to prepare himself or herself to speak in public must engage in a process of gathering, evaluating, and choosing material that is well-suited to the speech. Always remember that *the principal standard for judging whether or not material is relevant to begin with is the standard of purpose: the specific purpose designates the audience response, and material that helps to achieve that response is relevant material.*

GATHERING INFORMATION: AN OVERVIEW

The speaker can find the sources of relevant material in himself or herself, in others, and in published sources.

In Chapter 2 we discussed *the speaker as a resource* for his or her own speech. A person who is going to speak will have some ideas, some knowledge, and some very specific kinds of information about the topic upon which he or she will talk. In searching for relevant material, then, the speaker starts with himself or herself. He or she begins to think systematically about what information is readily available from his or her own experience.

Although this self-analysis is very important and necessary, the speaker must be very careful in avoiding two extremes. He or she can't rely exclusively on what he or she knows, on one hand, or, on the other hand, dismiss the topic because not enough is known. Speakers sometimes think that they already have a speech in their head and that they don't need to know any more than they do. They will assume that, somehow, they should be able to get up and talk without preparation, and that is a mistake. Furthermore, they will find that the process of preparing themselves to speak becomes a useless exercise if they do not grow intellectually during that process. On the other hand, some speakers will discard a topic because they think they don't know enough about it. All this is to say that *one needs to assess one's own personal experience, but not to rely on it exclusively.*

Relevant material can also be gathered through contact with other people, either by writing to them or interviewing them. As with all other aspects of the communication process, the speaker must first establish a clear specific purpose before any interviewing takes place or inquiries are made. It would be foolish, for example, to go to a University Registrar and say, "I want to give a speech on grades. Please tell me what you think about grades." That is such a vague and broad request that will probably produce either too much information—much of which is extraneous—or no information at all. The speaker has to be prepared with specific kinds of questions designed to elicit specific information needed to accomplish the specific purpose. If a speaker has a set of tentative ideas, then what he or she is looking for is *information that will help make those ideas more believable or understandable.* The speaker must also address himself or herself to the right person, the person who has the kind of information needed. Other people can serve as important sources, then, but the speaker must be careful to choose the right people and to know exactly what he or she wants to get from those people.

Published sources will, of course, provide most of the material that a speaker needs. Anyone who wants to prepare himself or herself to speak must learn to use the resources of the library. Popular periodicals—newspapers and magazines, for instance—will provide a variety of types of evidence that a speaker can use to support ideas. Specialized publications in a wide range of academic and technical fields can also provide information on specific topics. The library's card catalogue should be used to find books of general interest on a topic, and collections of special publications such as U.S. government reports should also be used as an important source.

One learns best how to gather supporting material by actually doing it. *The more one uses the library, the more one learns how to use it efficiently.* As one searches for relevant material, one should remember the stipulation that relevance is defined by purpose, so that the hundreds of articles, documents, or books on a general issue should be examined and possibly used only to the extent to which they will promote the speaker's goal. Furthermore, as speakers search the relevant material, they will find specific kinds of evidence that will help them to communicate more effectively, that is, specific kinds of support for which they should look as they sift through all the relevant material. The precise nature of that support is the topic of the following two chapters.

There are also intellectual and ethical considerations in selecting and evaluating sources for a speech. An article written in a magazine or periodical is not a speech. Simply to stand up and tell what's in a story in a recent Reader's Digest, for example, is, first, intellectually limiting. Retelling a printed story does not involve the speaker at all in the real process of preparing to speak (and the audience might well have read the piece and thus will learn nothing new or original). Second, such a practice is ethically unacceptable, since it is essentially plagiarism, stealing the ideas and material from the original author. Third, repeating what is in an article is not likely to be effective as communication, since the article is not adapted to those real, specific people sitting in front of a speaker. The article is addressed to a wide general audience with much more varied experiences, tastes, interests, needs, and so forth. Furthermore, relying on one article or relying on someone else's summary or digest of an article or series of articles is likely to bias the speaker in a way in which he or she might not be aware. Only when the speaker herself has looked at the wide range of sources available can she appreciate and understand the differing points of view about a particular issue. Only then can she begin to make independent and informed judgments.

There is a saying that everyone has a right to an opinion. In a free society that is true, but it is true in the sense that everyone has the right to be stupid, or everyone has the right to be ignorant without being arrested for it. Although we all have a right to an opinion, we have no guarantee that the opinion will be regarded as sensible or will be taken seriously. *Only an informed opinion is worth considering.* The speaker has the responsibility to survey sources in such a way as to be able to form such an opinion; the listener has the responsibility to weigh opinions carefully, discarding those that are based on unreliable or insufficient sources.

With this overview of research in mind, let's consider specific ways to go about gathering the material that a speaker needs.

INTERVIEWING: GATHERING INFORMATION FROM OTHERS

What is the key to a successful interview? The key is planning carefully, knowing what you want to do and how to do it. Here are some guidelines for carrying out a successful interview.

1. *Know what it is you want to find out.* Remember that you have a purpose in speaking. You are not going to "talk about grading practices." You may want your audience to understand what rules must be followed by all instructors giving grades or how criteria for grades vary, or you may want your audience to agree that a new grading system is needed. Depending on your purpose, you will find information that may or may not be relevant; you will not really care about the technical problems of recording, distributing, changing grades, and the like, if you want your audience to understand how criteria are applied to a student's work in order to determine grades. If you were advocating setting up an entirely new system, however, you might want to examine such considerations. So, it's important for you to determine what kind of information you're after before you talk to anyone.

2. *Plan questions that will help you get at what you want.* It is fatal to an interviewer to ask vague, rambling questions or to ask questions that lead the interviewee to "yes" or "no" answers. Questions such as, "What do you think of the grading system?" or, "Is the present system fair?" are not likely to be answered with specific information or informed opinion. Questions such as "What criteria are used to determine students' grades?" or, "Are criteria applied in the same way to all students?" may be much better in getting you the kind of information you want. You need to think of questions that elicit information that you need. What you are trying to do can also help you determine to whom you can talk.

3. *Interview the person who will be most likely to give you what you want and need.* Again, your purpose should help you here. If you want to know about the problems of recording grades and sending them to other institutions, the Registrar may be a useful source. The Registrar, however, will not be very helpful in addressing such academic questions as how standards for grading are applied in different sections of the same course. In that case, a department chairperson or several instructors might be better people with whom to talk. If

there is someone available to you who is an expert in some aspect of the question (perhaps a professor in Education has written a book on the problem of grading), such a person could be useful to you. Before you interview anyone, you should try to find out something about the person in relation to your topic. Some departments, for example, may have lots of sections of the same course, so chairpersons of those departments could give useful information on the problem of standardizing grades. If you interview an Education professor who is an expert, read his or her book first. Sometimes, you may not be sure who is to be interviewed. In such cases, talking first with a friend from another department or an instructor you have had for a course might be a useful way of identifying potential interviewees.

4. *Be sensitive to the possible reactions of the person you are interviewing.* Use common sense in arranging and carrying out the interview. Matters of courtesy should be observed, such as making an appointment for the interview ahead of time; telling the person what the interview is about; asking his or her permission before the interview if you may tape record it; being on time for the interview; ending the interview within the allotted time. You would be well advised not to use a famous investigative reporter as your model. Although you should press for the information you want, asking follow-up questions for clarity or for additional information, you should, at the same time, maintain a generally neutral stance. This means that you will avoid an argument with the person being interviewed or not take actions or put questions in such a way that the person will be overly defensive or hostile. Such questions as "Why can't instructors in English try to be fair to all students when they grade essays?" and "Why is grading in this department always so subjective?" and "Why can't the Registrar get grades to students faster?" are not designed to elicit the most information, put the interviewee at ease, and make him or her more cooperative.

In order to be sensitive to the person you are interviewing, you need to listen very carefully. Make sure you understand what he or she is saying. Restate ideas and get confirmation if you're not sure. Check exact quotes, if you plan to use any, with the person. One thing that is crucial to remember is that *the interview is one means of gathering information; it is not a way to confirm your own prejudices.* Listening, then, also implies keeping an open mind. Maybe you will learn something that can change or modify your own position.

5. *Review your notes (or tape recording) as soon as possible after the interview is over.* All of us have lapses in memory over time. A short-hand note we make may not be clear when we read it later. Get the important points down clearly on paper when the interview is over and determine where the information you have gathered fits in the speech in relation to your purpose.

USING PUBLISHED SOURCES

Keeping in mind the point made previously that the speaker is searching for material that will help him or her achieve the specific purpose of the speech, we will review some of the questions you need answered as you carry out your research and some of the most common published sources that are available to you.

Information can be gathered from direct interviews as well as from published sources.

HOW DO I FIND OUT WHAT HAS BEEN WRITTEN ON MY TOPIC?

You can consult the card catalog. Entries in the card catalog are by author, title, and subject. So you can look under the subject heading for materials.

You can consult special guides and bibliographies. When consulting guides, *The Reader's Guide to Periodical Literature* is a very important source. There are also specialized bibliographies on most topics. You can consult a guide such as Besterman's *Bibliography of Bibliographies* to get lists of specialized bibliographies. There are encyclopedias of all kinds; most students have looked at the general ones such as the *Encyclopedia Americana* or the *World Book*, but there are many others that deal with specific topics such as art, music, religion, philosophy, or education. Most of these will give you bibliographical material at the end of articles as well as specific information that could be useful.

HOW CAN I GET SPECIFIC INFORMATION THAT RELATES TO MY TOPIC?

You can look at special indexes. Besides the *Reader's Guide*, which lists articles from more popular literature such as magazines, there is a special index for most subject areas. The *Education Index*, for example, would be a good one to consult on the grading topic. There are also indexes in such areas as medicine, agriculture, business, and art. Newspaper indexes are very helpful when you are looking for stories on specific topics and getting precise information on how events happened. The most widely circulated newspaper and the one with an index that goes back the farthest is probably the *New York Times*, but several other papers around the country have indexes and are held by libraries.

You can look at books that summarize facts. *Facts on File* is an especially useful source that summarizes news events on a weekly basis and is put together annually in a *Yearbook*. Almanacs such as the *World Almanac* or the *Information Please Almanac* also provide useful specific information.

You can check sources about specific individuals. There are many biographical sources that will tell you about people in whom you are interested. *The Dictionary of American Biography* and *Who's Who* in America will provide biographical information on Americans from the past and in the present. There are several other such guides to biographies, such as *Current Biography,* a weekly publication that is also collected annually, that will give you much information on public figures. The *Biography Index* will help you find special-ized biographic material.

HOW CAN I FIND A SPECIAL SOURCE THAT I NEED?

Try the card catalog again. If you have an author or a title to look up, you can probably find it here. If, for example, you want to read what an education expert has written about your topic before you interview him, go to the card catalog.

IF I GET STUCK OR AM CONFUSED ABOUT WHAT TO DO NEXT, WHAT DO I DO?

Ask the librarian. This is simple advice that is worth repeating: *ask the librarian!* Librarians are professionals who are there to and who are willing to help you. They don't expect you to be knowledgeable; *their* job is to be knowledgeable. Of course, *your instructor* will also be willing to help. But, he or she is not right there on the scene and will not be as well informed about specific sources and their availability as the Librarian would. But your instructor should be able to answer questions about the relevance or adequacy of material that you are gathering.

PREPARING YOURSELF THROUGH RESEARCH

Surveying all the possible starting places for gathering information for a speech may seem overwhelming to a beginning speaker. But, there are two important ideas to keep in mind.

First, research gets easier as you do more of it. When you begin to learn such simple things as where materials are located, and what you can and can't find in the card catalog, and when you have consulted different indexes a few times, the process itself will become smoother.

Second, adequate researching of a topic is hard work. Remember that preparing yourself to speak is not a quick and easy task. There are no shortcuts in acquiring knowledge and using it properly. As you do research you learn more about your particular subject. Gathering information may even cause you to change your position on an issue. And gathering information takes time. You just can't let yourself think that if you reserve a few hours on the night before the speech is to be given, you'll be able to prepare yourself. You won't. If you have been reading this book carefully, you will know by now that giving a public speech doesn't just mean getting up and talking about something. Giving a public speech means getting yourself ready, and an essential part of getting ready is gathering material.

RELEVANCE AND INTEGRATION: PUTTING WHAT YOU HAVE LEARNED TOGETHER

In order to make what you have gathered most useful, you need to keep it in a useful form, decide what needs to go into your speech and what doesn't, and put what you have in a sensible order. There are many systems for recording material you have gathered. Most commonly, index cards, with pertinent information on them, are used. You arrange information according to the way you work, but here are some suggestions:

1. *Put a heading on the card that will quickly tell you about the relevance of the information.* One of the best ways to organize card headings would probably be according to ideas you will develop in the speech. For instance, in the hypothetical speech on grading that we've been using as an example, you might have such card headings as Objectivity and Subjectivity in Grading; Grades and the Job Search; and Different Grading Systems. The purpose of your speech should always be kept in your mind, and that purpose will help you develop appropriate headings. Of course, as you go on with your research, you will probably develop new headings and change others.

2. *Record accurately and completely the information you want.* If you are summarizing a point made, you should do so clearly so that you will remember it when you later use the information. If you are directly quoting someone, be sure to indicate that you are, so that you will know that this information can possibly serve as testimony, and so that you will not appropriate the words of someone else as your own. Be sure that you get all the necessary information on the source as you use it—author, title, date, and page are necessary—and you shouldn't waste time by having to go back to anything (if you can find it after the passage of time).

You must keep careful track of what you have so that you will be able to determine what to do with it. Tidiness is not one of the most sublime virtues, but it certainly helps when you are doing research, since sloppy recordkeeping will cause you more work and more grief than you need and can lead you to be less prepared than you should be.

Let's assume you have done a good job in gathering and recording the material you will need. How do you determine what precisely to use in the speech and where it will fit? This is partially answered in our previous discussion of purpose: what is relevant is what advances the aim of your speech. However, you still need to know more before you can determine what is most useful to you and exactly where it ought to be in the speech. This subject is covered in the next three chapters, and you should probably read them carefully before you begin research or as you are doing it. In looking ahead, we can partly discern the answer to the question: What do I do with all this material? Briefly put, you, the speaker, should use your material to make ideas understandable and believable through a reasonable argument and by involving the audience. To do so, you should carefully structure material so that ideas are supported and so that each piece of evidence used fits into the total scheme of the speech. The following chapters will help you to understand how to accomplish this task.

PRINCIPLES INTO PRACTICE: A SUMMARY

HOW TO DO RESEARCH ON YOUR SPEECH TOPIC

This chapter has stressed the importance of thorough research and has laid out procedures for carrying out that research. Gathering information is both a learning experience for the speaker and a means whereby he or she can be more effective as a communicator. If it is done well, research can provide the raw material out of which the speaker fashions an intellectually respectable and communicatively effective piece of work. In doing research for a speech topic, a speaker should take the following steps:

1. Carry out a realistic assessment of your own resources.
2. Interview people who have knowledge, experience, or both, related to your speech topic.
3. Carefully and thoroughly examine printed sources.
4. Use a system of note-taking that will indicate to you the relevance of the information you gather.
5. Record information accurately and completely.

CHAPTER 6

PREPARING A REASONABLE ARGUMENT: SUPPORTING IDEAS

After studying this chapter you should understand:

- What the principal types of communicative evidence are: examples, statistics, testimony, and comparisons.

- How to test communicative evidence.

- How to use the communicative methods of repetition, restatement, and visual presentation effectively.

- How to determine when an argument is rhetorically sound.

- What the relationship is among premises, evidence, and conclusions.

- What the difference is between *reasoning* and *rationalizing*.

MAKING IDEAS UNDERSTANDABLE AND BELIEVABLE

Supporting ideas is something that we normally do every day. When we urge a friend to see a movie that we've seen by telling him that it is very good, we are likely to add something like, "It's your kind of humor," or "It has a lot of action," or "Harry was with me, and he thought it was great, too," or "It's as funny as a Woody Allen film." If we're recommending a specific course to someone we know, we'll probably tell the person something specific about the course, such as what readings are required, indicating why such a course would appeal to that person. If we're explaining to a friend how to get to our house when he comes to visit during the school vacation, we'll probably draw him a map. If someone has borrowed a book and you want that person to understand that she must leave it at a place that is easily accessible to you, you might repeat the directions two or three times just to make sure that the person has it right.

In other words, in our routine communication situations we develop ideas—we bring in material to make those ideas believable or understandable—when we feel that it is necessary. The necessity for the material depends on the situation, the audience, and the complexity of the idea itself.

COMMUNICATIVE EVIDENCE

In the previous chapter on gathering relevant information, it was pointed out that the speaker is searching for information that will help him or her achieve the desired response to the speech. Let's turn now to specific kinds of material that will be helpful to the speaker in achieving the specific purpose of the speech.

There are four major kinds of evidence that are useful in supporting ideas: *examples, statistics, testimony, and comparisons.*

EXAMPLE

One of the very real problems faced by a speaker is how to take an idea or a concept that is abstract and make it concrete, how to take something that is generalized and make it specific. Using examples is one of the most effective ways of doing just that.

Examples are used naturally in informal kinds of communication settings. If you were to say to a friend that a particular course is very interesting or very boring, very relevant or very removed from your experience, very difficult or very easy, you would quite normally use an example to explain what you meant. You might describe a test, the content of a lecture, or an anecdote told in class or another bit of information that would make the generalization clear and understandable.

The use of an example to make abstractions real is the basis for much of the artistic and practical communication that exists. Often a novel or a play, for example, will attempt to describe how people live, how they think, or how they react to crisis by creating specific kinds of characters that take on a symbolic function for a whole group of people. One can talk about the atrocities committed during World War II by indicating the numbers of people killed or imprisoned. The enormity of the crime, however, becomes more apparent through the experience of reading books or watching film versions of real and fictional accounts such as *Playing For Time,* or *Sophie's Choice,* or *The Diary of Anne Frank.* Characters are seen as people; Anne Frank, for example, is not a number but a person who hid for years from Nazi persecutors only to be discovered at last and die in a prison camp. In this case, a real little girl—an example, if you will—makes the abstraction of numbers a concrete thing. Charitable organizations often use the example as a way of translating the abstractions of poverty, distress, and misfortune into reality; they might use such specific examples as a specific family made homeless by a flood, a specific child who will not get enough to eat, or a specific person stricken with a crippling disease.

There are two principle kinds of examples that a speaker might use to support ideas: the specific example and the hypothetical example. Either kind may be extended or brief.

A specific example deals with a real case; it is something that actually happened that can be pointed to by the speaker directly. The following excerpt from a student speech shows the use of a specific example.

> Fad diets not only waste your money, they can be dangerous. Last semester a girl in our dormitory tried to live on nothing but water and eggs. One day she passed out in a class and had to be taken to the hospital. Not only had the diet done her body a great deal of harm, but she had broken her arm and knocked out a tooth when she fainted and fell against a chair in the class.

Political figures who want to demonstrate to an audience that the generalizations they make are translated into the lives and by the experiences of ordinary Americans, often turn to specific examples. Ronald Reagan, for example, in his speech accepting the nomination for president in 1980, gave a series of specific examples designed to support his assertion that the Carter administration had a "sorry" record in foreign affairs. He mentioned that:

> A Soviet combat brigade trains in Cuba, just 90 miles from our shores.
>
> A Soviet army invasion occupies Afghanistan, further threatening our vital interests in the Middle East.
>
> . . .
>
> And incredibly, more than 50, as you've been told from this platform so eloquently already, more than 50 of our fellow Americans have been held captive for over eight months by a dictatorial foreign power that holds us up to ridicule before the world.

One can see specific examples spun out in persuasive settings in order to make wide-spread problems more concrete, as when people who have suffered under present circumstances testify before Congressional committees considering specific legislation. When President Clinton signed the Family Leave Bill, standing at his side was a woman whose testimony before Congress served as a persuasive specific example of the need for legislation: in her committee appearance she had described how she lost her job because she had to take time off to care for her child dying of cancer.

A hypothetical example is one that represents an action or an event that could very easily and plausibly take place in the way it is described, but the example is not of any particular incident or event. Although it is in a sense a made up example, it must not seem exaggerated or distorted in order to be effective. The following shows the use of the hypothetical example.

> Everyone has suffered from careless and irresponsible actions of others. Imagine how angry you would feel, for example, if you got up one morning, hurrying to get to an early class, only to find that someone had parked and blocked your car; or how you would react if you got out of that somehow, managed to arrive at class just in time, and discovered that the instructor didn't show up. It's when these kinds of things start happening to us that we begin to wonder if there are any unselfish people left in the world.

Angelina Grimke (whose speech may be found in the Appendix) sought to characterize the experiences of Northerners who refused to condemn slavery based on their contact with southern slave holders. She did not single out any particular persons; rather, she pictured a hypothetical group who exemplified their reactions. "Many persons go to the South for a season," she said, "and are hospitably entertained in the parlor and at the table of the slaveholder. They never enter the huts of the slaves; they know nothing of the dark side of the picture, and they return home with praise on their lips of the generous character of those with whom they have tarried."

Another instance of the use of the hypothetical is found in FBI Director William Webster's speech (also in the Appendix) when he explains the test for entrapment in hypothetical terms: "If based upon the facts the jury determines that the defendant had a preexisting willingness to violate the law, the entrapment defense will fail." He is not discussing here a specific case; he is explaining what happens in a hypothetical one.

Because things that are real are so much easier with which to identify, the example, then, can be a very potent means of support. Accordingly, the speaker must use examples properly and the listener has to exercise a great deal of care in evaluating arguments supported by examples. An example must be tested in order to determine whether or not it is really doing what it says it is doing. *The best test of an example is the test of typicality.*

If a speaker is trying to support a specific generalization by the use of examples, then a listener must ask himself or herself whether these examples really do represent *the normal course of events.* If someone were to describe, as a specific example, a newspaper article that he had read in which a student was arrested for shoplifting and then argued from that example that students didn't have any values, the listener should be very skeptical. Such a specific example simply does not support such a sweeping generalization. It would be as if one argued that because one college professor was arrested for hit-and run driving, all professors were criminals. Actually, such distortions of the use of the specific example produce stereotyping, in which an entire group is said to behave in the same way as one member of that group behaved on one specific occasion. It is up to the listener, then, to look very carefully at the relationship between an example and the conclusion to which that example leads.

The listener should also feel compelled to make a judgment about the importance of an example, as well as typicality. That is to say, sometimes an example will demonstrate that certain actions can take place but not necessarily that they will frequently take place; yet that might be enough to support a generalization. If, for instance, one argued that a cafeteria in a dormitory should be closed pending a thorough investigation by the Board of Health, and if one supported that assertion with three specific examples of students who had suffered from ptomaine poisoning in a week, then whether or not those cases were typical might be a secondary consideration. Even if only 3 out of 500 were poisoned, the seriousness of the matter would be more crucial than the number of representative cases.

STATISTICS

Statistics are a way of demonstrating *how some things are related to other things.* They may tell us the typicality of an occurrence and thus validate the examples used. In a speech dealing with the problems of rehabilitating criminals, for instance, a speaker gave an extended example dealing with the experience of a young man who left prison only to become a repeat offender and return to prison. This example was coupled with statistical information demonstrating how frequently this kind of experience was repeated.

Statistics also might be used to show *cause-to-effect relationships,* or at least correlations between certain phenomena, as in a speech dealing with the relationship between smoking and health, for example, that used statistical information to show that the incidence of lung cancer increased as the number of cigarettes smoked increased.

Statistical information can be helpful in pointing out *trends over time.* For example, we can appreciate better how quickly and significantly the price of building a new home has increased if we can see the year-by-year costs. The contention that crime is becoming a more serious problem in suburban and rural areas demands that the crime rate over a period of time be presented and specific information on the number of crimes committed contrasted. The contention that medical science has made significant strides forward in the last decade calls for use of supporting material that demonstrates changes in such matters as life expectancy, control of communicable disease, number of hours lost from work due to illness, and so forth.

Statistics, then, are one important way of making ideas more understandable and believable; they should, however, be used responsibly by the speaker and viewed critically by the listener. One should not assume that a statistic "proves" something conclusively. It is part of the total structure of evidence and should be considered in the light of other supporting material. *The speaker and the listener both must recognize that statistics can sometimes be misleading.* "Average," for example, is a notoriously vague concept, even though it seems to give an air of statistical weight when it is used. Averages can be computed in different ways, such as by adding up a list of figures and dividing by the number of figures (the mean), by choosing the figure that occurs most often (the mode), or by choosing the figure that is the midpoint between the two extreme figures (the median). These three methods of computing "average" may lead to quite different conclusions.

Assume, for example, that there are two small businesses in a town and that the owner of each is trying to get a bright young person to go to work in that business. Mr. Brown could argue, "Since the average salary at my store is $1600 per year more than at Smith's store, you had better come work for me." Mr. Smith might tell you, "My employees make, on the average, $2000 more per year than do Brown's, so you'd be better off working for me." Who is telling the truth? Well, the distressing thing is that, strictly speaking, they both are. But they are using different methods to calculate "average," and only when you find out the way they have arrived at their conclusions can you begin to tell which statistic gives you a better idea of what's really happening, and who might be misleading, although technically "true." Let's look at the list of salaries for each business, the first in both cases being the salary of the owner himself:

BROWN	SMITH	
1. $35,000	1. $20,000	
2. 10,000	2. 12,000	
3. 8,000	3. 10,000	
4. 7,500	4. 9,000	
5. 7,500	5. 9,000	
Mean = $13,600	$12,000	
Median = $ 8,000	$10,000	
Mode = $ 7,500	$ 9,000	

Mr. Brown took the *mean* (by adding all the salaries up and dividing by 5) as the average and therefore came out with a comparison of $13,600 to $12,000 in his favor. Mr. Smith took the median (the salary in the middle; as many above it as below it) as his average and came out with a $2000 advantage in his favor. He could also have taken the *mode* (the salary that occurred most often) and fared even better: a $2500 advantage. When you examine the data, it becomes clear that Smith's workers really do better; they obviously make more money on the whole than do Brown's workers, and Smith's median average seems most clearly to state the real comparison. Brown has given a mathematically accurate "average," but it is a misleading one.

During the 1992 Presidential campaign, both candidates tried to use statistics to bolster their own views of how the economy was faring. There was particular controversy over what Governor Clinton claimed was the success he had had in creating jobs in his own state of Arkansas. The Governor, using statistics derived for the last two years, pointed to the dramatic increases in jobs while the Bush campaign, using statistics covering a ten-year period, claimed that Arkansas had fared worse than the rest of the nation. Now, both sides were "right." But both sides were using a different set of figures to prove their point. The media consistently pointed out that the two campaigns were projecting how much programs would cost, whether or not they would lead to tax increases, how many people would be employed, and the like, based on statistics that each side had carefully selected to reinforce its own positions.

All this shows that *statistics must be approached cautiously*. If the listener can ascertain where the statistics came from and how they have been computed, he or she will have a much better idea of how seriously to take them. If, as will be the case most of the time, this is not possible, both the speaker and listener should evaluate carefully the place of statistics in the total pattern of evidence.

TESTIMONY

The impact that a speaker's ethos or personal appeal can have on an audience was discussed in Chapter 2. One effective way of making ideas persuasive is, in a sense, to borrow the ethos of someone to whom the audience responds positively.

Again, this is a common practice in everyday communication settings. For example, if you are studying with a friend for an exam, and you disagree over a specific point, the disagreement could be settled by one of you asserting that, "Jack (who is generally regarded as the best note taker in class) let me copy this from his notes, so I'm sure it is right." In public speaking, *testimony by authority* is one of the most frequently used forms of support when one is dealing with issues. For one thing, it is literally impossible for most of us to make very well informed judgments on many issues. We just don't or can't take the time to study all the available information, and we often don't have the necessary technical background or personal experience to make a reasoned judgment. In that case, we rely on those who we regard as experts or on those in whom we have some particular reason to trust.

When his opponents raised the question of whether or not a man who had not served in the military was capable of being the Commander-in-Chief, Governor Clinton brought out a retired Admiral and former Chairman of the Joint Chiefs of Staff to testify that the Governor was qualified to hold that position. When opponents of lifting the ban on gays in the military tried to thwart the new President's plan, they relied heavily on the fact that the military experts—the Joint Chiefs—were against the move.

The speaker, then, calls on the writings and statements of such persons to influence his or her audience. It is, of course, essential that the authority being quoted be considered an authority by the audience. It is all very well to use the testimony of a brilliant nuclear physicist regarding the future of scientific research. If the audience, however, has no recognition of the name, its impact will not be very great. One has heard stories of the unscrupulous, and not very bright, debater who felt he needed a quote at a specific point in his presentation and simply asked his roommate to say, "I support this plan strongly," and then inserted in his speech, "Harry Jones says that he supports this plan strongly." This type of verbal sleight-of-hand is really not very effective, or honest, because the audience simply does not respond to Harry Jones.

The listener needs to evaluate carefully testimony that is presented by a speaker. The listener evaluating testimony should raise certain questions about its nature in order to determine whether it is or is not persuasive.

The first question that might be asked of testimony is: *How timely is it?* People's ideas change as a situation changes. For example, a political figure may have commented on the relations between the United States and China in 1956 in a way that would not represent that person's views in 1993. We've all probably had the experience of finding that an initial impression we had about a person, an event, or an experience in our lives has changed over time. Perhaps the first few months you were at school might have been an unhappy time for you. If asked then about college life, you might have testified negatively. A year later, as the situation changed, you might have testified quite differently. It is important, therefore, to understand the situation in which testimony is given.

A situation might include not only time, but another aspect, which raises another question: *What is the context out of which the testimony comes?* Suppose, for example, a noted financial expert had written this: "Mining stocks are generally a good investment these days as long as one avoids any association with companies that have been in business for less than two or three years." Any speaker, even one representing a company that had been in business for six months, could say that according to the noted financial expert "Mining stocks are a good investment these days." Now, the financial expert did say this, but the context out of which it grows clearly suggests a meaning that does not support the speaker's contention that his company's stock is a good investment.

Perhaps the most critical factor in evaluating testimony is the nature of the authority. The question to be asked is: *Is the person being quoted a relevant authority?* One of the most common misuses of testimony by authority in public communication occurs in advertising. Often someone who is an authority in one field is used to give testimony in a field in which he or she has no particular expertise or experience. A famous tennis player, for example, may know a great deal about the best kind of equipment to use for tennis, but he or she does not necessarily know more about what kind of toothpaste is best to use or what kind of razor blade shaves the closest. This sort of *shift of authority* occurs frequently and should be avoided by a speaker and received critically by a listener. A person may have won a Nobel Prize in physics, which would make him an expert in certain scientific areas and his testimony in those areas particularly relevant. But that Nobel Prize does not necessarily qualify him to be an expert commentator on political events. If, on the question of technical problems associated with limiting strategic arms a speaker wishes to use scientific testimony, the opinion of the Nobel laureate could be entirely appropriate. However, when the speaker calls on the views of the same scientist to support her position on whether we can or cannot trust the Russians to live up to obligations, then the question has shifted to a historical and political one, and that might be a question on which the scientist cannot give the most pertinent expert testimony.

In all these areas of concern, it might not always be possible for the listener to make an informed judgment about testimony. The listener might not always be able to tell when the testimony was given, what the total context was, or even how expert the authority was. However, the listener's goal in this case as in all cases in which evidence is evaluated should be to view the evidence with some skepticism and accept it tentatively pending more information.

COMPARISON

One of the principal ways that human beings learn things is by comparison. We compare the unknown to the known. We look for similarities between a new experience and an old experience. We try to see ways in which new problems that need to be solved are like old ones that have been solved.

One of the most frequently used ways to make ideas more understandable or believable is *by comparing the familiar with the unfamiliar.* If a speaker, for example, were giving a speech in which she hoped to help the audience understand styles of architecture, she would be well advised to compare an unknown but famous architectural example with a more familiar one from among the buildings on campus or in a nearby city or town. Or if a speaker were discussing some national financial problems, he might compare these with a type of personal financial problem that college students normally face. One of the most striking uses of comparison occurred in the 1992 presidential campaign. Ross Perot, in countering the Clinton campaign's focus on how well the Governor had done in Arkansas, told voters that to claim one who had succeeded in running Arkansas would likewise succeed in governing the United States was like comparing the successful management of a "Mom and Pop" grocery store to overseeing Wal-Mart.

If a speaker wished to condemn a course of action, he or she might well compare that course of action with one taken in the past that led to unhappy results. Again, the 1992 presidential campaign affords good examples of this tactic. The Bush campaign constantly harked back to the election of Jimmy Carter in 1976, arguing that the election of another Southern Democratic governor with little national experience would lead to the economic and foreign policy problems that Republicans claimed marred the Carter Administration. On the other side, Clinton supporters reminded the electorate that George Bush had made promises before ("Read my lips. No new Taxes.") that he had failed to keep—with devastating effects on the economy.

Comparisons are often made in order to *simplify difficult concepts*. We have all experienced traffic control first-hand. We've seen and found it relatively easy to understand how a policeman at an intersection manages the flow of cars. In some ways, this management is like certain kinds of functions performed by the brain. A speaker who wants to explain the process by which the brain controls specific action might compare it with the way in which the traffic policeman controls traffic. Sometimes a complicated organizational system may be compared to the better-known system of a tree, with its roots, a trunk, branches, leaves, and so forth.

Although the listener may find comparisons very helpful and potentially persuasive, he or she should be particularly careful to consider the basis of comparison. That is to say, the speaker must ask himself or herself: *Are the things being compared really comparable in essential ways?* Some objects, events, and ideas may be similar in obvious or superficial ways, but comparison on such bases could be misleading. Assume, for example, that a speaker is urging the rejection of a plan (Plan B) because it is similar to a plan the group has already rejected (Plan A). The nature of the similarities is very important if the comparison is to be a valid one. If Plan A costs $5000 to put into operation and Plan B also costs $5000 to put into operation, and if Plan A was rejected because no money was available for the operation, the comparison is a good one; Plan B like Plan A is too costly and therefore should be rejected. On the other hand, if Plan A and B are similar in that both call for the expenditure of time on the part of the members of the organization, both call for quick action, and both have been proposed to the group by the same people, yet if Plan B does not involve any expenditure of funds, then the comparison is not a good one because financial considerations are central. The speaker who urges a particular form of government for one country by pointing out that form of government has worked so well for another country might be setting up a false comparison if the histories, cultures, and values of the two countries are not similar. So, care must be exercised in using comparisons. *The speaker and each listener should try to satisfy himself or herself that the two things being compared are really similar in ways that are essential to the argument being made by the speaker.*

COMMUNICATIVE METHODS

In addition to the specific material used to make ideas believable and understandable, certain methods of presentation of those ideas and the supporting material can be very effective. *Principally through repetition and restatement and through the use of visual aids can ideas be further supported.*

REPETITION AND RESTATEMENT

As attractive as the prospect might sometimes be, one cannot turn off a speaker. He cannot be halted and moved back to repeat a paragraph nor can he be slowed down or speeded up by the listener. When one is reading a book, one can move at one's own pace. If the reader begins to daydream, she can go back to the page, reread the part that the daydream obscured, or quickly scan the last few pages to remind herself what is happening. With the speaker, of course, all this is impossible. *So what the speaker needs to do is to provide for the less than 100 percent attention of the audience.*

A speaker who wants to make sure that the audience follows him remembers what is said and sees the direction in which he wants to go, is prepared to say things more than once, and says things in different ways. We have all used these communicative devices of repetition and restatement; for example, how many times have we given directions in which we repeat crucial elements in order to make sure that the listener goes the right way? If we want her to turn right and then left, we will most likely tell her to go to the corner, turn right, proceed for eight blocks, and then turn left at the white house, and we will follow this with "Now, do you have that? It's right at the corner, eight blocks, left at the white house."

Certainly in a speech the speaker would do the same type of thing as the direction giver. The following section from a speech is an example. Note the way the speaker presents the idea and restates it. After the idea has been developed, the speaker repeats it once more before going on to the next idea.

> The best way to defend yourself from attack is by being prepared. Yes, if you know what to do beforehand, you can defend yourself. So, we've seen that preparing for an attack is the best defense. Let's consider what you would do if actually faced with an assault.

VISUAL AIDS

In helping the audience to follow and to remember, and in attempting to be persuasive, *the speaker will do well to engage as many of the senses of the listener as possible.* The fact that we talk about the audience as "listeners" indicates that the principal sense that the audience members employ is sense of hearing. But the speaker has ample opportunities to employ the audience's sense of sight as well. What he or she does to engage the audience visually can be very simple or very complex.

Some of the most obvious and easy to use visual aids are often neglected by the speaker. For example, every classroom and many meeting rooms contain a blackboard. The simple device of listing the major ideas on the blackboard as one talks about them can help an audience; such a process can simply make it easier for the audience to follow the speaker as he or she moves from one point to the next. The blackboard can also be very useful when one is trying to demonstrate how a particular process works; one can do this by adding one step at a time as the process is explained. It should be noted however, that using the blackboard takes a certain amount of skill and that the speaker who ends up talking to the blackboard rather than to the audience distracts from, rather than adds to, the communicative effect.

It is better to make some preparations beforehand, and the very simple and easy-to-prepare chart is most likely the best technique to use. Often an example can be made more dramatic through the use of a visual; statistics can be made more clear and more vivid through the use of a chart or a diagram; and comparisons can be made more understandable when they are represented visually. Figures 6–1 to 6–7 are examples of visual materials that have been used in student speeches. They were presented very simply on a chart or a blackboard and proved very helpful to the speakers.

In some cases, more complex and more technical means of visually representing ideas and their support are available. Sometimes certain types of technical equipment are absolutely necessary for a speech to make any sense and have any impact at all. If, for example, a speaker is talking about the history of jazz in America, it is inconceivable that he would not play a tape or record of examples of the music. A speech on how films are made certainly seems to call for some films to be used during the speech. Other kinds of equipment such as *slide projectors, opaque projectors, and overhead projectors* all provide ways of

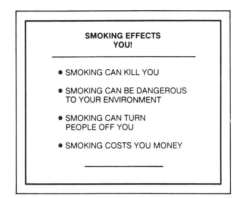

FIGURE 6-1

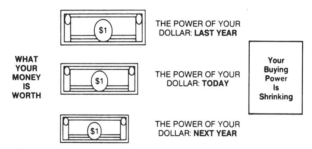

FIGURE 6-2

presenting material visually to an audience. In some cases, even videotaping facilities are available and videotape may be used. *Ways of visualizing ideas, whether very simple or very sophisticated, should be incorporated into the speech whenever it is appropriate to do so.*

Speakers often do not fully exploit the potential of visual material and do not realize how important it is and how frequently it can be used. Almost no speech cannot benefit from a type of visual aid, and the speaker should always keep this in mind. There are, however, certain commonsense rules that ought to be followed when using visual aids.

First, visual aids should be used because they support an idea directly and not because they just provide an effect. A visual aid has the added benefit of

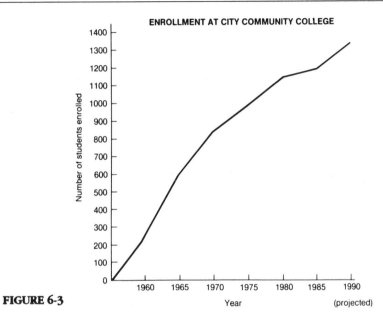

FIGURE 6-3

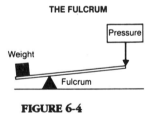

FIGURE 6-4

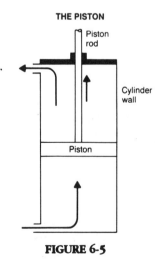

FIGURE 6-5

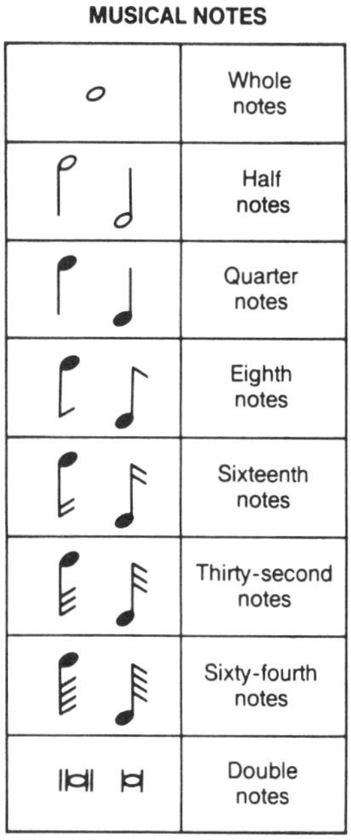

MUSICAL NOTES

○		Whole notes
		Half notes
		Quarter notes
		Eighth notes
		Sixteenth notes
		Thirty-second notes
		Sixty-fourth notes
		Double notes

FIGURE 6-6

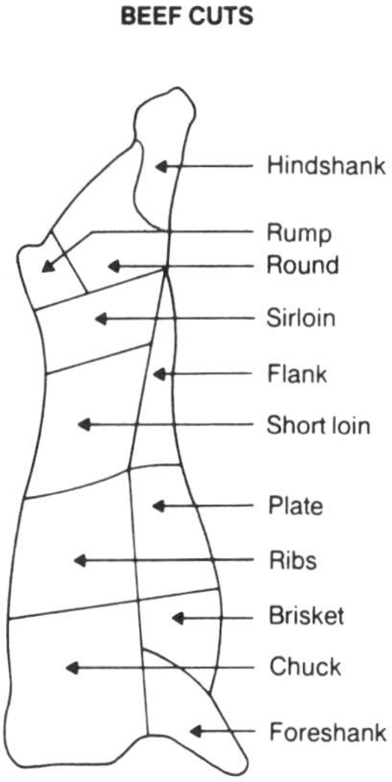

BEEF CUTS

- Hindshank
- Rump
- Round
- Sirloin
- Flank
- Short loin
- Plate
- Ribs
- Brisket
- Chuck
- Foreshank

FIGURE 6-7

adding interest and attention, but it should never be used for this alone. A visual that does not support an idea can end up confusing, misleading, or distracting an audience.

Second, the visual should be as simple and as clear as possible. Visual material should never be cluttered with nonessentials. Only what is important to the speech should be part of the visual. And the speaker must always keep in mind that no visual is useful if an audience cannot see it and understand it. Speakers have actually gone in front of an audience and held up for the audience's inspection a piece of ruled notebook paper with a diagram in pencil on it and expected this to help them understand the point.

Third, a visual should not in any way distract the audience from where its attention should be. A visual aid that is put before an audience too soon, for

Chairman of the Joint Chiefs of Staff, General Colin Powell, points to a map of the Middle East during a Pentagon briefing. Visual aids help the audience to follow and remember what has been said.

example, can be distracting. A chart put up for an audience to look at long before it is necessary might engage their attention when the speaker wishes them to focus on what she or he is saying. Furthermore, the chart becomes dull and uninteresting when the speaker finally does get to it. The problem of distraction is also the one inherent in handouts. When someone passes a picture or an article around in the audience, it usually engages each individual auditor's attention as it is received, which thus distracts the listener from the point the speaker is making at the time. In order to be effective, handouts ought to be given out with enough copies for everyone and should be used as soon as everyone receives a copy. *The speaker needs to think very carefully about the impact of his or her visual material on the audience so that it promotes rather than hinders clear communication of the idea.*

Fourth, the speaker should practice using his or her visual aid before doing so. Equipment can malfunction; a place on a phonograph record or tape can be difficult to find; and a chart can be difficult to refer to while one is speaking. Practice in using material will enhance both the speaker's confidence and his or her skill in handling visual aids.

DETERMINING THE QUALITY OF ARGUMENT

We all know that there are good and bad arguments. Too often we tend to decide which is which on the basis of how closely those arguments match our own opinions or beliefs; a "good" argument is one with which we agree. Of course, anyone who stops to think about it knows that he is not always right; at times he may have been convinced that something should be done only to find that it was the wrong thing. All of us have been "talked into" something that proved to be disappointing, unpleasurable, or even disastrous. The process of "talking someone into something" is the process of arguing. Accordingly, the ultimate judges of whether or not an argument is good are the speaker and the listeners. But because listeners can be actuated on the basis of an argument that leads them in a direction they did not wish to take, one should realize that arguments that seem to be sound ones can be flawed. For an argument to be a good one, there must be a recognition of its worth by the participants in the rhetorical situation as well as by the neutral observer testing the "logic" of the argument.

THE RHETORICALLY SOUND ARGUMENT

An argument moves from a *premise* that an audience can accept through a variety of kinds of *evidence* to a *conclusion.* Let us consider each of these parts of the argument.

The premise is an acceptable generalization that grows out of the context in which the public communication occurs. The first test of the premise is whether or not it makes sense to an audience. There are certain values in our culture or in our social group that are supported without much serious question. But such fundamental ideas are audience-specific. In our society most listeners might agree that everyone is entitled to fair and equal treatment under the law; in other societies listeners might assume that power and rank automatically assure one of the right to circumvent the law. We might feel confident that an audience in our society would accept the idea that individuals are important as human beings and should be protected in their rights, whereas other people might not question the assumption that individual rights have to be sacrificed for the good of the whole community. And even within our culture, certain listeners will need no proof for the assertion that education is important for everyone, whereas other listeners will be not at all convinced that education is worth spending time or money on.

Quite often premises are not even stated by the speaker; they are invisible underpinnings like the pilings sunk into the ground to support a bridge. Like the pilings, they need looking after, inspection to make certain they can sustain the weight (of an argument). The speaker has a responsibility to test the firmness of these foundations. Indeed, the speaker, unless he or she is very careful, might not even be aware of what these premises are. Such a lack of awareness is probably a mistake, for part of what the speaker wants to do is to be absolutely sure of the integrity of his or her own thinking. Similarly, the speaker, as well as the neutral observer, should seek to know and question the premise. Take, for example, the following excerpt:

> I have consistently argued for a reduction of the budget. Five years ago, it was the committee that I headed that was responsible for reducing a variety of social service payments and costs by almost 20 percent. The Citizens for Tax Relief have judged my performance to be an outstanding one. There can be no doubt in anyone's mind that I have always stood for good government.

Now, that argument is based on a certain premise. The premise could be stated like this: Good government is that which is economical. The speaker in this case is obviously arguing that his frugality is the critical ingredient in determining whether he's for "good government." The speaker, in this case, is arguing as if such a premise were beyond question. Many, however, would question the premise, that economy is the basic ingredient of good government.

Assuming that a premise is valid, we note that *the conclusion of an argument rests on the strength of the supporting material.* We already discussed in this chapter the principal kinds of communicative evidence and ways to test them. It is important here to say that *a sound argument is one in which the evidence is both qualitatively and quantitatively adequate.* That is to say, the evidence passes the tests (that the examples used are representative; that the statistics are accurate; that the testimony is by an authority; that the comparisons of objects or ideas that are indeed sound, and so forth), and are quantitatively sufficient to provide ample justification for the conclusion. Perhaps the best way to summarize and conceptualize the structure of an argument is to look at it operationally. Many students of the communicative process and of the reasoning process have done this. It might be most advantageous here to consider a simplified diagram that shows what we have been saying: *A premise comes out of the total context; on the premise is built specific items of evidence, and these items of evidence in turn support the conclusion of the argument.*

The best argument, then, is one in which the conclusion is most adequately supported by the evidence and which grows out of an intellectually and emotionally acceptable premise. We noted that the best argument is not always the most effective one, just as the best product is not always the one that sells the most. Unfortunately, consumers—consumers of products and consumers of arguments—can be and are being duped. Incensed by the fact that our foods can poison us, that extremely expensive machinery wears out in a short time, that gadgets fall apart in our hands, that services are promised us which are never performed, we as consumers have begun to rise up against the hucksters who would exploit us. Intellectual hucksters are just as harmful, and probably more dangerous to us. *The absolute responsibility of the speaker is to apply carefully the principles that demonstrate the proper use of evidence; and of the listener, to evaluate carefully and critically the relationship between evidence and conclusions.*

We have all been in a situation where our real "reason" for doing something is not what we publicly express. We might, for example, go to meetings or participate in activities that we say we are interested in; in reality, our attraction to postage stamps, traveling, bowling, or scuba diving may be caused by the fact that a person in whom we are very interested happens to be attracted to those activities. Similar kinds of situations abound in our lives; we might, for example, buy something that is very expensive because we want it, because we like it, or because we want to indulge ourselves, and then later explain to a friend or parent that we bought it because it would save us money in the long run. We've all probably told ourselves that taking a break in the middle of studying by going to a movie we want to see is really therapeutic—it will help us study better in the long run. Or we might have decided that we just had to study tonight because we really did not want to go out with a person who asked us. A popular cartoon once showed a character, a young boy, writing a letter to a medical school. After going through a long section in which he attested to his desires to help others,

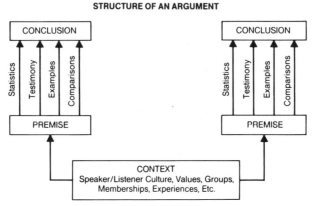

FIGURE 6-8

his feeling of being useful in society, his need to serve the community, he ended up with something like, "and besides all that, I really want to make a bundle." Most of us are not that candid, but most of us "dress up" our real reasons and motivations in "clothing" that will be more acceptable to the outer world or even to ourselves.

Public communication, of course, affords numerous examples of this process at work. Speakers, for example, will often give lofty, highly principled and highly abstract reasons for promoting policies or plans that are less idealistic than they sound. For example, there have been times in our past when speakers have appealed to the purity or integrity of the constitution, urged us to launch a campaign to check the rising tide of crime in the street, or urged us to adopt policies that promote self-help as opposed to government aid. Sometimes these speakers have been honest and straightforward in their arguments; at other times, at the other extreme, they have used such arguments to mask the most determined kind of racism: "law and order" could be translated into "zap the blacks." Speakers have been known to promote schemes to reform taxes, to guarantee that everyone pays a fair share, or to preserve the rewards of one's labor—all of which are commendable. But sometimes these are merely acceptable ways of arguing on behalf of those who want to pay as little as possible to support the needs of society.

Advertising, of course, provides other examples of public communication that substitutes acceptable reasons for real ones. A mother, for example, may want to buy a type of cereal for her child simply because that child likes to eat it since it is coated in sugar and tastes good. But she must be assured by that manufacturer that it is also good for the child, that it is fortified with vitamins, that it is part of a balanced breakfast, and so on. Interestingly enough, advertising also provides examples of the awareness on the part of persuasive communicators that underlying reasons for buying a product exist, and that these had better be appealed to. One of the most fascinating examples is toothpaste advertising. It seems obvious that brushing one's teeth is primarily a way of preserving and protecting those teeth. Advertising that is directed mostly to parents appeals to this reason; it argues that a brand of toothpaste reduces cavities, keeps teeth healthy, and so on. As the advertising begins to aim at a more mature audience, it recognizes that brushing one's teeth for health purposes is somewhat secondary to brushing one's teeth for social purposes. Some advertisements recognize a dual purpose and discuss how their toothpaste will both make one attractive to the opposite sex and keep one's dentist happy. In this case, it might well be that the most potent reason for buying the product is to be attractive to the opposite sex, whereas the appeal to keeping one's teeth healthy makes the toothpaste respectable by adding to its cosmetic value a health value. In some cases, however, toothpaste is frankly advertised as making one's teeth white so as to make one's mouth more sexy. Here, the underlying reason has emerged most blatantly.

The process that we have been discussing—that of finding good or acceptable reasons for taking action or believing ideas that one is inclined to take or believe in any case—is called *rationalization*. Rationalization is adding stated reasons in place of the underlying real reasons.

Why do we rationalize? *We probably do so because of the way we believe certain public arguments will affect our images, images that we have of ourselves and images that others have of us*. For example, if we like to think of ourselves as practical and hardheaded, we many not wish to admit, even to ourselves, that we bought a new car because we especially like the color. In such a case, we would want to be armed with the salesperson's arguments about gas mileage, record of repair, and comparative costs. We could thus preserve for ourselves our image of ourselves. Or we might have bought the car so that we could show off in some way, perhaps gloat a little that it's a better car than the one owned by a neighbor or a friend; it would enhance our perception of our own prestige. Of course, it would be rather awkward to admit—perhaps to ourselves, but certainly to others—this real reason for buying the car. So, again, the salesperson's arguments are necessary for us.

It's also quite conceivable that people will want to do things that they perceive as being in contrast to the norms or practices of the group with which they identify, and so they will try to find reasons for that behavior that are acceptable to that group. One professor, for example, who identified himself with what he considered to be the moderate-to-liberal intellectual community decided to vote for a gubernatorial candidate who was conservative and decidedly not intellectual (some even said exceedingly dull), and whose outlook was extremely parochial. The real reason for this choice may well have been that the opposition candidate was personally distasteful to the professor, or that the professor was really much more conservative than he would admit. And so he justified his action by asserting that the candidate of his choice was a great friend to education in the state. If one judged by the candidate's support of the basketball team, this was true; by almost any other criterion, it was not. In this example, of course, there is no way of saying whether or not the specific candidate should or should not have been elected. The point is that the professor perceived his vote for the candidate as being something that had to be justified in terms of the accepted norms of the group to which he perceived himself as belonging. Sometimes a person would rather go to a play than go bowling, or vice versa, and finds it difficult to justify such a decision in light of the attitudes and behaviors of his or her group. In such a case, the person would feel pressured to say that her choice is based on the necessities of the moment, on parental pressure or pressure from a teacher, on the demands of some friends, on mistaken information, and so on, preferring to hide the fact that she would rather go to a play than bowl.

This process of rationalization has the most profound and far reaching implications for both speaker and listener. For the speaker, as has been pointed out in a previous chapter, one important task in understanding the audience is understanding the kinds of allegiances, loyalties, and associations that audience members have and subsequently the kinds of motivations and pressures to which they might be subject. As the speaker prepares to speak, he or she must be aware that audiences may demand a good sound argument, not only to be convinced or to be motivated—they may be that already—but, in a sense, to be armed with weapons necessary to defend their decisions. The lifelong Democrat, for example, may be ready to switch parties because he feels this would be in his best economic interest; yet he hesitates to abandon long-professed principles for what he fears might appear to be crass or selfish reasons. In short, a speaker recognizes that rationalization is likely to take place and that it is his or her responsibility to provide the audience with a good, sound, sensible argument.

For the listener, the most important fact about rationalization is that he or she does it. Rationalization is simply a part of our behavior. It is a way in which we manage the world around us. There are times when we must rationalize in order simply to cope with our lives. But in a public-speaking situation, the more we can understand about our own reactions to messages, the better off we are bound to be in judging and acting upon those messages. As we respond, we should try to understand the basis of our response. Ultimately, we may decide that it is not politic, polite, or safe to explain to others the real reasons of our actions; we may never want to tell someone that we bought a car because it was fire-engine red. Nonetheless, *we can make more informed kinds of decisions if we at least recognize the basis of each decision.* Maybe if we say honestly to ourselves, "I really want to buy that car because of that color," we might give ourselves a chance for internal rebuttal, a chance for another part of ourselves to say, "Is the color worth the gas guzzling?" How we resolve that question can depend on many factors, such as our perception of environmental problems, our commitment to improving the ecological situation, our realistic assessment of our own finances, or our basic value system. Rationalization is, after all, a way of smoothing over conflict. The listener who will make the best decision often encourages conflict within himself or herself.

Undoubtedly, any discussion of rationalization raises ethical questions. On the most basic kind of level there can really be no question posed such as: Is rationalization right or wrong? Rationalization simply *is*; it is a psychological process. *The real question is whether or not rationalization can be misused or misdirected by speakers and listeners in the public-speaking situation.*

All of us know that at times people are offered what appear to be "good reasons" in order to encourage them to do things that are harmful or socially undesirable. Sometimes people tend to act on the basis of prejudice, ignorance, and narrowmindedness, grasping at more "respectable reasons" for doing what is essentially wrong. Other times people have basically good instinctive feelings which direct them to act in ways that are beneficial to the community in which they live. These people may need to be assured that their instinctive responses are, indeed, good ones. The resolution of such issues will hinge on how speakers or listeners see themselves and the world in which they live. That is, their personal values will ultimately determine the way in which rationalization is used.

In the context of this chapter, however, there is one rule related to ethics and rationalization and generally to reasoning that seems sensible: *A sound argument is one that is clearly thought out, well developed, and supported by evidence, and one that reaches a sensible conclusion.* An argument that obviously is an effort to promote reasonable and logical thought could hardly be conceived as being unethical. However, an argument that is unsound, that is based on faulty or insubstantial evidence, and that comes to a conclusion that is misleading or myopic obviously does not promote rational thinking and is clearly an unethical way in which to participate in the process of public speaking.

PRINCIPLES INTO PRACTICE: A SUMMARY

HOW TO PREPARE GOOD ARGUMENTS FOR A SPEECH

The speaker who has considered his or her audience and the situation in which public communication will occur and who has determined a reasonable purpose is then ready to invent and develop the ideas of a speech. In constructing good arguments, a speaker should take the following steps:

1. Devise clear, complete ideas that support the specific purpose.
2. Support the ideas, to make them more understandable and believable, with

   - Specific or hypothetical examples that are typical and important.
   - Statistics that show how things are related and what trends have occurred over time; they should not be misleading or inaccurate.
   - Testimony that is authoritative and timely, and in context.
   - Comparisons of the familiar with the unfamiliar; comparisons that

simplify difficult concepts and that compare things that are essentially similar.

3. Use repetition and restatement to help the listeners follow and remember what is being said.

4. Use visual aids that support ideas, are clear and simple, and do not distract the audience's attention.

5. Maintain a sound, logical relationship among the premises of an argument, the evidence and ideas that are built on those premises, and the conclusions reached in the speech.

This chapter has been concerned with reasoning tactics designed to promote ideas to an audience. Other closely related and overlapping tactics may be designed to involve the listeners in the speech. They are considered in the next chapter.

CHAPTER 7

INVOLVING YOUR AUDIENCE: MAKING IDEAS MEANINGFUL

After studying this chapter you should understand:

- Why emotion is important in involving audiences.

- What the important listener needs are and how the speaker might appeal to them.

- How to appeal to listeners' beliefs and values.

- How to involve listeners emotionally.

- How to employ factors of attention and interest.

- Why establishing common ground is important and how to establish it.

- What the effective ways are to introduce and conclude speeches.

EMOTION AND INVOLVEMENT

Students of public speaking are sometimes suspicious of emotion. We have all heard the comment that a speech we listened to, a story we read in the newspaper, or a comment reported by the news media was not very "logical." Perhaps we've had the experience of thinking that someone we were talking to was becoming too "emotional," getting too excited or involved. One of the sexual stereotypes preserved over the years was that women are emotional and men are logical. As was generally true of such stereotypes, they were designed to put women in an inferior role, since emotion is seen as being inferior to logic. Indeed, many people believe that logic and emotion can't exist at the same time, that a person must be either logical or emotional.

Furthermore, emotion is sometimes confused with bombast; the shouting, sweating, arm-waving speaker, lacing his message with appeals to fear, prejudice, or superstition is seen as the ultimate "emotional" communicator. Such perceptions of emotion tend to obscure the very important realization that

Audience must be emotionally engaged to be involved in the speech.

emotion, whether its effects are good or bad, is absolutely essential to successful public speaking.

Emotion is, after all, an experience of strong feeling. It is being roused from an impassive, impersonal state to one of *involvement*. Perhaps we've had the experience of being in a communication situation in which we have no emotional involvement at all. For example, television commercials, for products we couldn't possibly use or in which we aren't remotely interested, as insistent as these messages may be, usually fail to gain our attention and, consequently, do not motivate us to absorb information or take action. Perhaps you've sat in lectures and wondered why on earth you were taking that particular course. Feeling completely detached from the content of the message, you might have found it very difficult to understand and retain information.

If you were asked to give money to a cause that neither interested nor affected you, if you were asked to vote in an election whose outcome you believed could have no bearing at all on your life, if you were asked to learn a precise and technical procedure for repairing a piece of machinery that you had never even seen, heard of, or anticipated using, or if you were asked to spend time engaging in an activity that you believed did not form a part of your experience, feeling as you do that they don't make any difference to you, you probably would not do them. *For someone to take the time, expend the energy, or make the effort to understand, to believe, to act, that person must have some feeling of identification with or involvement in the recommended knowledge, belief, or action.*

Much has been said concerning the evils of apathy. Apathy certainly is one of the primary forces that works against successful public speaking. And surely apathy is the reverse of emotion; it is a lack of any strong feelings—it is simply just not caring. The speaker who would accomplish his or her purpose must not only appeal to the reason of the audience, but also involve the audience emotionally.

Reason and emotion should not be thought of as incompatible; one does not have to cancel out the other, and a speaker does not have to choose one or the other. The speaker is under an obligation to himself and to his listeners to make as sound an argument as possible. But he must recognize that even the most sound argument has little persuasive or informative potential unless someone attends to it. *Listeners will not be motivated to respond to planned purposes if they perceive the desired response as being irrelevant to them.*

A speaker, for example, who has as a specific purpose, "I want my audience to understand the operation of a rocket engine" needs to consider ways in which he or she can point out to an audience why such information is important to listeners. The speaker who would urge her audience to take action against pollution needs to make certain that the audience feels strongly that such effects are a direct and personal threat to them.

The problem that the speaker faces, then, is how to directly involve the listeners with the topic. The ways in which a speaker can promote emotional involvement on the part of listeners are varied. The following specific ways in which the listeners may be emotionally involved will be discussed in this chapter: by *meeting the listener's needs, by appealing to a listener's beliefs and values, by directly engaging the emotions of the listener, by capturing the listener's attention, and by establishing common ground between the speaker and the listener.*

MEETING LISTENERS' NEEDS

The psychologist A. H. Maslow has described basic human needs in terms that will be helpful in understanding and developing tactics for listener involvement. Let's consider here those that are relevant to this discussion.

SATISFYING BASIC PHYSICAL NEEDS

Basic to all human life is the need to be physiologically secure. We all need food and drink, clothing, shelter, and sexual gratification if we want to feel comfortable and to avoid the discomfort of pain, sickness, injury, and so on. These needs are "basic" because, in a sense, they preempt or obliterate all other needs if they are not met. Groups such as the Salvation Army long ago recognized that those who are in the deepest and most serious distress can hardly be called on to live up to their full potential as human beings if their most basic needs are not met. And so such organizations provide food, clothing, and shelter and only then make an appeal to people to fulfill other kinds of needs. Most of the audiences, however, to whom we will talk will usually have had their basic needs met. Freed from the preoccupation of satisfying these needs, most listeners will be more successfully appealed to on the basis of the "higher" needs.

ASSURING THEIR PERSONAL SAFETY

People like and need to have a safe environment in which to live. That is, we all need a secure and predictable world. A certain amount of routine, order, or predictability protects us from dangerous, surprising, and unfamiliar situations that threaten our safety. This does not mean that people have a basic drive for dullness. Even the mountain climber wants the security of knowing precisely how his or her equipment will function, and the scuba diver does not want to be surprised by an unexpected flow of the tide. However, just as physiological needs do not unduly preoccupy most of those who are members of our audiences, so do the normal needs for safety seldom dominate listener's minds. There are routine ways in which safety is guaranteed in any organized society. We have a police force to protect us from crime; we have a fire department to protect us from a disaster; and we have many departments and agencies dedicated to make sure that gas lines do not blow up, electric wires do not break, buildings do not crumble beneath our feet, or highways do not disintegrate under our automobiles. There is a "defense establishment" designed to protect us from potential enemies abroad, and government bureaus to protect us from being poisoned at home. Our safety is the concern of many people and groups.

Most of us go through our lives assuming our own safety. It is only in periods of crisis, such as war or natural disaster, that we seriously question how safe we are. Nevertheless, there are times and places when our personal safety appears to us to be seriously threatened, and such fears may influence an audience. In many large cities, for example, people, particularly older people, feel very unsafe. Both their physical preservation from attack and their financial security are perceived as being definitely threatened. In such a setting, *a speaker who would like information to be understood, action to be taken, or beliefs to be modified would be well advised to consider how such purposes would meet the very important safety needs of the audience.*

FEELING LOVE AND A SENSE OF BELONGING

The love that exists between people—a father and a son, a husband and a wife, a boyfriend and a girlfriend—fulfills a very important human need. Furthermore, in a larger sense, there is a distinct human need to be loved or at least to be accepted, wanted, or identified with groups. People join clubs, maintain close family or ethnic ties, associate themselves strongly with a church or religious movement, or take great pride in their nationalistic feelings toward their country. All these things help them to meet the need to be an accepted and cared-for part of some identifiable group.

Listeners are likely to be more emotionally involved when they believe that a speaker is advocating a proposal that will either be of direct benefit to those whom they love, reduce their feelings of isolation, or help them to be secure as a part of an admired group.

FEELING CONFIDENT IN THEMSELVES AND APPRECIATED BY OTHERS

"Esteem needs" stem from a person's desire to feel that he or she has some worth and importance. People like to feel that they control to some extent their destiny, that they are not constantly under the thumb of other people, and that they are in some way recognized as being good or important human beings by others. We all like to have some attention paid to us and be thought of as "good" in one way or another.

This need can frequently be translated into a desire for *status,* a desire to be better than other people; the symbols of status, the indicators of what makes one person "better" than another, are significant. In many ways, this need for prestige is the most obvious one appealed to in public communication. Assuredly, it is the basis of much advertising that would have us believe that smoking a certain type of cigarette, driving a certain type of car, or wearing a certain brand of shoes will help us acquire the status we long for; we will then be admired as people fashionable and wealthy enough to do just the "right" thing.

STRIVING TO REALIZE THEIR OWN POTENTIALS

The concept of "self-actualization," as Maslow calls it, recognizes that human beings want to make the most of themselves. Most people are in the process of becoming. We tend to strive for something; we tend to have goals toward which we work. Most people, if they feel striving is worth it, will continue to do so and will probably never be completely self-actualized. Not everyone, of course, will have the same ideal or the same ambition. Nevertheless, the speaker who realizes that people want to achieve the full extent of their capabilities will appeal to this very important need.

Any tactic or set of tactics designed to help an audience meet their needs is bound to promote emotional involvement, and will thus contribute toward the achievement of the purpose. Yet, along with needs to be met there are also beliefs and values that will shape the nature and degree of emotional response in an audience.

APPEALING TO LISTENERS' BELIEFS AND VALUES

As we go about our daily lives we are constantly called on to make decisions. We make these decisions on a variety of bases. We have, in other words, a set of standards that shape our behavior. These standards, or values, we carry around in our heads, and they provide a means whereby we can make decisions in situations in which these standards apply. The standards could be moral or ethical ones that will help us decide matters relating to such things as our sexual behavior, the type of political candidates we might support, and the extent to which we will use other people or other people's work in preparing what is supposed to be our own original work. Standards that we internalize may also help us make practical types of decisions. If we value efficiency and common sense, for example, we will tend to value those solutions that seem to us to best exhibit such characteristics.

Listeners derive their values and beliefs from many sources. Certainly the country, the part of the country, the city, or the rural area we live in all affect our value systems; our religious affiliations, our political allegiances, the types of clubs or organizations to which we belong, and the types of friends we have all shape our values and beliefs.

Let's look at a historical example of a situation that produced a great American speech that dealt with values. In the 1950s and 1960s when blacks were struggling to achieve civil and economic rights, Martin Luther King, on August 28, 1963, gave what was to be his most famous speech, the "I Have a Dream" speech. In this speech Dr. King asserted that his dream was "rooted in the American dream." What Martin Luther King attempted to do in that particular speech was to show that what he and other black leaders was asking for was nothing more than the same rights and opportunities as other Americans. He appealed to what he hoped were commonly held values in America—the values of fair play, of equality under the law, and of equality of opportunity. But as King and other black spokespersons knew, appeals to such values do not automatically bring positive responses. Just because great disparities between the values we profess and the practices we engage in are pointed out, doesn't mean that those practices will be immediately or radically changed.

The values of our country, our group, or our individual selves may not always be very easy to live up to. Indeed, we may never live up to some values that we profess to hold. The whole situation is complicated by the fact that values often can be in conflict with one another. At one time we can hold two values that simply don't fit together. Americans, for example, have long been under the strain of trying to live up to a set of ethical or moral ideas while at the same time experiencing the very strong urge to succeed. Let's examine in detail this particular tension between two values as an example of what problems both groups and individuals can face when they try to live up to their own values. This should help the speaker better understand that just pointing out a value and supporting it isn't always enough to move an audience.

Americans are often thought of as expedient people. In our politics we generally tend to promote compromise in order to get along, and we end up with two major parties and not twelve or fifteen splinter parties, as so often happens in political situations in which principles aren't flexible. At the same time we seem to want to succeed, to get ahead, and to compete successfully with others. One famous football coach was supposed to have observed that the reason football was so popular was because "football is life." In many ways that might be true. Americans are supposed to be able to show a certain amount of stamina, determination, and enthusiasm in order to score and to win the game. Sometimes, winning might also involve punching someone in the face when the referee is not looking. We can be very upset or puzzled when we hear that behaving fairly, honestly, and equitably is the right thing to do and yet, at the same time, see that some people who behave very unfairly are rewarded by material success.

Another obvious way in which Americans are pulled in opposite directions is when our feelings about individuality and conformity conflict. If one looks at or listens to much public communication, one can get the feeling that we believe that each individual has certain rights and privileges. We believe that individuals ought to be protected by the government and not sacrificed to a larger good. In short, individual people—each and every one—have some real worth. At the same time, and again this is evident in the content of public communication, one quickly realizes that there are strong pressures in this society to conform. On one hand, we are urged to make up our own minds, to be our own masters, to determine our own fate; on the other hand, we are urged to be part of the team, to cooperate, to do what everyone else is doing.

Anyone planning a public speech needs to remember that there are commonly shared values to which members of his or her audience will react strongly and feelingly, and that these values may be in conflict with each other. *As the speaker attempts to engage emotions, he or she will try to develop tactics that will make the listeners care about the message, identify with the message, be associated with the outcome of the message, and be interested in the results of the message.* As the speaker plans such tactics, he or she must make an estimate of the intensity and importance of the values held by the audience.

Much of what is being said here relates to what was previously discussed concerning ways in which the speaker should go about studying the audience. We return to one point: *All listeners are not alike, and a speaker can never assume that all listeners are like him or her.* The speaker needs to think very carefully about how his or her speech bears on the types of standards that the culture or the region develops, or that the listeners' group associations develop. Take, for example, the question of the nature and role of higher education. For a long time, those people who urged that colleges and universities should receive more financial support based much of their argument on the recognized value of *success.* They maintained that going to college would help someone make more money as a result. Earning a college degree would also contribute to the person's success by enhancing his or her ability to move onward and upward in a chosen profession. When the economic realities changed drastically, and, for a time, college graduates had more difficulties in getting jobs, the rationale for higher education became rather shaky. Indeed, the success value seemed to be working against college graduates and against increased support for educational institutions.

Or take, for example, the speaker who urges certain zoning changes to be made in a community so that a section of town can be torn down and a new shopping center put up. That speaker has to contend with many conflicting values—probably held with different intensity by different listeners—as he goes about trying to accomplish the purpose. Some people may value progress very much and think that building new buildings is progress. Others may value efficiency and practicality and say that the land can be much more useful when developed as a shopping center. Others, and particularly those in the neighborhood, may stress their individual rights to privacy, peace, or simply the right to keep their own property and live where they have always lived. Because such values become engaged in these kinds of controversies, they become so emotionally charged to those who participate in them.

Listeners responding to public speaking respond emotionally if their values are truly engaged. Consumers of public speaking, if they are truly touched by a speech, will measure its effects against their value structure. They will have to cope with the problem of incompatible values that is sure to arise. In such a situation, the listener's ability to be open with himself or herself is of paramount importance. An intelligent response demands that the listener order his priorities, that he recognize conflict and deal with it in a way that is most honestly compatible with his own feelings or beliefs and with his own judgment of the reasonable aspects of the case as well.

Listeners, then, have needs to be met and they have values to which they adhere. A question naturally arises. What types of techniques or procedures can be employed in public speaking that will best relate these needs and values to the communication event by engaging the emotions of the listeners?

ENGAGING LISTENERS' EMOTIONS

The speaker who wants to engage the emotions of listeners must begin with his or her own emotional involvement. Listeners tend to respond to a speaker in an emotional pattern similar to the speaker's. The speaker sets the *mood,* as it were, for the speech.

One of the speaker's basic assessments must be of his or her own feelings. The speaker who hopes to excite an audience, to interest an audience, to direct an audience's anger against an injustice, or to fill an audience with pride over a laudable practice or program will have a very difficult time in doing so unless she feels such emotions herself. It is always best for the speaker to choose to speak about those things for which he or she can generate *genuine* feelings. It is absurd to try to feign emotion. There are, of course, highly skilled professional actors who are able to project emotional states. But for most public speakers to attempt to do such a thing would be futile and foolish, to say nothing of unethical. It is always best to be genuine, sincere, and honest with an audience; if listeners sense indications that this is not the case, efforts to communicate successfully will likely fail.

This does not mean that the speaker shows no emotional restraint. The nature of the audience, the setting, and the total situation dictate certain limitations on both the speaker's and listener's emotional responses. In one public-speaking class, for example, a student was talking about the destruction of wilderness lands by commercial industries. The student felt very strongly on this matter and during the course of the speech became very angry, repeatedly pounding his fist on the lectern. In the small classroom with a small audience, his reaction seemed much too extreme. The audience literally jumped each time he pounded the table and soon became uncomfortable and restless. The genuine emotion had deteriorated into excessive emotionalism that distracted from rather than contributed to the message.

Another speaker in a beginning public-speaking class suddenly stopped in the middle of her speech and said, "I can really see that nobody here seems to be terribly interested in what I am saying. It's probably because I haven't convinced you about how important and how real and how terrible the disease I'm talking about is. As a little girl I watched my grandmother die. Recently I learned that my sister also has this disease. This is a very real and very terrible thing to me, and the only reason I am talking about it is because it could happen to you. I'm not talking about something rare or unique. I'm talking about something that I've had to cope with and something you might have to cope with." Such an insertion in the speech, if it had been an "emotional outburst," could have been embarrassing or disruptive. In this case, it was so genuine, and yet so calmly stated, that it deeply impressed the audience. When the speech was over, one of the listeners said, and many of her fellow listeners agreed that "This was the first time I really concentrated on what was going on in a speech. I really heard it. She made me stop thinking about what was going on in my life and think about what was going on in hers. She really made me feel that it could be me."

Listeners' emotions may be engaged when the premises of argument are clearly recognizable as being need- or value-based. Some types of controversies seem to generate much emotion, and these arguments apparently do so because they are perceived by an audience as being directly relevant to their deepest interests. For example, there often are heated controversies over the selection of textbooks in public schools. These controversies are so emotionally engaging because arguments often are based on premises such as these:

"Schools should reinforce the prevailing religious views of the community."
"The role of the schools is to expound the truth."
"The role of the schools is to promote and equip students for free inquiry."

All of these premises engage important values for different segments of the audience. They also relate to human needs such as those that deal with the listener's self-actualization, with his or her need to be appreciated by others, with his or her feelings of love and protection for others and, even in some cases, with his or her real fears that arise from what is perceived as being a threat to personal safety. In order for us to understand the basis of emotional response and to stimulate emotional response, the premises of arguments sometimes need to be made explicit if they are not obviously so in content of the controversy. In this example, listeners might not tend to get involved in this issue if they perceive the argument as being a purely pedagogic one, that is, one that centers on a question such as: "Is a specific textbook employing the most worthwhile techniques for promoting learning?" The tendency in such a situation might be to think, "Leave it to the experts." Whereas, if the listeners perceive the issue to be related to a very basic premise dealing with religious values, then they could well be expected to respond with deep and intense emotional reactions.

Listeners' emotions may be involved when needs and values are related to the stability and comfort of the known. Change can be a very frightening thing. All of us experience some degree of stress when we are put in new and different kinds of situations. Often we have a tendency to defend ourselves against the distressing feelings that change can provoke by looking back on what has been and by trying to recapture it. Again, our own history affords us a good example. In 1933, when President Franklin Roosevelt was inaugurated, he faced a country in the throes of a disastrous economic depression. The world seemed to be going to pieces everywhere and each change brought more bad news. Under these circumstances, the President was about to ask for many, many more changes, changes that would come in rapid and surprising succession. In his efforts to rally the American people, he foretold these changes in the context of a return to that which was good. "We face the arduous days that lie before us," he said, "with the clear consciousness of speaking the old and precious moral values."

Sometimes an appeal may seem to be couched in escapist terms; the urge is to return to "the good old days" that somehow seem much safer than the present. In other words, as is true in almost any aspect of public speaking, such a method may be useful and may legitimately direct our emotions in order to make the most of what we have, or it may simply be a way of using our emotions to delude us.

Listeners' emotions may be engaged through the language used in public speaking. This topic will be touched on again as we discuss style and language, but it is important to point out here that the words that a speaker chooses to use can trigger emotional responses. *Words do not, in and of themselves, have meaning; they only have meaning as we put that meaning into them.* A word in a foreign language that we do not understand might simply be to us a collection of sounds. Translated, that same word could insult, amuse, anger, or excite us. Stories are often told of people being given something to eat which they report to be quite good, only to become physically ill when some name or label is attached to it (rattlesnake or candied fish eyes, for example). Little children may chant that while sticks and stones will break their bones, words will never hurt them; but words do hurt.

Language can be a weapon. The use of epithets to taunt people can make them angry. The use of soothing and loving words can make them feel good. The words we choose reflect perceptions we have, and a speaker's choice of words can influence the perceptions that a listener forms. A person whose ideas usually, when expressed, lead to an extended discussion in the group, could be described by his or her superior as "provocative," or as "one who raises important issues." The same person could be described as "quarrelsome," or "a troublemaker." In both cases the actual behavior might be the same, but the person labeling that behavior obviously interprets it differently and communicates a different interpretation.

Speakers have been known to use *language in place of argument,* to dismiss an idea not by dissecting it, analyzing it, or examining its weaknesses or strengths, but simply by calling it something that is undesirable: the idea is too "socialistic"; the idea is too "radical"; the idea is too "conservative." Sometimes, a speaker can use language that has a strong negative emotional connotation for a listener, and the speaker may not be at all aware of it. In an interview, for example, a young man walked in and said to the interviewer, "That dude that just left said I should come in next." As it turns out, the interviewer reacted very negatively to the word "dude." He associated it with nonbusinesslike slang. He perceived it as being a type of country-and-western "hick" way of speaking that prejudiced him against the interviewee immediately. Some listeners are extremely offended by what they consider to be obscenities or "bad" language. They find the message obscured by their identification of the speaker with the contravening of important values. Both the speaker and listener must recognize that language in context can produce strong associations with needs and values and thus can arouse emotions. To be unaware of that can lead the speaker to make blunders and can lead the listener to act on the basis of emotionally triggered responses to language alone.

   The listener's emotions are often engaged through the use of vivid description of pleasant or unpleasant situations. The use of a specific example was discussed earlier, and that discussion is relevant here. It was pointed out that telling a story about real people tends to promote identification between the audience and the subject. The simple telling of a story can make us feel ashamed or angry. A student, for example, once began a speech by describing in vivid detail an automobile accident. She went on to explain how the victims of the accident were rushed to the nearest hospital and how one of the victims was examined very quickly, put on a stretcher, and left in a hallway unattended. She described the patient's condition as the hours passed, and how doctors and nurses hurried by, some occasionally stopping for a quick look and then going on. As she told the story, the sense of frustration, surprise, and anger in the audience was apparent. Everyone wondered why on earth something wasn't being done for that patient. The speaker concluded her story by explaining that the accident, which took place several years ago, involved a black woman who had been taken to a white hospital. Actually, the example was so vivid and the emotions aroused so real that the speaker had very little more to do to finish her speech on the evils of racism. There is no doubt that listeners who are exposed to a careful and detailed narrative description have a strong likelihood of identifying their own needs and values within the context of that description and therefore of responding positively.

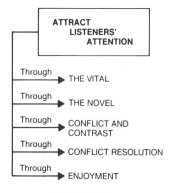

FIGURE 7-1

Thus far, we have been talking about listeners' emotions, their relationship to needs and values, and some tactics designed to engage these emotions. It remains for us to discuss two other important tactics designed to involve the audience: attracting attention and establishing common ground.

ATTRACTING ATTENTION

There are several factors of attention and interest that can be used to heighten the involvement of an audience in a particular topic. Let's consider the most important of these.

1. *Listeners attend to things they perceive as being vital.* A worker who has heard that his plant might close down within a few days and throw him out of work will go to a union meeting and listen carefully. He will attend to what's going on because it is very important to him and he knows it. A student who wants to find a part-time job and goes to listen to a career officer talk about immediate openings will be likely to give full attention to the speech because what is being said is so critical to her. Sometimes there are matters that are important to listeners but the listeners will not be fully aware of the importance. Under those circumstances, the speaker's job is to promote attention by stressing the importance of the topic.

2. *Listeners attend to the novel and to that which arouses their curiosity.* One student speech, for example, was exceptionally well received by an audience that listened very carefully because the speaker succeeded in arousing curiosity. He began by describing in vivid detail the way a traveler would have first come onto the pyramids along the Nile. The speech, which was an informative one, was designed to promote understanding about the construction of the pyramids. This is not a topic that would seem on the surface to be greatly important to students or one that they would feel a great need to know about. It was, however, very interesting in and of itself and succeeded in satisfying the listener's curiosity about these engineering miracles.

3. *Listeners attend to messages that are characterized by conflict and contrast.* As anyone who reads the newspaper or watches a television news program knows, conflict is a basic element in much of what is reported. Vivid, dramatic interactions capture and hold our attention. They also tend to contrast with our normal daily routine. If we walked down the street in the summertime and saw someone coming toward us wearing a large fur-lined coat and hood, with corduroy pants and high boots, we would undoubtedly notice that person; he or she would certainly draw our attention. If we walked down the same street in January, that person wearing the same clothing might pass us scarcely noticed. In the first instance, his or her clothing would have been in such contrast to everyone else's and in such conflict with the needs of the environment that we would have attended to him or her. A wise speaker would not wish to provoke conflict between himself and his audience anymore than he would want the audience to feel that the speaker's ideas, behavior, or attitudes were in direct contrast with the listeners. What the speaker *does* hope to do is to enhance the dramatic or conflicting elements within his material, to demonstrate to the audience, for example, that the topic at hand is one that provokes different and intense reactions.

4. *Listeners attend to messages that tend to resolve conflict.* Just as conflict interests us, we are also interested in establishing a kind of equilibrium in our lives. If things are somehow unbalanced, out of phase, or incomplete, we like to find ways of bringing about some balance, some completion. A speaker who carefully and clearly recognizes and identifies a problem that her listeners sense, or a void that they need filled, and proposed to resolve this difficulty is most likely to be assured of getting attention.

5. *Listeners attend to messages that afford them a measure of enjoyment.* The speaker who begins the speech with an anecdote or a story that is truly funny and then relates that story to the message that follows usually captures the audience's attention. There are dangers inherent in the use of humor, however; humor is a very difficult thing to carry off. Often, what seems very funny to one or two people might not seem so to an audience. Some people think they should begin by "telling a few jokes." Even if the jokes are funny and well told, if they don't relate to the speech they will only serve the most fleeting use as attention getters. For if they don't have anything to do with the speech, funny stories will become ends in themselves. It is quite possible that listeners will only listen for other jokes and not for any more serious types of messages. Nevertheless, we do attend to what we find enjoyable, to that which helps us escape from realities that we may find depressing, that which might release us from current concerns or worries. Although this method of gaining attention must be approached cautiously, it does help listeners attend under the circumstances.

ENGAGING EMOTIONS

- Be emotionally involved.
- Develop argument on need/value-based premises.
- Relate needs/values to the familiar.
- Use appropriate language.
- Use vivid descriptions.

FIGURE 7-2

ESTABLISHING COMMON GROUND

Speakers and listeners tend to become involved with others as they perceive similarities between them. Such similarities can promote understanding. When a speaker and a listener speak the same language, have the same kind of cultural background, and share the same social and educational experiences, they naturally understand each other better. In such cases, the speaker would use examples that involve either people or experiences with which both speaker and audience would be familiar; would understand what types of comparisons would be most appropriate for the listeners; and would rely on the same authorities to bolster arguments as would listeners.

Furthermore, *we tend to find people who are similar to us to be attractive.* In spite of the old adage that opposites attract, in reality, listeners often find themselves being more attentive and more involved with speakers when they perceive those speakers to be like them. Listeners even tend to minimize differences and exaggerate similarities when such attraction results. With people that we find to be less attractive, we tend to respect and trust them less.

Now, despite all these tendencies for listeners to be involved with and to respond positively to a speaker who they perceive to be similar to themselves, not everyone is always moved to act, to believe, or understand simply because the speaker is like the listener. Nevertheless, we should realize that perceived similarities tend to facilitate the kind of communicative response that is desired.

The process of establishing common ground involves both recognizing similarities and using those similarities in the preparation of the speech. For example, a speaker may wish to emphasize similarities in experience and background that are relevant to the topic as he or she begins to talk. The speaker may wish to point out clearly what substantive similarities exist; that is, what values, ideas, or specific kinds of proposals on which both the speaker and the audience agree. Most likely, the speaker will want to take his or her listeners a step further than they are. He or she will want to either change or reinforce positions that listeners hold. It is likely that the speaker will encounter areas of disagreement with the audience, but if the common ground can be established first, then areas of disagreement can occur within a general context of agreement. Common ground is a way for a listener to say to an audience, "We are not opposite people. We do not see the world in an entirely different way. Instead, because we are alike, because we share the same kinds of concerns, and because we want the same kinds of things, we can work out a good solution to our problems or come to a type of agreement on what the best way is for us to proceed together."

Common ground is also promoted when membership ties are exposed. The speaker who belongs to the same types of groups (social groups, political groups, ethnic groups, economic groups, and so forth) as do his listeners may promote a responsiveness on the part of the listeners depending on the extent to which such memberships are considered relevant.

Common ground, then, grows out of a shared experience between the listener and the speaker. The speaker should think very carefully and thoroughly about specific ways to establish common ground. This does not mean, however, that commonalities that don't exist should be created or false impressions given. Such ground would be very shaky indeed. As well as being totally unethical, such a practice would be very dangerous to the speaker if an audience sensed his or her insincerity. *At its best, the establishment of common ground is an effort to bring the speaker and the listeners together* as well as to bring all the potential listeners themselves together. A good example of an attempt to establish common ground in American speechmaking was during Thomas Jefferson's inaugural address. After a long and bitter political campaign, Jefferson hoped to promote unity among those who had lately fought one another so doggedly and determinedly. The whole tone of his speech was one of conciliation. It was mostly an attempt to establish common ground, as is exemplified in the memorable passage, "But every difference in opinion is not a difference of principle. We have called by different names brethren of the same principle. We are all Republicans. We are all Federalists."

Involving the audience with the speaker and the speaker's message is, of course, a process that goes on throughout the entire speech. But it also does take on particular significance as the speech is introduced and as it is concluded. Let's now consider those tactics that could prove most useful in promoting the listeners' identification with the speaker and the speech as the message is begun and as it is ended.

INTRODUCTIONS

The principles that govern audience involvement have already been discussed in this chapter. It is helpful here, however, to consider them as specific tactics to be used in the introduction. Of course, all these methods will not be used in every speech, but the speaker should consider the entire range of possibilities as he or she plans a speech.

1. *Listeners can be told of the significance of the topic.* Basically, listeners' attention can be attracted by answering the question, "To what extent and in what ways will the content of this speech meet listeners' needs?" The speaker

needs to consider the ways in which his or her topic will promote the listener's well-being—financial, social, and emotional. If what the speaker is about to say will save the listener money, then the listener should be made aware of that right away. If what the speaker has to say will make the listener healthier, then the listener ought to know that. The speaker's responsibility is to consider very carefully the ways in which his or her topic will touch on the lives of the listeners and make sure that the listeners understand these ways. Of course, the wise and careful listener will both help the speaker by trying to discern the ways in which the topic can influence the listener's life and will evaluate carefully whether or not the significance suggested by the speaker is real or strained simply to fit the case.

2. *Listeners can be challenged by a striking rhetorical question.* The unusual and the arresting can immediately capture listeners' attention and make them want to hear more. One student, giving a speech on the need for universal safety and first-aid training began his speech with the question, "Have you ever sat hopelessly by and watched your best friend die?" He went on to say that this is exactly what happened to a young man who had pulled his drowning friend out of the water but then didn't know what to do to save the friend's life. It should be clearly understood that every question is not necessarily striking or interesting. Just raising a rhetorical question does not automatically engage an audience's interest. The speaker who began his speech with the question, "Did you have breakfast this morning?" probably felt that he was using an acceptable device to start his speech. Such a question, as important as it might be to the speech or to what will follow, is hardly striking. Also, in raising questions, as in performing every other aspect of the speech, the speaker needs to remember that the speaker's and the listeners' interests are not identical. One speaker, beginning his speech with a question, totally ignored the fact that everyone in the audience was not caught up, as he was, in a specific sporting event. After he began his speech by saying, "I suppose you are wondering, How would I go about pole vaulting?" the result was slightly ludicrous. The *significant question is one that challenges the audience to respond;* one that starts listeners thinking and feeling about the subject.

3. *Listeners can be drawn into the topic through the use of an extended example.* Speakers who begin with a story, whether it be humorous, exciting, or horrifying, usually gain attention immediately and lead the audience into the

speech itself. Of course, *any example or story used needs to be relevant*. A "good" story is not good at all if it doesn't make precisely the point the speaker hopes to make. This is why just telling jokes is not a good way to introduce a speech. One student began her speech by telling a very pertinent story of her friend Craig. In detail, she explained how Craig had a serious financial problem and was afraid he would have to drop out of school. She told of the day when Craig went to register and asked for a deferred payment only to be told that he had to have a voucher from the student aid office in order to do this. She explained Craig's long wait to see the student aid officer, Craig's recounting of his problems, and the student aid officer's response: certainly Craig could get a voucher promising financial aid as soon as he produced his enrollment cards that demonstrated he was a student! Craig's travels between the registrar and the student aid officer were elaborated upon as the speaker continued her opening story. By the time she finished, the audience was both amused at the foibles of the bureaucracy as well as indignant that a student should have been put through such difficulties. Listeners had begun to identify with the student and certainly to be interested in both the nature of the problem and the way it might be solved.

   4. *Listeners can be interested by provocative quotations or statements.* There are times when someone has stated a thought particularly well, or when someone has made a statement that is bound to arrest the audience's attention, or when someone with whom the audience strongly identifies has commented on the topic at hand. In all these cases, it makes sense to begin the speech by quoting the appropriate passage. One speaker, for example, began her speech to a largely black audience with this quotation from Malcom X: "So, I'm not standing here speaking to you as an American, or patriot, or flag-saluter, or flag waver, no, not I. I'm speaking as a victim of this American system. And I see America through the eyes of the victim. I don't see any American dream; I see an American nightmare." Such a quotation served the dual purpose of coming from someone with whom many in the audience may have strongly identified, and of serving as an unusual, interesting way of expressing the strong sense of frustration felt by many members of the audience. Another student speaker began a speech in which she used statistical information to form a provocative statement, pointing out that psychiatrists predicted that 1000 college students would kill themselves in the following year, that another 9000 would try and fail, and

that 90,000 would threaten to commit suicide. She added that the suicide rate for college students was 50 percent higher than that for the general population. Bearing in mind that all material used must be relevant, the speaker can select carefully either from the words of others or from unusual or different kinds of information that will help to engage audience members' interest and attention and involve them with the topic of the speech.

5. *Listeners can be reminded of a specific situation out of which the speech grows.* Obviously the goals of an organization sponsoring the meeting at which a speaker appears, or the reason for calling the meeting, or the national, local, or campus situation out of which the speech grows can all be referred to in order to interest the audience. Furthermore, in the immediate situation, such things as the content of previous speeches may also be incorporated into the introduction. One student speaker, for example, combined the emphasis on the significance of the topic with the use of immediate situation when he began his speech by saying, "All of you have sat here for the past several class meetings patiently and politely listening to speeches. Many of you, I'm sure, would have rather been somewhere else, some of the time. I appreciate the fact that you've all come to listen to my speech even though you don't have a speech of your own to give. I hope that today your patience and endurance is really going to pay off for you. Because today I'm going to tell you something that is going to save you money—a lot of money, and it's going to begin saving you money right away."

6. *Listeners can be prepared for the content of the speech.* Listeners can sometimes listen and follow a speech much better if they, in advance, have an idea about what's going on. For example, a speaker can, in the introduction of his or her speech, help the audience to understand and follow the message, and therefore help the audience become more involved, either by stating the main point of the speech or by presenting a type of initial summary of the speech in which the major points are laid out. Such a "preview" of a speech should help keep the listeners with the speaker as he or she progresses through the speech.

CONCLUSIONS

The conclusion to the speech is the speaker's last word. This is his or her final chance to leave a positive impression with the listeners. Essentially there are three important considerations for the speaker to keep in mind as the message is brought to a close.

1. *Listeners should be left with the overriding feeling of the speech.* The speech has, one hopes, created a strong mood that the speaker hopes the audience will feel. For example, the speaker who began her speech with the story of Craig's battle with the bureaucracy wanted to leave her audience with a feeling of indignation. After developing her main points, she went back in the conclusion to the story of what happened to Craig when, as a result of red tape, he finally gave up his college education and found himself having real difficulties getting a job. Feelings that a good person was wasted, that technicalities upset someone's life, left the audience angry about the system and insistent that something be done to change it.

We should realize here that just as the mood of the speech can be sustained, it can also be completely destroyed. Some speakers seem not to conclude but just to stop. This often leaves the audience with the feeling that somehow the speech hasn't been closed properly. Many television programs will end with a short epilogue of sorts, which in a few minutes resolves the loose ends of the story and reinforces the tone of the program. Many viewers would feel disoriented if this final short session did not occur, just as listeners would feel if the speech were not properly concluded. A weak, ineffectual, or rambling ending, as well as no ending at all, will contribute to the destruction of the feeling the speech should project.

2. *The listeners should be left with a clear idea of the content of the speech.* After all the points have been made, the speaker can help the listener considerably by going back and either restating or reiterating the major point, or by summarizing and reviewing the main ideas. The conclusion is not the place to introduce new and different material; this can be confusing and misleading for an audience; it may well be the place for the speaker to tie the whole speech together by a quick review of what has been said already. We should remember here the point that was made earlier, that a listener does not have the opportunity to stop a speaker and go back as he would to stop a book in the middle of a page and go back to the previous one. The listener must depend on the speaker alone to fill in any gaps in comprehension and to emphasize what the speaker wants emphasized. A concluding summary is usually very helpful in doing just that.

3. *The listener might be left with concrete suggestions for action.* If the speaker has successfully aroused the concern of listeners, if he or she has convinced them that there is a certain wrong that needs to be righted or that there is a good solution to an important problem, the listener will naturally look for something to do about it. The last word the speaker leaves with the audience, in those situations in which it is appropriate, could well be a direct suggestion. The speaker would then give the audience a way to follow through on the message that has been delivered.

PRINCIPLES INTO PRACTICE: A SUMMARY

HOW TO INVOLVE YOUR AUDIENCE

We have considered here the task of finding ways to involve the audience so as to promote the purpose of the speech. In order to do this, the speaker should take the following steps:

1. Gather and assemble evidence and material that will demonstrate to listeners how their needs might be met.

2. Gather and assemble evidence and material that will appeal to listeners' values and beliefs.

3. Engage the emotions of the listeners through:
   - Their own emotional involvement
   - Identification of the needs and values of the audience with argumentative premises
   - Demonstration of stability
   - Proper language choice
   - Vivid description of experience

4. Devise tactics to increase attention and interest by:
   - Showing the vital relationship of the topic to the listener
   - Making use of the novel
   - Uncovering elements of conflict
   - Pointing to ways to resolve conflict
   - Searching for that which the audience will enjoy

5. Establish common ground between the speaker and listener through the presentation of shared experiences.

6. Plan an introduction that involves audiences by:
   - Stressing the significance of the topic to the audience
   - Challenging the audience through a rhetorical question
   - Using an extended example
   - Stimulating the audience by using provocative quotations or statements
   - Reminding listeners of the specific situation out of which the speech grows

7. Plan a conclusion that leaves the audience with:
   - The overriding feeling of the speech
   - A clear idea of the content of the speech
   - Suggestions for action

As we have looked at the public-speaking process thus far, we have considered the audience and the speaker and their relationship, the importance of a clear purpose, ways to gather relevant material, and ways to promote successful communication by making ideas believable and understandable to listeners. Now it is time to consider in more detail the means whereby the speaker can integrate all these concerns by giving a coherent structure to the speech.

CHAPTER 8

STRUCTURING YOUR SPEECH: ORGANIZATION

After studying this chapter you should understand:

● What constitutes a good idea.

● How ideas can be patterned:
  - Chronological
  - Topical
  - Spatial
  - Problem-solving
  - Causal

● How transitions and internal summaries function.

● How structure and form affect the clarity and persuasiveness of ideas.

● How you should respond to structure as a listener.

THE RELATIONSHIP OF IDEAS TO PURPOSE

Ideas are the foundation of rhetorical strategy, because they hold the entire speech together and carry the weight of achieving the specific purpose. That is to say, *if* the audience accepts ideas, *if the ideas are understandable and believable to the listeners, then the purpose is accomplished.*

Consider, as a simple example, someone who wants to sell a washing machine. The specific purpose would be very obvious, it would call for the direct action involved in buying the machine. As the salesperson has learned about the machine himself, he or she has gathered specific information that can be used to develop a set of ideas that are intended to move the buyer to action. The salesperson might likely come up with the following set of ideas:

    I. This machine costs less than comparable models.

    II. This machine uses less water than others.

    III. This machine has a variety of settings to meet every washing need.

    IV. This machine gets clothes exceptionally clean.

    V. This machine comes in a wide range of colors.

Such a set of ideas, given that the situational factors are right and the potential buyer really wants a washing machine, seem likely to accomplish the speaker's purpose.

But consider a more complicated example, one that might very well illustrate the kind of speech that you would give. You may wish to have your audience agree that the university should abolish the current grading system.

If this were a speech that you were going to give in class, you would have a different kind of audience from the one you would face if you were going to give the speech to the faculty senate. The *different audiences, then, would mean that you might develop different ideas designed to further your purpose.* Or it might be that for some ideas you would emphasize them for one audience and de-emphasize them for another. In other words, certain ideas might need to be proven more for some people than for others. If the speech were to be given in class, you might devise a set of ideas such as these:

    I. Abolition of the grading system would encourage students to be more adventurous in what they choose to take.

II. Abolition would reduce competition among students and promote cooperation in its stead.

III. Abolition would improve faculty-student relations.

Furthermore, in a speech of this type, the speaker would need to be aware of counterarguments and build into the speech those ideas that would rebut competing ideas in the minds of the audience.

Anyone thinking about the problem of grading would know that there are many people who argue that the abolition of grading would make it difficult to distinguish in any way among students. This, critics of abolition would argue, would make it impossible to reward excellence. Furthermore, in a more practical vein, it would clearly be impossible for graduate schools, professional schools, and employers to make any judgment about the quality of work the student has performed while in college. Now the speaker, given this obvious negative to his or her idea, might develop a fourth idea: the current system of standardized examinations (such as those required for admission to law school or the Graduate Record Exam, coupled with a system of on-the-job training and probationary hiring periods) would make it possible to distinguish among students for advanced education or jobs. Now, unlike the more simple washing-machine example, the results in this case are much more problematic. But, in both cases, the results *will be influenced by the way the particular ideas are stated and developed.* Simply enumerating the main ideas, of course, does not guarantee that the purpose will be accomplished, but delineating clearly those ideas is an essential first step in the development of the message.

What the speaker does, then, is to invent the ideas out of what he or she knows about the audience and situation, out of the needs dictated by the specific purpose, and out of the nature of the subject itself. This invention process is one that the speaker must go through early in his or her speech preparation. Assume, for example, that a student is giving a speech on the constitutional amendment process. She has decided that her audience needs to know precisely how the U.S. Constitution can be amended before she can try to persuade them in subsequent speeches that the process should be made easier or harder, or to try to get them to take direct action in support of specific amendments being debated nationally.

So, her specific purpose would be, "I want my audience to understand how an amendment to the U.S. Constitution is adopted." She might begin by reading

Article V of the Constitution, which describes the amendment process, the amendments themselves, and the commentaries on the way amendments are adopted. Further specific information about how amendments have been dealt with in the past can be gained from historical accounts and newspaper stories written at the time. As this information is sifted through, the ideas—and the material that will serve to enlarge and support those ideas—should begin to emerge and be brought into focus. With the purpose of gaining understanding, the speaker will shape those ideas that seem best designed to promote that understanding. Such questions as how the process begins, who has responsibility for proposing amendments, how they are ratified, and how long the whole process can take will need to be answered if the audience is to understand exactly how amendments become part of the constitution. Accordingly, the ideas generated will address themselves to such concerns. In this case, they might be something like this:

I. Constitutional amendments often arise out of public controversy or controversial situations.

II. The Constitution provides that Congress propose amendments or call a convention for proposing amendments if enough states request it.

III. Amendments passed by Congress or in convention must be ratified by three-fourths of the states.

IV. There is no set time limit on how long it may take for an amendment to be ratified.

As the speaker develops the speech, these ideas may, of course, be modified, discarded, or replaced by others. But the likelihood is that they will form the skeleton on which the body of the speech will be built. Given the fact, then, that ideas are at the heart of the speech, let's consider carefully *the worth of ideas, how ideas affect one another in a speech, and what ideas can mean to those who listen to them.*

DETERMINING WHEN AN IDEA IS A GOOD ONE

Ideas, when taken together, should further the speaker's purpose. So, when deciding whether or not an idea is a good one, a speaker should consider how well it is designed to get the desired response. There are, however, other factors that help determine how good an idea is: a good idea is one that is *clear,* one that is *simple without being oversimplified,* one that is *appropriate to the demands of the situation,* and, above all, one that makes sense. Let's consider each of these characteristics.

CLARITY OF IDEAS

There is a strong relation between language and thought; the way we talk and the way we say things can tell us a lot about the way we think. All of us have probably been guilty at one time or another of saying something like, "Well, I know the answer to that but I just can't put it into words," or, "I understand myself, but I just can't explain it," or, "I know what I want to say, but it just doesn't seem to come out right." All of these comments are, when you think about them, just ways of fooling ourselves about what we really do know. *If you can't say it, you don't know it; if you can't explain it, you don't understand it.* If one is to be successful at communication one has to admit the facts to oneself: *putting an idea into accurate, correct, and clear language is the only way to be sure that the idea is truly understood.* Now even if this were disputed on some theoretical level, it is certainly true in the practical sense; an unexpressed idea cannot be a full-blown idea.

So clarity, then, depends on the way in which language is used. One of the first implications of this proposition is that an idea, in order to be clear, must be complete. That is to say, *language fragments do not convey complete ideas; a full sentence is the best way to insure that an idea is stated in its most fully developed form.* Such phrases as "the economy," "unfair taxes," "ways to improve," or "the future" are not clearly expressed ideas. Such words written on a card might be reminders to a speaker, but what we are discussing at this stage is how ideas are developed. It is crucial, when inventing ideas to support the purpose, that we leave no room for doubt as to the precise meaning of those ideas. Ambiguity at this stage is deadly. What the speaker must do is to *be sure that the idea is fully stated so that she or he can test that idea against the purpose.* If one hopes to get an audience to agree that the best way to stimulate and improve the economic situation is by reducing taxes, for example, then one must be sure that he or she has clear ideas that promote that purpose. "Jobs" is *not* an idea designed to this whereas, "By providing consumers with more money to spend the government will thereby stimulate the economy and provide more jobs" is an idea.

Take, for example, a student who was giving a speech on the benefits of space exploration. The specific purpose was: "I want my audience to agree that substantial funds should once more be channeled into space research." On the initial outline the main ideas read like this:

    I. Accomplishments
    II. Medical
    III. They will advance
    IV. Space relation to earth
    V. Altering environment

It is quite obvious, in the light of the foregoing discussion, that these are not clearly stated ideas. Points I and II are simply one-word notations that don't convey any meaning in and of themselves. In order to be a complete idea, point I might read:

    I. In the past, space research has resulted in very practical benefits.

If this were the idea, it would immediately become apparent that the speaker's job here would be to prove how beneficial the program had been in the past. In this case, the speaker reconsidered his initial thoughts and realized that this one idea could be the entire speech; he decided he could reasonably go back and change his purpose. On the other hand, he did not wish to neglect the fact that he was arguing for future policy and therefore had to demonstrate in some way that positive good would come out of the program in the future just as it had in the past. This caused him to think that he would develop ideas that followed just such a line of thought. He would rewrite his specific purpose in this way: "I want my audience to agree that the space program has benefited all of us and will continue to benefit us if funds are provided." He then looked at the remaining four notations on his outline and began to develop those in the light of his restated purpose, so his first idea became:

    I. In the past, space research contributed considerable knowledge of how the human body functions.

Under that point, he could develop all his information about the medical advances made as a result of space research. He then decided that points IV and V as listed could be consolidated into one idea:

II. Our increased knowledge of space has contributed to our understanding of earth itself and its environment.

The point that he had listed before under III, "They will advance," is a complete sentence, but it is obvious that it is not a clear idea. What the speaker had in mind here was that, in the areas in which some knowledge had been gained in the past, there would be even greater advances in the future. He finally developed this notion into a third main idea:

III. The kinds of knowledge that can be gained by continuing research could be of direct practical advantage to us as inhabitants of earth.

After having gone through this process, the speaker was still faced with the problem of developing each of these ideas, still faced with other types of factors that in the future might cause him to limit those ideas or to expand them. But at least he now had a set of ideas that were clear in themselves and related to the purpose of the speech. A comparison and restatement of the two sets of statements should clarify the evolution from notation to idea:

I. Accomplishments *becomes*
I. In the past, space research contributed considerable knowledge of how the human body functions.
II. Medical *becomes*
II. Our increased knowledge of space has contributed to our understanding of earth itself and its environment.
III. They will advance *becomes*
III. The kinds of knowledge that can be gained by continuing research could be of direct practical advantage to us as inhabitants of earth.

The same process could be applied to develop the two final points to determine whether or not they fit appropriately in the speech as determined by the purpose.

SIMPLICITY OF IDEAS

Audiences, of course, must understand ideas if they are to respond to them. *On the one hand it is important that an idea be directly and simply stated, while on the other hand it is important that an idea not be distorted.* The speaker's problem is to establish this *balance*, that is, not to communicate inaccurate ideas and yet not to complicate ideas so that an audience is baffled rather than enlightened.

With the specific purpose in mind, the speaker must ask himself or herself whether the idea is as basic as it can be and whether it is as unencumbered as it can be. If a speaker thinks that an idea cannot be made simple, that it is very complex, then he or she needs to determine whether or not such an idea will be understandable to the audience. *If an idea cannot be simplified in order to be understood, then the speaker may very well wish to reexamine the specific purpose to see if it is appropriate to the audience.* It may be that the speaker is trying to do too much in the time allotted and needs to focus more sharply.

Furthermore, *speakers often try to include too much information or even a whole series of ideas within one idea.* The idea is, after all, the essence; it is what the audience must grasp, must respond to, in order for the purpose to be achieved. Each idea will be developed fully in order to make it understandable or believable, but the idea itself is the basic thought unit. Let's take two examples.

The speaker has as his or her purpose the following: "I want my audience to become involved actively in political campaigning." The first idea reads like this:

I. College students who take an interest in politics can restore idealism to the process as well as learn valuable skills themselves and make a practical impact.

This idea tries to fit too much in. It is not, in reality, a single idea. It is a complex and interrelated set of ideas. What the speaker needs to do is to sort out the idea from the material necessary to develop that idea. A revised form of this might be:

I. There are direct benefits to society when college students participate in politics.
II. There are direct benefits to each person who participates in the political process.

The speaker is saying, then, that if he can induce his audience to agree that there are both social and personal benefits to be gained from participating in the political process, he will have achieved his purpose. His next task, of course, will be to develop the ideas, that is, to enumerate the benefits that come from participation, to demonstrate that they are indeed beneficial, and to make them real and motivating for an audience. Thus, the speaker will develop specific, convincing tactics to further the overall strategy promoted by the main ideas as a part of the total structure of the speech.

To take one other example of a main idea that could be improved through simplification, consider the speaker who is giving a speech with the specific purpose, "I want my audience to understand the roots of our American legal system." In this speech, she will be discussing aspects of English history that bear on our own legal development. She begins her speech with this idea:

   I. Since Charles I was defeated by the Parliamentary forces, English monarchs have been deemed to be accountable to the law.

This idea as it is stated is accurate and perhaps clear enough. However, it presents certain problems that could be solved by simplification. First, it obscures the major point that the idea hopes to make by burying that point within a historical context. Second, in doing this, the speaker has emphasized certain specific historical elements with which the audience might not be familiar and which might tend to distract them from the point that she is making. One way to recast this idea would be the following:

   I. The principle that no one is above the law was established in England in the seventeenth century.

This statement emphasizes the point—no one is above the law—and does not obscure it with historical detail. What the speaker wants is for the audience to understand what basic principles have been formed in history that shape our own legal system. This idea complies with that purpose. Now, certainly, as the speaker develops the idea she will explain in detail the historical situation that brought it about, but the historical situation is subordinate to the idea she wishes to promote.

Simplicity, then, goes hand in hand with clarity as being a basic characteristic of a well-stated idea. Of course, clarity and simplicity are sometimes relative concepts, and it is necessary to remind ourselves that *the ideas in the speech, just as other elements, grow out of the rhetorical situation.*

SITUATIONAL CONSIDERATIONS

We have already considered at some lengths the proposition that a speech is designed for an audience and that the speech is also influenced by the occasion that prompts it and the setting in which it occurs. Remember, the ideas of the speech are ones to which the listener must respond, and therefore they must be appropriate to that listener and to the context in which he or she will listen. The level of complexity of any idea will be significantly influenced by the audience's relationship to the topic.

If one has as his purpose, "I want my audience to understand the types of scientific data that are gathered by the exploration of Mars by an unmanned satellite," one can further that purpose by using ideas that are highly technical, sophisticated, and complex. A speech to a colloquium in the Astronomy Department might call for exactly those kinds of ideas; a speech in a beginning public-speaking class would call for a different set of ideas.

IDEAS THAT MAKE SENSE

In Chapter 6 we discussed in detail the question of what makes an idea a reasonable one, pointing out the relationship between the basic conclusions embodied in an idea and the evidence used to support those conclusions. As the speaker prepares, he or she must consider the initial impact of an idea on the audience as well as its intrinsic sense. The speaker must first ask himself or herself whether an idea is a sensible one and then consider how an audience might view it. Speakers have sometimes proposed as main ideas those that are just not sensible. For example:

1. Most people would probably like to learn to throw the javelin.
2. Whether or not you subscribe to the student newspaper will be one of the most important decisions you will ever be called upon to make.
3. People who participate in college athletic programs need special tutoring, since they do not have the intellectual abilities of other students.

These ideas just don't make sense. Perhaps if the speakers had thought more carefully about the ideas and had considered their implications—had tried to imagine how an audience might react—they would have avoided them. These ideas, as stated, are not sensible because they (1) confuse the speaker's own interests with those of the audience, (2) seriously overstate the case, and (3) over-generalize on the basis of popular stereotypes.

Sometimes ideas will also seem not to be sensible to listeners if they appear to be romanticized, sentimentalized, or idealized, or if they seem too cynical or pessimistic. For example, the idea that students come to college primarily to develop and sharpen their intellectual and artistic powers may not seem sensible to the average college audience. Many in the audience may know either from their own experience or from that of others that many people come to college in order to get better jobs, to kill time until they decide what they want to do with their lives, and to comply with parent or peer pressure. Now, this kind of an idea is a little more difficult to deal with because it does not state some obvious misconceptions. Perhaps what the speaker is talking about is what he or she believes college students *ought* to do, or what he or she believes the true goals of a university ought to be. The speaker could keep the concept behind the idea intact but would need to rephrase it considering how sensible the audience would think it to be.

A good idea, then, is clear, simple, grounded in the situation, and sensible. Let's now consider how an idea once developed relates in very specific ways to other ideas in a speech.

HOW IDEAS RELATE TO ONE ANOTHER

IDEAS AND PATTERNS

When one has developed a good idea or a series of ideas, one must face the problem of how to put them together. We all know that there are times when we would like to say everything at once. We would like to present a whole picture so that our listeners can see a totality that would make all the parts more understandable. Unfortunately, we talk in a linear fashion. That is to say, one word comes after another, and one idea must come after another.

If, for example, you were taking a course in literature, it would be nice to understand the basis on which you could best judge and interpret a book that you read. On the other hand, rules or standards for judging the quality of one book would be meaningless and difficult to understand unless one had read several other books. So what should one do first? Probably the best thing would be to do two things simultaneously, but that is impossible. The same thing is true for the speaker.

A speaker might like to say everything at once, but ideas have to be taken one at a time. This means, of course, that they have to be put in a type of order. The process can be totally random—whatever pops into the speaker's head—or carried out in such a way that it will help the audience respond as the speaker

Informative Speeches

hopes they will respond. The speaker, then, must decide which idea should come before which other idea, *and to develop a sensible order, he or she must develop a pattern of ideas based on the subject matter itself and on the demands of the situation.*

When a speaker is faced with the problem of taking a set of ideas and making it reasonable and coherent for an audience, he or she will want to put the ideas together in a way that is best designed to accomplish the specific purpose of the speech. Let's consider the basic patterns of organization: chronological, spatial, topical, problem-solution, and cause-effect.

1. *Ideas can be arranged in a logical time sequence.* This is often called a *chronological pattern.* If the subject matter of a specific speech deals with historical development or if it involves a step-by-step, one-after-another approach, then a time sequence is sensible. If, for example, a speaker wants her audience to understand the events that have led up to the American Revolution, she could very easily use a chronological approach that traces the occurrence of events through time. If one explains how a skilled craftsman has woven a rug, he probably begins with the first step that the worker has undertaken and follows the process in time, step by step, to the actual completion of the rug. The following is an example of ideas arranged in a chronological pattern:

Specific Purpose: *I want my audience to understand the rise of Nazism in Germany.*

I. The Treaty of Versailles that ended World War I created several serious problems for Germany.

II. Financial crises encouraged the National Socialists, led by Hitler, to attempt an unsuccessful coup in Bavaria in 1923.

III. By 1930 the National Socialist Party, campaigning on a platform of opposition to the Versailles Treaty provisions, emerged as a major political party.

IV. The violent election campaign of 1933 and the burning of the Reichstag resulted in the necessary political power for the National Socialists to establish the Nazi dictatorship.

2. *Ideas can be arranged in a sequence governed by space relationships.* This is often called a spatial pattern. When a topic is by its nature geographical, for example, or when a topic demands progression that moves from one

physical area to another, then this kind of pattern is a very sensible one. If, for example, one were describing the facilities that are available to students at the University library, one could quite profitably do this by telling them where they should go from place to place from the main entrance to the very top floor. The following is an example of ideas sequenced in a spatial pattern.

Specific Purpose: *I want my audience to agree that democratic institutions are threatened in Europe.*

    I. In Great Britain, the power of the unions over economic life could lead to a proletarian dictatorship.

    II. In Italy, the political success of communism threatens the existence of other political parties.

    III. In Spain, the new spirit of moderate liberalism could lead to violent reactions from both the right and the left.

    IV. In France, dependence on Middle Eastern oil could stifle criticism of government foreign policy.

    3. *Ideas can be arranged in a sequence that emphasize distinct topics.* This is called the *topical pattern.* If the speaker is advocating a specific position that offers several benefits to the listeners, those benefits could well form individual topics: for example, if one were giving a speech on the benefits of higher education, one could develop ideas related to the intellectual, social, or economic advantages of education. In other words, these topics, which are interrelated, suggest independent ideas. The following is an example of the main ideas of a speech arranged topically.

Specific Purpose: *I want my audience to register and vote at the next election.*

    I. The results of the election could influence the amount of taxes that you and your parents pay.

    II. Aid to higher education could be affected by the outcome of the election.

    III. A whole range of other issues related to your everyday life could be settled by this election.

    IV. The process of registering and voting is a simple one.

    V. Your vote can make a difference.

4. *Ideas can be arranged in a sequence that leads from cause to effect or from effect to cause.* This causal pattern is a useful one for speakers who want an audience to understand the development of a specific idea, event, or phenomenon, or for speakers who want to suggest modifications in a chain of relationships that will bring more desirable outcomes to an audience. If, for example, a speaker wants his or her audience to understand why urban violence occurs, he or she may arrange ideas so that they will show the relationship of an event or circumstance to another event or circumstance, thus forming a chain of events that has as its final link the violent behavior the speaker hopes to explain. The following is an example of ideas arranged in a causal pattern:

Specific Purpose: *I want my audience to agree that a better system of traffic lights and signs is needed in this community.*

    I. Three children have been killed or seriously injured in the last year on First Street while attempting to cross an unguarded crossing. *(Effect)*

    II. At the crossing on the bypass, several accidents have resulted when oncoming traffic has failed to stop for the red light. *(Effect)*

    III. Traffic jams causing long delays and increasing psychological stress on drivers occur every weekday during the rush hours. *(Effect)*

    IV. Directions showing lanes in which to turn, speed limits, and so on, which are painted on the street, are completely worn away by the end of the winter. *(Effect)*

    V. Something must be done about the poor traffic-control procedures in this town. *(Cause)*

5. *Ideas can be arranged in a problem-solution sequence. The problem solution pattern* is one that lends itself to particular topics. It appeals to an audience that wants a careful, logical, well-grounded approach to a perceived difficulty. This kind of a pattern of ideas suggests itself when there are many ways to deal with a problem and when one way may not necessarily be purely advantageous but may have certain drawbacks. Through a problem-solution pattern a speaker may be able to demonstrate that a solution with drawbacks is still the best possible solution to a difficult problem.

In this pattern, the speaker's first idea would deal with the nature of the problem itself, what it is and who it affects; his or her second idea would establish the criteria for solving the problem; his or her third idea would encompass the possible solutions to the problem; and his or her fourth idea would offer the best possible solution. It should be emphasized that the speaker using this kind of a pattern needs to make explicit the relationship between the criteria for solution and the best possible solution. After all, the solution that most nearly meets the criteria will be the best one. The following is an example of ideas that fall into a problem-solution pattern.

Specific Purpose: *I want my audience to agree that prostitution should be legalized and regulated by law.*

I. Illegal prostitution raises serious legal, moral, and health problems.
II. Any solution to these problems must take into account the sensibilities of the community, the difficulties of law enforcement, the protection of the public, and the individual rights of those involved.
III. Prostitution could be kept as a totally illegal act, as it is in most places now; it could be kept illegal and enforcement made stricter and punishment more severe; it could be legalized without any restraints; or it could be legalized only under careful government supervision.
IV. Legalization under supervision is the solution that best meets the needs of society and speaks most directly to the more serious aspects of the problem.

The above list of possible patterns is not exhaustive, but it does include the principle ways in which a speaker can sequence his or her ideas so that coherent patterns suitable to his topic and appealing to an audience can be constructed.

SEQUENCING IDEAS

The five basic organizational patterns discussed above *(chronological, spatial, topical, problem-solution, cause-effect)* are the principal ways that ideas are put into a coherent structure in a speech. The pattern the speaker chooses is selected because he/she believes that it is the pattern that best suits the topic, purpose, and audience. The pattern constrains the speech: a chronological pattern must be governed by when things happened, problem-solution must identify a problem and show how it can be solved, and so forth. Even so, the speaker has some other options within the organizational patterns chosen.

The speaker can sequence ideas within the pattern in ways that reflect audience characteristics, predispositions, knowledge, and the like. There are three particular sequences that a speaker can find useful in adapting her/his ideas to an audience: the *directional sequence,* the *climactic sequence,* and the *contrastive sequence.*

1. *Ideas can be arranged in either a direct or an indirect sequence.* This directional sequence is based on the speaker's assessment of what the audience knows, believes, and expects. When discussing a controversial issue, for example, a speaker may wish to lead gradually to a conclusion by an indirect development rather than arouse the audience's hostility or antagonism before the opportunity to present the evidence is given.

On the other hand, a speaker's position may be well known or the audience may be strongly in agreement with the speaker, and, consequently, the speaker may wish to lay out the rationale for the position very clearly so that the audience's own feelings and beliefs will be reinforced by what is said. Consider the following examples of a speech in which a topic developed both directly and indirectly.

Specific Purpose: *I want my audience to feel more strongly that collective bargaining by faculty would improve faculty performance and benefits.*

    I. The regulation of professional matters related to such factors as class size, teaching load, and adequate and comfortable office space would help instructors to do a better job.

   II. Regulation of qualifications for technique would result in the upgrading of instruction.

  III. Financial security and job security would relieve unnecessary psychological stress and create a better climate in which teaching could be carried on.

Specific Purpose: I *want my audience to agree that collective bargaining by the faculty will result in an improved educational system.*

    I. A good educational system depends on getting the best performance possible from the best faculty.

   II. Faculty can do the best job when the conditions under which they work are designed to promote learning.

III. Faculty can do the best job when they can direct their energies to solving educational problems.

IV. Securing a good faculty and providing conditions under which they can work well can best be done through collective bargaining.

2. *Ideas can be arranged in a sequence that goes from simple to difficult, from least important to most important, from emotionally neutral to emotionally intense.* This *climactic sequence* very much reflects audience needs and pressures. If, for example, a speaker is addressing a topic with which the audience is not at all familiar, he or she might want to start with a very simple idea first so that the audience is not puzzled or confused. The speaker might also, as he or she assesses the battery of arguments to be used, decide that it would be best to leave the audience with the strongest argument. In this case, the speaker would arrange ideas so as to build up to that argument.

Considerable difference of opinion and conflicting research results exist as to whether or not this weak-to-strong indirect method is a good one. A good case could be made for the proposition that it is generally better to start with the best argument, follow through with other arguments, and then return briefly to review the best one again. At any rate, the ideas should all be sound ones, and therefore should not suffer too much by an indirect approach. Furthermore, a speaker, like a playwright, may wish to build on his listeners' interests and attention until he or she reaches a climactic moment. That is to say, a speaker may wish to arrange ideas so that the audience becomes increasingly absorbed and interested in those specific ideas until the moment is reached when the audience can most strongly identify with what the speaker is saying. The following are examples of ideas that can be patterned climactically. The first example goes from least to most important with rising emotional intensity, and the second from simple to complex.

Specific Purpose: *I want my audience to agree that action to stop environmental pollution must begin now.*

I. Pollution of air and water in this community has direct consequences for your health and your pocketbook.

II. Pollution effects can drastically alter the standard of living in this country.

III. Pollution can ultimately lead to the destruction of human life on this planet.

Specific Purpose: *I want my audience to understand the basic operation of an automobile engine.*

    I. The gasoline-fueled automobile functions through the combined process of compression and combustion of the fuel in the piston cylinder.

    II. The power that the engine produces is the result of many small but quickly timed explosions.

    III. The essential parts of the engine for this process are the carburetor, piston and piston cylinder, spark plug, crankshaft, and fuel mixture.

    IV. The sequence of the piston strokes is intake-compression-ignition/combustion-exhaust/power.

3. *Ideas can be arranged in a sequence in which those in favor of a proposition are contrasted with those opposed to it.* This contrastive sequence is suited to a speech that deals with the acceptance or the rejection of a specific program, policy, or idea. If, for example, a speaker were discussing a Constitutional amendment to limit government spending, that speaker could use this contrastive patterning of ideas to lay out the arguments for the amendment as opposed to the arguments against the amendment. Through a process of weighing both sides of an issue, the speaker would then come to a decision for or against it based on the pros and cons as he or she has laid them out.

This method is one that should be used, as well as reacted to, with some caution, since it often gives a speaker the appearance of impartiality without the reality of that quality. On the other hand, there are times when failing to recognize arguments on both sides of the issue might suggest to an audience, particularly an audience familiar with those arguments, that the speaker is overlooking, ignoring, or deliberately trying to hide arguments that would be disadvantageous to his or her case. The following is an example of the way in which ideas could be arranged contrastively:

Specific Purpose: *I want my audience to agree that the best kind of state-sponsored student loan program is one that provides for 100 percent state guarantee.*

    I. The state Senate and the House of Representatives have passed two different student loan bills, one that provides a 100 percent guarantee behind loans and one that provides a 95 percent guarantee.

II. The 100 percent plan would make more loans available to more students and would qualify the state for 100 percent federal reimbursement for any defaulted loans.

III. The 95 percent bill would make financial institutions more cautious in lending and could result in savings of tax dollars.

IV. But the drastic reduction in loans that would result from the 95 percent plan would defeat the purpose of the program, and many worthy students would be unable to raise the money to attend college.

TRANSITIONS AND INTERNAL SUMMARIES

It is the speaker's task to do the best he or she can to help the audience apprehend the relationship of ideas to one another. The way the ideas are put together is, of course, crucial. *But it also is very important for the speaker to plan carefully the ways in which he or she will progress from one idea to another.*

A transition is a type of bridge whereby the speaker moves from one idea to another. After all, the audience cannot be expected to be paying 100 percent of their attention to the speaker, nor can they be expected to understand the sequence of ideas as clearly as does the speaker. This information is all new to them, so the speaker must alert her listeners to prepare for a new idea to be introduced and developed. The bridge can be a very simple one, as when a speaker says, "Now that I have laid out the principle advantage, let me turn to the disadvantage." Or it can be a simple enumeration, "And now consider the second way in which money can be raised."

Sometimes getting from one idea to another may be accomplished in an elaborate fashion because the complexity of the material warrants it. For example, a speaker may employ an *internal summary.* That is, he or she may very briefly go over the points made so far before moving to the next one. The speaker in such a case might say, "We've seen how the Stamp Act in 1766 aroused the first successful organized resistance on the part of the colonists to the British government and how British attempts to deal with the problems of taxation and defense, coupled with a growing spirit of independence in the colonies, caused an ever-widening breach between North America and Great Britain. Now let's see how the events in the months preceding the Declaration of

Independence led the young colonies to a final break with the mother country." That kind of statement is, in essence, a short summary of what has been said. It helps keep the audience mentally on the track.

A good transition, then, helps the audience to look back on what has been said and forward to what will be said; thus, it will help the audience to follow more closely the speaker's pattern and see more clearly the connection between ideas.

THE WHOLE SPEECH AND ITS PARTS

STRUCTURE AND THE CLARITY OF IDEAS

As the speaker begins to impose structure on his or her ideas, he or she should be able to determine the strengths and weaknesses of the entire speech in promoting the purpose. In other words, the structure gives a type of clarity to the whole speech that only becomes evident when all the ideas are carefully articulated and when their relationships are very clearly understood and uncovered. It is only when the speaker can discern a clear pattern that he or she can appreciate breaks or distortions in the pattern.

A speech is often said to be "crafted." Like anything that is individually made or built employing the skills of a creator, the speech must present a symmetrical and balanced whole. It must be intellectually complete. It is only when the structure is fully formed that the speaker can truly apprehend how well he or she has organized ideas.

FORM AND THE PERSUASIVENESS OF IDEAS

We have all learned the truism that the whole is greater than the sum of its parts. What this means is that when individual characteristics or parts or pieces are held up and examined by an observer, they may not suggest the total impression that will be given when all of these are put together. When a speaker is structuring ideas, he or she should realize that the combination of ideas or the cumulative effect of ideas may be different from or greater than each idea taken individually. Consider, for example, items of behavior that might be called, in and of themselves, trifles: one forgets to put a stamp on a letter that is being mailed; one addresses the letter to the wrong place; one cancels an appointment that should not have been canceled; one sends out a letter without indicating who it is from; or one misfiles a document. These are minor mistakes. When put together, however, they may give a strong impression of inefficiency or carelessness. In a similar manner, the way ideas are structured and developed may strongly suggest that a certain person, object, or idea be perceived in a certain way; that is what we would refer to as the "form" of the speech.

Certain communicative forms can emerge, also, from different messages if those messages are structured similarly. For example, during 1976, President Gerald Ford's movements were reported in detail. Often these reports included a physical malfunction or minor error on the President's part, such as tripping when alighting from a plane, or falling down when skiing, or being a passenger in a car that collided with another car. The repetition of these incidents, and the way in which they were structured as part of the event as reported by the media, tended to project a particular form. That is to say, that the idea of a fumbling or bumbling President could easily have emerged from the structure of the individual messages. So when a speaker puts a series of ideas together, he or she needs to consider not only the impact of each of those ideas but the combined impact of all of them as they appear in a single message.

LISTENER RESPONSES TO PATTERNS OF IDEAS

A speaker uses structure to promote the persuasiveness and clarity of his or her ideas. The listener needs to both exploit and evaluate structure as it relates to his or her needs. That is, the listener must do everything in his or her power to try to *understand the structure, to use it in order to follow ideas clearly, and to get from it a true sense of the speaker's purpose.* The listener must also be aware of the criteria for determining a good idea: he or she must test the idea to make certain that it is *clearly stated, that it is simple but not oversimplified, that it is addressed to him or her, and that it makes sense.*

As the listener begins to see a pattern of ideas, he or she must be prepared to evaluate that pattern through an understanding of what it is doing. For example, although the pattern of a speech may suggest that a speaker is evaluating both sides of an argument, the listener needs to ask himself or herself if that really is the case, or whether a veneer of objectivity is simply being applied. Although a speaker may follow a problem-solution pattern, the listener needs to exercise some caution in accepting the speaker's criteria for arriving at the best solution While the speaker may assert that certain events are the cause of later effects, the listener must demand that such a link be proven conclusively. In other words, *the listener, as he or she experiences a speech, must be aware and actively critical of the structure of the speech and the form it suggests.*

PRINCIPLE INTO PRACTICE: A SUMMARY

HOW TO ORGANIZE YOUR SPEECH

At this point, the speaker should be able to generate ideas that strongly and clearly promote her purpose The listener can use the structure of the speech to further his understanding of the ideas and their relationships, but he needs to be skeptical of the impact of structure on his own conclusions.

The speaker should take the following steps in organizing the speech:

1. Support the purpose by developing ideas that are
   - Clear to the audience
   - Simple without being oversimplified
   - Sensible to the audience
   - Related to the situation

2. Sequence ideas in appropriate patterns that suggest the desired form oroverall impression of the speech, choosing from among.
   - Chronological pattern
   - Spatial pattern
   - Topical pattern
   - Problem-solution pattern
   - Causal pattern

3. Plan carefully how transitions will help the audience follow the movement of one idea to another.

4. Plan internal summaries to make the transition from one idea to another when the material is complex and needs to be reviewed for the audience.

The tool that is most helpful to the speaker in finally putting together all the material that he or she has gathered into a sensible structure is the outline. In fact, *as the speaker goes through all the steps that have been discussed thus far in this book, he or she is already constructing an outline.* Since preparing a good outline is crucial in the process of preparing yourself to speak, the next chapter is devoted to considering this device in detail. Following that chapter is a set of sample outlines that illustrate the organizational principles that have been discussed in this chapter.

CHAPTER 9

PUTTING IT ALL TOGETHER: OUTLINING

After studying this chapter you should understand:

● How outlining is related to the process of preparing yourself to speak.

● How to construct a good outline.

● How to evaluate preparation by consdering:
  • Purpose
  • Main Ideas
  • Supporting Material
  • Introduction and Conclusions

OUTLINING AND PREPARATION

When a speaker tries to understand the nature of the audience and the situation, tries to devise a sensible, reasonable purpose that will generate sound ideas, and attempts to put those ideas together in a meaningful way, he or she is participating in a process that will ultimately prepare him or her to speak. *This process of preparation can be visually represented through an outline.*

Sometimes speakers think of an outline as something to be done after the speech is prepared—a sort of formal partitioning of the speech. Still others think of the outline as a set of notes to be used in delivering the speech. Actually, the outline is neither of these things. It is the *tangible representation of the process of speech preparation.* It is built as the speaker goes through the intellectual operations necessary to get ready to speak to an audience. What has been discussed so far should be used in generating a type of skeletal outline of the major portion of the speech.

The speaker who has defined a clear purpose, designed ideas to further that purpose, and arranged ideas in an effective sequence has actually begun to outline. His or her next consideration is to find ways in which those well ordered ideas can be developed in order to make them understandable or believable for an audience. That is to say, the ideas must be supported. Support for ideas, gathered through research with the intention of uncovering the type and amount of material that will build a good argument and involve listeners, takes its final shape with the help of the outline. *An outline shows clearly the supporting relationships that exist within the speech.* It should demonstrate for the speaker how his or her purpose can best be carried out using the evidence that is available.

THE PROCESS OF OUTLINING

A few years ago, a beginning speaker introduced his first classroom speech by saying, "How many times have you either gone to class, or to work, in the morning and heard somebody say, 'Boy, I must have slept on the wrong side of the bed last night, my neck is killing me.'?" The introduction thus dispensed with, the speaker went on to raise the rhetorical question, "What is Super Marvel?" and answered it with the information that Super Marvel is a mechanical muscle relaxer that has been on the market for fifty-three years. He continued by explaining that Super Marvel, unlike other treatments for aches and pains, is not a greasy cream or ointment and needs only an electrical source to operate. Producing a Super Marvel from a bag, the speaker asserted that it could be used for mechanical muscle massage or converted for an electrical impulse treatment. He concluded, "The next time you go to the store looking for relief from common body ache, don't ask for a cream or an ointment, ask for the Super Marvel."

Would you? Probably not; as most of the speaker's listeners probably would not. There is a lot wrong with the speech. The strategic considerations of purpose, structure, and form do not appear to have been given much thought; the tactical choices designed to make ideas understandable and believable and to involve the audience are severely limited. The speaker obviously did not prepare himself well. He took some time (but not very much) and he made some effort to put a message together. The fact that his preparation was inadequate is demonstrated by his outline.

THE SUPER MARVEL

Specific Purpose: *To introduce the audience to one of the most successful treatments of the common body (muscle) aches.*

INTRODUCTION
How many times have you either gone to class in the morning (or work) and heard somebody say, "Boy, I must have slept on the wrong side of the bed last night, my neck is killing me."?

BODY
1. What is the Super Marvel?
   A. A mechanical muscle relaxer
   B. Has been on the market for fifty-three years
2. Advantages of the Super Marvel over common treatments of aches and pains
   A. No greasy ointments or creams involved
   B. No side effects
   C. Only need an electrical source to operate

3. Demonstration of the Super Marvel
   A. Showing muscle massage
   B. Showing electrical impulse treatment

CONCLUSION

The next time you go to the store looking for relief from a common body ache, don't ask for a cream or ointment, ask for the Super Marvel!

BIBLIOGRAPHY

No sources but myself.

It should be obvious to anyone who has read this book that the "Super Marvel" outline is evidence of poor preparation. The point to be emphasized here is that it is the preparation that is being faulted, because *the outline should be the result of the way the speaker prepares himself or herself to speak, and not just a division of the speech into sets or categories.*

Outlining is a process. The outline grows as the speaker gets ready to speak. The outline is not something that one does as the final link in the chain of events leading to the speech. Nor is it a set of notes to be assembled just before practicing for the speech. It should emerge as the speaker goes along. Let's consider the Super Marvel outline in some detail as an example.

The first strategic choice involves purpose. As the speaker develops his or her purpose, he or she will be creating the first, crucial determinant of the outline. Remember, from the purpose, structural strategies emerge as the speaker decides what ideas will further the purpose and how they should be put together.

It is apparent that the Super Marvel speaker made initial errors. First, he did not formulate clearly his purpose in terms of audience response. "To introduce the audience" to something does not describe the response. Accordingly, there is some confusion about whether the speech is essentially an informative or a persuasive one.

This initial ambiguity helps to explain the problem in conceptualizing the main ideas and forming them into a coherent structure. The first idea should not be a question, "What is a Super Marvel?" but rather, an answer to that question, something like, "Super Marvel is a mechanical muscle relaxer." If the purpose is "I want my audience to understand what a Super Marvel is," then that is probably a good first idea.

The second idea is not correctly stated either; it is a heading for a list of advantages and not what the audience should believe or understand. Again, there is a problem here because the purpose is not clear. What the speaker probably has in mind is a persuasive purpose, such as, "I want audience members to agree with me that the Super Marvel will improve their health," or "I want my audience to buy Super Marvel." These purposes could generate different structural and ideational strategies.

If the purpose is to get an audience's adherence to the proposition that the device may improve health, the first idea should probably deal with the relation of the device to well-being, such as, "Pain resulting from tension or muscle fatigue can be reduced or eliminated through electric massage." The same idea could begin a speech with the second purpose, buying the device, but would more likely result in a set of ideas that stress the advantages the speaker mentions along with several others that should be devised dealing with matters of cost, safety, and so on.

The speaker planned, as his third point, a "Demonstration of the Super Marvel." Now, that is not an idea. What purpose does the demonstration serve? The idea might be that the Super Marvel is easy to use, and one way to make that idea believable is to show the audience. But whether or not this is an idea that should be in the speech at all depends on the strategic considerations of purpose and structure, and in this case these considerations are too vague. So, the fault with the outline at this stage is a fault in preparation.

The outline illustrates preparation problems related to supporting material as well. A quick examination of the outline shows that there is almost no effort made to make ideas believable or understandable or to develop them, nor is there conscious effort made to involve the audience in the subject. Of course, what tactics are used will depend on what strategy is chosen, so if there is no clear purpose and structure, it will be impossible to provide enough supporting material, or even to know what kind of supporting material should be provided. But if one takes what is in point II and restates it as an idea, "Super Marvel is the most effective way to treat common aches and pains," then one can see how inadequately the speaker has planned to support that idea. One appeal is obviously to cleanliness, showing that no messy creams and ointments are used. There is a reference to "no side effects," but that makes one raise the question, What side effects are caused by other remedies? And what are the other remedies, anyway? The only common treatment mentioned is the use of creams and ointments. The final piece of support given the idea is that it needs only an electrical source. But, since creams need no electricity at all and thus could be used anywhere, and since they call for no expenditure of energy, the Super Marvel's need for an electrical source might be said to be a disadvantage.

This illustrative discussion of the outline should indicate that things went very wrong as the speaker got ready to speak. The communication process itself may be seen as constructing and applying a model of information and appeals—the construction and use of strategy and tactics—that the outline evidences. So one does not construct an outline as if it were an additional technicality to satisfy a critic. One builds an outline as one prepares himself or herself to speak. The result is concrete; not only something for an instructor to criticize and react to, but also a tangible map of experience that a speaker can use as a tool for self-criticism and self-regulation as he or she prepares to speak in public.

An excellent way to begin to see and understand preparation problems and avoid them as one participates in the speaking process is by developing an awareness of and sensitivity to what constitutes a good outline. This is often very hard to do just by looking at samples in textbooks. The remainder of this chapter presents two real outlines—those turned in by beginning speakers in a public-speaking class—and illustrates some of the ways their shortcomings might have been avoided. This is followed by an explanation of guidelines for evaluating outlines that should help you evaluate your own preparation.

OUTLINE I: The Zodiac

Specific Purpose: *To explain how zodiac signs got their names.*

INTRODUCTION

I. The Zodiac is an imaginary belt in the heavens that extends for several degrees on either side of the path of the sun.
   A. This path is called the ecliptic.
      1. The ecliptic is divided into twelve sections of 3 degrees.
      2. These sections are known as the Houses of the Zodiac.
   B. The sun takes a year to travel through the twelve houses.
      1. These months are not the ones we are familiar with.
      2. They are periods from the twenty-first of our months to the twentieth of the next (approximately).

    C. The beginning of the zodiac year is when the sun enters the house of Aries.

       1. From this time, the days are longer than the nights and are increasing in length.

BODY

II. The first sign is Aries.

    A. The constellation of Aries is a group of three very bright stars visible to the naked eye.

       1. The brightest is referred to as the ram.

    B. The Babylonians and the Chinese gave great prominence to Aries.

       1. Aries was believed to have occupied the center of the heavens.

       2. The symbol for Aries is the ram.

       3. In early religions, the symbol of sacrifice was the ram.

III. The second sign is Taurus.

    A. This constellation is a beautiful cluster of stars.

       1. The constellation's name is Hyades, from Greek meaning "rain."

       2. Its influence is believed to be conducive to rain.

    B. Taurus was named after the seven daughters of Atlas.

       1. Because of their great virtue and purity, were rewarded by a place in the heavens as a constellation of stars.

       2. The symbol of Taurus is the bull.

IV. The third sign is Gemini.

    A. In the earliest zodiacs, this house was symbolized by two kids.

    B. The Greeks substituted twin children.

       1. The sons of Jupiter, Castor and Pollux.

    C. The myth of Castor and Pollux.

       1. Castor was killed in battle, and Pollux, overwhelmed at his loss, asked Jupiter to restore his brother to life or make them both immortal.

       2. As a reward for and in recognition of their noble deeds when on earth, Jupiter turned the two brothers into the constellation Gemini.

V. The fourth sign is Cancer.

    A. Cancer, the crab, was placed in the heavens as a reward.

       1. The goddess Juno rewarded Cancer for the sacrifice of its life, which it lost in an attack on Hercules, in her service.

VI. The fifth sign is Leo.

    A. In Greek mythology, the lion is said to represent the monster who was the terror of travelers in the forests of Nemaea.

       1. He was slain by Hercules in battle.

2. To commemorate the great combat, Jupiter gave it a place amongst the stars.

VII. The sixth sign is Virgo.
   A. In mythology, Virgo was represented by Isis.
      1. She was the goddess of harvests and fruits.
      2. She is said to have invented the arts of husbandry.
      3. Previous to this, humanity existed on a diet of acorns.

VIII. The seventh sign is Libra.
   A. Libra is symbolized by a pair of scales.
   B. Libra was not included in the earliest zodiacs, and it has not yet been determined how it got its name.

IX. The eighth sign is Scorpio.
   A. According to Greek mythology, the scorpion was placed in the heavens by Juno, queen of the gods.
      1. Scorpio carried out Juno's wishes by stinging Orion.
      2. Orion had offended the goddess by boasting that he could subdue the wildest and fiercest beast.
      3. Orion died from the effects of the sting.

X. The ninth sign is Sagittarius.
   A. This sign is named after Chiron, the son of Saturn.
      1. Chiron studied medicine and became a skilled physician.
      2. Chiron was also a famous astronomer and scientist.
      3. He was the instructor of Achilles and Hercules.
   B. Chiron became a zodiac sign by accident.
      1. Chiron dropped one of Hercules' poison arrows on his foot.
      2. Being born of immortal parents, he could not die.
      3. He was released from his pain by becoming a zodiac sign.

XI. The tenth sign is Capricorn.
   A. Capricorn is usually seen as half goat and half fish.
   B. This is explained by an adventure of the god Pan.
      1. Pan, while feasting on the banks of the Nile, was attacked by the monster Typhon.
      2. In order to escape, Pan jumped into the river and took the form of a fish for the lower body and a goat for the upper half.

XII. The eleventh sign is Aquarius.
   A. It is not really known how Aquarius got its name.

       1. It is believed Aquarius got its name from the ancient Chinese, but no one is sure.

XIII.   The twelfth sign is Pisces.

     A. In ancient Grecian mythology, it is recorded that two fish were placed in the heavens by the goddess Minerva.

       1. To commemorate the escape of Venus and her son Cupid from the monster Typhon.

       2. To escape, Venus and Cupid transformed themselves into fishes and plunged into the river which took them to safety.

XIV.   There are a lot of books on zodiac mythology.

     A. It makes for very enjoyable reading.

BIBLIOGRAPHY

William Thomas and Kate Pavitt, *The Book of Talismans, Amulets, and Zodiac Gems*. London: Rider & Company, n.d.

ANALYSIS OF "THE ZODIAC"

To begin with, *the purpose of this speech is not stated as audience response:* "To explain" is a speaker-centered description and not an audience-centered one. Probably, the speaker wants to have the listeners understand how the zodiac signs were named. If that is his purpose, *the structure that has been used is a very poor one.* Each sign is named as an "idea," giving twelve "ideas" that don't help to accomplish the purpose. Looking at the main ideas will not provide many clues as to how the signs were named at all. The structure that is suggested by the purpose should be one that would help the audience first to know just what the zodiac signs are, the differences between "signs" and "constellations," and then to see relationships between the signs and their names.

The *introduction* to the speech seems really to be the first main idea, one that tries to explain what the zodiac is. The ideas that follow, however, do not promote understandings of the origin of the names. As the speaker was preparing himself, he should have asked: Did the signs get their names in different ways? What were these ways? In fact, the outline taken as a whole makes it very difficult to see exactly how any of the signs got their names. The speaker probably was thinking about "saying something interesting" about each one of the signs instead of focusing on the audience's response. Some of the signs seem to have been named for animals and some for gods or goddesses in Greek mythology, but *how* were they named? Were they named because they looked like specific figures to observers? The signs are often represented like the "connect the dots" games that children play, suggesting that by drawing lines connecting the stars, one can produce a picture that looks like a bull or a crab.

To develop the purpose as restated here, the main ideas for the speech might be:

I.   Some signs were named because their configuration looked to observers like the shapes of certain animals.

II. Some signs were named because their configuration suggested to some observers the shape of mythical characters.

III. The origin of the name of one sign is obscure.

Such a group of main ideas seems more likely to promote the specific purpose of the speech than the listing of twelve signs.

Of course, the tactics used to develop the ideas would now be different from those used in the outline. The speaker would need to uncover and arrange materials that would make the ideas more understandable and believable. In this kind of speech, examples—Leo looks like a lion, Cancer looks like a crab, and so on—would probably be the most frequently used form of support. Yet, if you look carefully at the original outline, you will see how careless preparation leads to difficulty as we attempt to reconstruct the outline. The speaker must know more about the subject than we, the critics, do. He should be able to determine the accuracy of certain information and its best place in the scheme of the speech. The speaker in this case has not supplied enough information for us to decide if a shape came first, and then a story made up to explain it, or if a story was made up to explain the constellation and then a "symbol" taken because of the shape. Look at Taurus. The speaker has not really prepared to deal with how that name came about. There are seven stars in the constellation, (a fact not mentioned), and mythology probably accounted for this fact more than for the fact that a line drawing would come out looking like a bull. So, this is somehow different from Leo or Cancer, the names for lion or crab. And then there is Aries, whose "symbol" is the ram, but whose name origin is never mentioned.

The organizational pattern that is suggested here might not be the best one if the speaker's purpose were not the one we hypothesized. Obviously, a lot of anecdotal material, examples of how Greek mythology accounted for the constellations, doesn't fit into this new outline devoted exclusively to the names of signs. What becomes apparent as we examine the outline in detail is that the speaker's preparation was governed by a deep misconception of purpose; the speaker seems to have come across a book about the Zodiac and intended to use it to tell the audience something about each sign. As a result, the speech will be very difficult to follow and generalizations very hard to remember, but a few assorted, but not integrated, facts may remain.

Furthermore, *there is no planned introduction or conclusion.* How can listeners be made interested in this topic? Does it relate in any way to their needs or values? There is no consideration here of the methods suggested for relating the audience to the topic and helping them to follow what will come. And in the conclusion there seems to be only a quick reference to a book. The speaker has not wrapped up this speech and not left the listeners with the overriding theme or mood of the speech.

This analysis shows more than the fact that the speaker "has not put the ideas together" correctly. It demonstrates *that the preparation began with a poor conception of purpose and form, and proceeded with a very limited and not appropriately focused set of tactics.*

OUTLINE II: From Sugar To Honey

Specific Purpose: *To persuade listeners to give up refined white sugar and to use honey as a substitute when necessary.*

INTRODUCTION

After a nice weekend did you ever wake up on that first day of the week with a disease called the "Monday morning blues"? Well you may think the sole reason is because you have to be in class at 8:00 A.M., but there may be another reason that can easily be eliminated if you would just give up refined white sugar and use natural sugar, such as honey. I'd like to tell you just what refined sugar is and how honey can benefit you, also how to substitute honey in your cooking.

BODY

I. Refined sugars are stripped of their nutritional value during the refining process.
   A. Grapes as an example on why this is done.

1. Will keep practically forever
2. Could have them in condensed form to put on the table
3. Could flavor food with their sweet taste summer and winter

    B. Result of refining process is a vitamin B loss

       1. Vitamin B is necessary to burn the sugars in digestion so it steals vitamins from vital organs, nerves, muscles, liver, kidneys, stomach, heart, skin, eyes, and blood

       2. Results of niacin deficiency: will make a strong courageous person cowardly, apprehensive, suspicious, mentally confused, and depressed

II.   Honey, as a nutritious, natural sugar, contains protein, calcium, phosphorus, sodium, potassium, nine of the ten amino acids necessary for human nutrition, and vitamins B and C.

III.   Calorie content of honey is less in proportion to sweetening power of sugar

    A. Need half as much honey as sugar

    B. Save 33 percent of sweetening calories

IV.   How to substitute honey for sugar

    A. Use half as much honey as sugar

    B. Dark honey

       1. Better on breads

       2. As syrup on pancakes

    C. Light honeys

       1. Come from early spring crops

       2. Suited for cakes, cookies, light breads, fruits, tea

    D. Use more flour or less liquid to get right consistency

    E. Oven temperature when making cookies and breads is 25 degrees less, because it will brown faster.

    F. Cakes and cookies cooked with honey are moister and fresher.

    G. In jams, jellies, and preserves, use half as much honey as sugar that the recipe calls for.

    H. Thin honey before adding to beaten egg white.

       1. Meringue

       2. Cake frostings

    I. How to thin honey

V.   It is easy to store in the refrigerator.

       1. Becomes hard to pour

       2. May crystallize and get grainy

          a. Just thin to return to normal state

          b. Will not hurt quality of honey or alter consistency permanently

CONCLUSION

I'm not suggesting you deliberately add honey to your diet, because honey is a carbohydrate and most of us get too much carbohydrated food in comparison to our protein consumption. But if you feel you need a sweetener on cereals or on fruit, by all means use honey instead of sugar; it is a healthy food which is easily substituted for sugar. Also, you need half as much so you save half the calories. You might like to know that when craving sugar that that is a natural way of getting us to eat vitamins and minerals, since they are tasteless; you wouldn't eat them if they weren't put in a sweet form, so when you are craving sweets, it is craving sweets because it needs those vitamins and minerals that come in the sweet form, and remember with sugar cane, they stripped away all the vitamins so you get calories and nothing else, so get sugar the way nature meant for us, eat foods with sugar that still have vitamins and minerals, and if you need sweetener use honey, and wake up on Monday morning with a smile.

BIBLIOGRAPHY

J. I. Rodale, *Health Builder*. Emmaus, Pennsylvania: Rodale Press, Inc., 1959.
"I'll Take Honey, Thank You." *Prevention*, pp. 132-137.

ANALYSIS OF "FROM SUGAR TO HONEY"

The speaker's purpose in this case is fairly clear; she calls for direct action on the part of the listeners when using sweeteners to give up refined sugar and substitute honey in its place. The purpose, however, could be more precisely stated to conform to the suggestions offered in this book: "I want my audience to give up refined white sugar and to use honey as a substitute when necessary." But the purpose is fairly clear and direct in this case.

To further that purpose, the speaker has come up with five main ideas. The first idea (refined sugars are stripped of their nutritional value during the refining process) is designed to show that refined sugars are harmful. This, of course, makes sense; if the speaker hopes that we will stop using the product, she certainly needs to make us believe that it is good for us to do so. The idea that the nutritional values are gone from refined sugars is supported by an example (which is not very clear as it appears in the outline and makes one wonder if the speaker is sure of the point to be made), and by an assertion that vitamin B is lost in the refining process. The loss of vitamin B is further amplified as the speaker describes what the body does to get necessary vitamin B, and as she gives one example of what can happen to someone who suffers a niacin loss.

There are many problems with the planning of this idea. Given the purpose, it is certainly a good and useful one, but it seems inadequately and incorrectly developed. Point I. B reads, "Result of refining process is a vitamin B loss." But the material that supports this assertion is a claim that, since vitamin B is necessary to burn sugar in the body, it is stolen from vital organs. Yet, the description of what happens in the body does not make clear how vitamin B is removed during the refining process. The material necessary to support point B is that which contributes to our belief that the vitamin is removed during refining and to our understanding of how it is done. What I. B suggests is that there is harm done to the body by the depletion of vitamin B; it is caused by the body's attempt to burn sugar. Such a point involves more than the matter of loss of nutritional value.

What is needed here are two main ideas:

I. Refined sugars are stripped of their nutritional value during the refining process.

II. Refined sugars can be directly harmful to the human body.

Now the speaker needs to consider how well she has planned to support each of these ideas.

The first point is supported only by the grape example, and the second point only by the assertion that sugar "steals" vitamins from vital organs. Obviously, for an audience to be convinced, more is needed. *Testimony* of nutritionists could be brought to bear on the question of the results of the refining process, and testimony of nutritionists and medical authorities on the point of refined sugar's damage to the body. *Examples* in the form of medical case studies or hypothetical descriptions of what could happen could be used to assess the effect of sugar on the body. *Statistical information* indicating the extent of the problem could be adduced. *Comparisons* between the effects of other harmful substances and sugar could be made. Indeed, if a speaker really hopes to get an audience to change its behavior, considerable preparation must go into amassing enough evidence to make a case beyond merely telling each listener that a substance is bad for him or her.

The point I.B.2 has not been considered so far. This point suggests that there is another main idea that the speaker should explore and develop:

III.   Refined sugar could, by creating certain imbalances, cause undesirable changes in behavior.

This is a point that requires additional evidence of a medical and psychological nature. The speaker instead has tried to cover in a very quick and superficial way what is really important in helping to bring about the change she desires.

The same criticism can apply to points II and III. These are totally unsupported statements that claim that honey, as contrasted with refined sugar, is good for you. Perhaps the two points fit together as one: Honey is a natural sugar and, unlike refined sugars, it is good for you. This point could then be developed by elaborating much more on the nutritional values of honey and on the advantages in terms of caloric intake. Here, too, the speaker would need statistical, testimonial, and comparative support, as well as specific examples that would involve the audience further in the extent and nature of the problem.

The main ideas IV and V both involve the ways in which honey can be used as a substitute; they could profitably be combined into one idea. "How to substitute honey for sugar" is not a complete sentence and may better be stated as "It is easy to substitute honey for sugar by making minor adjustments." This could be developed, perhaps, through a simple short list of reminders that touched on quantities, light versus dark, ways to store, and so forth. Given the nature of the audience—a beginning public-speaking class of undergraduates—the specific details on baking might better have been eliminated.

The speaker has made an effort here to plan an introduction that relates to the feelings of the audience and gives a brief summary of what will happen in the speech. But more is needed to involve the audience if they are to believe that this is a serious health matter. Perhaps some striking medical testimony, a surprising statistic that would dramatically illustrate the extent of the problem, or a specific example of a medical incident would serve to involve the audience.

The conclusion includes an attempt on the part of the speaker to cause closure by going back to the opening through the "Monday morning" reference. But there is a very jumbled quality to the conclusion that is partly a result of the initial problems in the ideas of the speech. A careful summary of the ideas as revised, coupled with a final word in the form of a quotation or an example, would end the speech on a sounder note.

PRINCIPLES INTO PRACTICE: A SUMMARY

HOW TO CONSTRUCT A GOOD OUTLINE

From all that has been written thus far, and from the examples just presented of ways in which one might begin to evaluate preparation, one can construct steps for a speaker to take to help himself or herself.

1. Clearly state the purpose as a desired response from the audience.
2. Create ideas that promote the purpose by moving the audience in the direction desired by the speaker.
3. Support ideas by including in the outline ample forms of communicative evidence such as examples, testimony, statistics, comparisons, and motivational materials which will involve the audience in the topic.
4. By using carefully planned introductions and conclusions, engage the listeners' interest immediately and help them to follow what will come in the speech; end on a note that ties the speech together, and leave the listeners with an appropriate sense of closure.

As one begins to work on an outline, it soon becomes apparent that performing the above steps is not simple. Following are a set of outlines that serve as good models; they exemplify the organizational principles and practices that have been discussed in this and the preceding chapters. Studying these outlines will help you to improve your ability to diagnose potential problems you may encounter as you prepare yourself to speak. The purpose of outlining bears repeating: an outline is the tangible representation of the process of preparation. The better a student is at building an outline, the better her chances are of coming to the speaking situation ready to communicate clearly and effectively.

SAMPLE OUTLINES

Following are outlines that exemplify each of the basic organizational patterns discussed in this chapter: *chronological, spatial, topical, problem-solution,* and *cause-effect.* Included are outlines for two *Informative Speeches,* and three *Persuasive Speeches: stimulate, convince,* and *actuate.*

SAMPLE OUTLINE: CHRONOLOGICAL

General Purpose: Speech to Inform
Specific Purpose: I want my audience to understand the situation in Somalia prior to American/United Nations intervention.
Organizational Pattern: Chronological

INTRODUCTION

I. American has intervened in Somalia, a country in chaos, to bring humanitarian relief.
   A. Keith Richburg reports the following story in the September 12, 1992 edition of *The Washington Post:* In the Somali town of Baidoa, "Each morning, a hospital worker pushes a bright blue wheelbarrow through the courtyard collecting the bodies of those who died the night before. Most of the dead are children, so the worker can lift several bodies into the wheelbarrow before wheeling it to a mass grave outside the hospital gates."
   B. When we hear stories like this one, we are forced to ask ourselves, Why is this happening? As concerned human beings, we must explore the answer to this question. And as Americans, we need to be aware of what's going on in countries where we have our troops engaged and our money invested. This is why I would like to talk a little bit today about how such a severe crisis came about in Somalia, a crisis that necessitated American and UN intervention.
      1. On a personal level, one reason for my interest in why our troops are in Somalia is that I have a very close friend who is training to be a Navy SEAL. The SEALs were the first to go into Somalia, and if he had been trained a few months earlier, my friend would be there right now.

Transition: While none of us has probably been the victim of an actual famine, we have all seen pictures of famines and have read and heard about famines all over the world. Every famine is horrible, but what makes Somalia's famine unique and especially devastating is its interaction with the civil war that is going on there. So today I'd like to tell you a little bit about how the civil war in Somalia started and then explain how the interaction of the famine and the civil war led to such a severe crisis. First, let's look at the main groups in the war and how they began fighting.

BODY

I. The civil war in Somalia came about due to clan rivalry.
  A. The history of the clans.
    1. Somalia broke from Italy in 1960, and in 1969, Muhammad Siad Barre took power during a coup.
    2. Although Somalia and neighboring Ethiopia had been somewhat at odds for a decade, in 1988, Ethiopia offered to return two Somali villages that they had captured and to stop arming and protecting the Somali National Movement, a group of rebels. In return, Somalia agreed to stop supporting Ethiopian rebels.
    3. While this may seem like a god deal at first, it created chaos, as the Somali Nationalists came home fighting. The July 9, 1988 *Economist* reports that "Within two months of the border agreement, its guerrillas were engaged in the largest insurgency Somalia has faced since it gained its independence in 1960."

Transition: So as you can see, the clan-based warfare began as President Barre and the Somali Nationalists exchanged bullets, granades, and bombs. We now turn to the question of why the SNM came home fighting Barre.

  B. The position of Barre
    1. President Barre acted as a dictator from the moment he seized power. For example, according to the June 25, 1988 edition of *The Nation,* Barre's government owns and closely censors the media, denies citizens basic rights, such as the freedoms of association, religion, and expression, and has abolished political parties.
    2. But in his efforts to maintain power, Barre has done even worse. Again, *The Nation* writer Neier reports that the government has been known to kill, rape, loot, and torture for the sake of "depriv[ing] the SNM of a civilian base of support."

Transition: It seems that President Barre will do virtually anything for the sake of power, but while he may seem like the "bad guy" in all of this, as we will see, the Somali Nationalists are no angels, either.

  C. The position of the SNM
    1. According to the August 22, 1988 copy of *The New Yorker,* the Somali Nationalists believe that they have been "excluded and discriminated against" by Barre.

2. *The Economist* adds that their movement is not a separatist one. They merely want to remove Barre from power. And it seems that they have succeeded, at least somewhat.

3. The SNM overthrew Barre in January, 1991, and then began fighting with each other. The two main warlords, General Mohamed Farah Aideed and President Ali Mahdi Mohamed, both claim to be the legitimate head of state, and both clans kill and loot for power.

Transition: So, with Barre overthrown, the clans led by Aideed and Mohamed are left to battle it out, along with numerous young gangs, who answer to no one. However, as we will see, the situation is still more complicated because of the interaction between the famine and the civil war.

II.   The civil war, in combination with the famine, produced a severe crisis.
   A.   The source of the clans' power includes both guns and food.
      1.   According to Keith Richburg's September 24, 1992 article in *The Washington Post*, "As rebels opposing Barre closed in on the capital, the artificial Somali state unraveled, and Somalis were left in essentially their pre-colonial condition—a collection of regionally based clans, newly laden with modern arms." So the clans now have the resources for inflicting more widespread pain and suffering.
      2.   But guns are only one source of power, and only the beginning of the problem. As Richburg reports in his August 30, 1992 *Washington Post* article, ". . . in a starving country, food becomes power." Those who can get food become powerful. And those with guns can get the food they want.

Transition: This is why the people who most need to be fed are starving to death. Clan members and other rebels loot and kill for food every single day. And the people are poor, weak, and unable to oppose the men with the guns, food, and power. I would like to try to give you a clearer idea of just how bad the crisis in Somalia is.

   B.   The famine and war have produced widespread hunger and death.
      1.   The August 30, 1992 edition of *The Washington Post* reports that, "an estimated 1.5 million people face imminent starvation." That's over twice as many people as live in Indianapolis, and over ten times as many as in Monroe County.

2. In Baidoa alone, 270 people starved to death in a single day.

3. And the October 23, 1992 *New York Times* reports an estimate by the director of the Somali Red Crescent Society, Hussein Dahir Ahmed that 25% of the population of Somalia has already died.

Transition: As you can see, besides the shootings, fighting clans are killing people by thousands, just by denying them food.

CONCLUSION

I. In summary, we have seen how the clan-based warfare originated in Somalia, and how this civil war interacted with the famine to produce a crisis in which food is power, in which those who most need to be cared for are receiving the least help, and in which people die by the hundreds each day from starvation, shootings, and other abuses.

II. The essence of the interaction of the civil war and the famine seems to be most strikingly and touchingly displayed in the following story, reported by Keith Richburg in the September 12, 1992 *Washington Post:* "[A] young man . . . lifted his shirt to show a reporter scars on his back from a beating by feeding-center guards. 'It's not fair,' he said. 'The poor people are not fed here.' [His] hand was in a makeshift sling, and the skin had peeled away from the bone, from a burn he said he suffered when guards at one feeding center pushed him into the open fire used to cook its rice and bean stew."

SOURCES

The Economist, July 9, 1988, p. 48-49.

The New Yorker, August 22, 1988, pp. 17-18.

Perlez, Jane. "Hungry Somalis Still Die but Crops Grow, Too," *The New York Times,* October 23, 1992, pp. A1 & A8.

Perlez, Jane. "Somalis Try a Food Center Without Gunmen," *The New York Times,* October 29, 1992, p. A7.

Press, Robert M. "Battered Somali Capital Tries to Restore Normalcy," *The Christian Science Monitor,* October 8, 1992, p. 5.

Richburg, Keith B. "Solutions for Somalia Complicated by Chaos," *The Washington Post,* August 30, 1992, pp. A1 & A33.

Richburg, Keith B. "Somalis Starve Despite Aid," *The Washington Post,* September 12, 1992, pp. A1 & A16.

Richburg, Keith B. "Can Battered Somalia Be Pieced Back Together?" *The Washington Post,* September 24, 1992, pp. A20 & A24.

Wallace, Bruce. "A Nation Behond Hope," *Maclean's,* September 14, 1992, pp. 28-31.

SAMPLE OUTLINE: SPATIAL

Title: THE MYSTERIOUS PYRAMIDS
General Purpose: Speech to Inform
Specific Purpose: I want my audience to understand the various parts of the
Egyptian pyramids and their functions.
Organizational pattern: Spatial

INTRODUCTION

I. The pyramids of Egypt are an architectural marvel that have fascinated human
beings for centuries.
   A. The ancient Greek historian, Heroditus, wrote of seven wonders of the
world; the pyramids are the only ones left today.
   B. There have been hundreds of articles and books written about the pyramids,
movies have been made about them or with them as the backdrop, and
thousands of tourists travel from all around the world each year to the
Egyptian desert to see them.
   C. Since I hope to be an architect myself someday, I have always been interested in this greatest architectural feat in human history.
II. Building the pyramids was a major accomplishment.
   A. The size of the pyramids is staggering.
      1. The Great Pyramid of Khufu at Giza, for example, was about 756 feet at
the base and about 480 feet high.
         a. That's taller than the UN Building in New York or, to take an example
closer to home, the pyramid was almost as tall as the Indiana National
Bank Building in Indianapolis.
         b. You could put St. Peter's in Rome, or Westminster Abbey in London
inside this structure; you also could easily fit the Hoosier Dome in it.
      2. About 2,300,000 stone blocks, weighing an average of 2.5 tons (although
some weighed as much as 30 tons) make up the pyramid.
   B. It is almost impossible to conceive how this was accomplished 4000 years
ago.
      1. Experts are still not exactly sure how the Egyptian architects managed to
build such structures with the technology available to them .
      2. Since the pyramids were built along the Nile River, it is fairly certain that
the stones were quarried up river and transported by rafts.
      3. Heroditus, who visited the pyramids in the fifth century B.C., claimed that
it took 30 years to build the pyramid, and that 100,000 workers were
employed in the building for all that time.

Transition: All of you, I'm sure, have seen pictures of the pyramid—there's even one on a one-dollar bill. Today, I would like to take you beyond that simple picture, and describe the entire complex in which the pyramid existed. It should be pointed out that all the pyramids were not the same and varied according to when they were built, as to size, etc., so what I will talk about today is the "typical" pyramid. As I mentioned, the pyramids were built along the river, and our tour begins there.

BODY

I. From the river a canal was dug leading to a landing quay before a small temple.
    [A diagram/map showing the layout of the pyramid complex will be referred to throughout the speech.]
    A. The canal was important in the building of the pyramid since the stones were transported by water.
    B. The pyramids were constructed as tombs for the pharaohs and were thus intimately connected with the afterlife, an essential part of Egyptian religion, so it was natural to have a temple at the outskirts of the pyramid complex.
    C. The small temple was at the foot of a long causeway, often roofed, that led to the pyramid itself.

II. Other structures were grouped around the pyramid itself.
    A. The complex of buildings, in which the pyramid was the center, almost always was in practically all cases located on the desert plateau overlooking the western bank of the Nile.
    B. This complex was enclosed by a wall and was meant to serve as the residence for the king in his life after death.
    C. Another temple was located outside the pyramid
        1. Earlier complexes located the temple to the north of the pyramid, after they were located to the east.
        2. In this temple the funeral rites were performed.
        3. The temple also contained special installations for slaughtering sacrificial animals and storage areas for offerings.
    D. Tombs of the King's cortiers were grouped around the tomb.
        1. The relationship between the monarch and his court was meant to continue after his death.

III. The pyramid, the royal tomb itself, was the center of the complex.
    A. The Egyptians took special care to hide the entrance so as to protect the tomb from grave robbers.

    1. Since the King was provided with food, wine, and a host of treasures for him to take with him in the afterlife, the graves were very tempting to plunderers.

    2. Several means were used to block or disguise the entrance.

      a. In some cases the entrance was sealed with large blocks that followed the surface of the pyramid in an effort to make the entrance invisible.

      b. In other cases hugh stones were lowered to block the entrance.

    3. These efforts were largely unsuccessful; most of the tombs opened in recent history had already been broken into by grave robbers.

  B. Past the entrance was a sloping passageway that eventually levelled out, leading to the burial chamber in approximately the center of the pyramid.

    1. Not all the pyramids were the same and vary as to the size, shape and number of rooms. Some contained reliefs cut into the wall depicting the king's life, some also contained sculptures.

    2. In many cases, again to thwart grave robbers, there was a chamber that was left empty—probably to convince the would-be robbers that someone else had gotten there first.

    3. In those rare instances when a tomb has been discovered intact (such as the famous discovery of "King Tut's" tomb) priceless works of art and artifacts of the king's day were found.

[Overhead projection of pictures showing some of the treasures found.]

Transition: As investigations of these 4000-year-old mysterious monuments goes on we will continue to learn more about the mysterious tombs built by the ancient Egyptians.

CONCLUSION

  I. Today I have tried to explain how the pyramids were really complexes, consisting of:

    A. A small temple joined to the river by a canal and to the pyramid by a long causeway, and

    B. A series of buildings (another temple, other tombs) surrounding the pyramid itself.

    C. In the center the pyramid housed the burial chamber and contained many treasures.

  II. Stories we have heard about mummies and ancient curses and what must seem to us the very strange customs and religious beliefs that caused such a preoccupation with death, are not the only puzzles surrounding the pyramids: how the

great Egyptian architects produced such marvels remains, for me at least, the
greatest mystery of all.

SOURCES

Edwards, I.E.S. *The Pyramids of Egypt*. rev. ed. New York: Penguin Books, 1985.
Mendelssohn, Kurt. *The Riddle of the Pyramids*. New York: Praeger, 1974.
Steward, Desmond, *ThePyramids and the Sphinx*. New York: Newsweek, 1971.
Tompkins, Peter, *Secrets of the great Pyramid*. New York: Harper & Row, 1971.

SAMPLE OUTLINE: TOPICAL

Title: EXERCISES FOR YOU

General Purpose: Speech to Persuade (stimulate)

Specific Purpose: I want my audience to feel more strongly that exercise is
good for them and to suggest three different means of exercising: step
aerobics, jogging, and swimming.

Organizational Pattern: Topical

INTRODUCTION

I. Just about everyone agrees that exercising is good for you.
   A. There are clear physical benefits to exercise; here are a few examples.
      1. According to an article in *U.S. News and World Report*, exercise that
         contributed to weight loss helps prevent arthritis.
      2. A Harvard Alumni Health Study found that males who burned off 1000
         calories a week in physical activity had half the risk of colon cancer
         compared with inactive men.
      3. Dr. Richard Terry of Stanford University asserts that weight loss by diet
         and exercise reduces the risk factors for heart disease.
      4. Writing in the *Philadelphia Inquirer*, Donald Drake summed it up:
         "moderate exercise is enough to achieve significant health benefits."
   B. There are also psychological benefits to exercise.
      1. Experts believe that physical exercise can combat depression and en-
         hance self-esteem; Elizabeth Birge writes in an article "There's No Excuse
         for One to be Out of Shape," that exercise reduces tension and stress.
      2. In "Banishing the Blues with Exercise," an article in a recent *Newsweek*,
         maintains that hundreds of studies have shown that people report vari-
         ous good feelings (less stress, higher self-esteem, less depression) after
         exercising and these psychological benefits are the result of improved
         cardiovascular and muscular endurance and an increase in energy.

Transition: All this, of course, is not news to you—we all know that exercise is good for us. It may be that many people don't exercise because they haven't found just the right exercise for them, so today I'm going to introduce you to three excellent forms of exercise; maybe one will appeal to you.

BODY

II. Step aerobics is a new trend in this popular form of exercise.
   A. Step training was developed by an aerobics instructor who was also a physical therapist and is based on therapy exercises used to recover from knee injuries.
      1. In this exercise, participants use a set of "steps" made from sturdy molded plastic; it is about 3-1/2 feet long and 14 to 16 inches wide, adjustable in heights of 4, 6, 8, 10, and 12 inches.
      2. Since I am a recreation major, I was able to borrow one of these, and I will quickly show you how it is used.
   B. Step aerobics can be a very effective form of exercise.
      1. In a study conducted at San Diego Stat U, the effects were compared with walking and running. They found that the intensity of running at 7 mph was about 3 times as great as walking at 3 mph. The intensity of step aerobics was the same as that of running, but the impact on the feet was like that of walking. This means that you can get the intensity of running but the low impact of walking.
   C. You can join a step aerobics class through the university's fitness program or at the local "Y."

Transition: Another kind of aerobic activity that is very popular and is beneficial to you, is running.

III. A running program offers many benefits.
   A. Jogging regularly helps in weight loss, firming up muscles, improving your general appearance, stamina and easing tension.
   B. A Baylor University Medical School study showed that jogging increases the amount of good cholesterol in the blood, regardless of diet.
   C. You can jog when and where you like—you are not dependent on others and you don't need special facilities and equipment.
      1. In bad weather you can jog on an indoor track on the campus or at the "Y."
      2. You can proceed at your own pace, jogging only as fast and as far as you want to.

3. Some people are solitary joggers and some like to have a jogging buddy.

Transition: Finally, let me suggest an activity that may be the most popular sport Americans participate in.

IV. Swimming is a beneficial and enjoyable way to exercise.
    A. Experts agree that swimming improves flexibility, coordination and strength, and ranks just below running for aerobic benerfits; Dr. Robert McMurray of UNC's Human Performance Lab, points out that swimming instantly increases blood flow to your heart.
    B. Dr. Eric Orwoll, chief of endocrinology at the VA Medical Center in Portland, Oregon, did a study in which he found that swimmers had more calcium and phosphorous in the spine and arm bones than did their sedentary counterparts and concluded that "Resistance exercise, like swimming, should give you the same kind of effect as weight-bearing exercise."
    C. A large number of people enjoy swimming as a sport: a Lou Harris poll reported that 26 million people swim three or four times a week.
    D. Those who have not been swimming for a while, or those who never learned will find it very easy to do so.
        1. The American Red Cross offers swimming courses with great frequency—they have issued more than 70 million water safety certificates.
        2. There is a poll on campus available to students at specific hours and the pool at the "Y" is available for swimmers at most times from 6 am to 10 pm.

Transition: We all know that exercise is beneficial if only we could find just the right kind of exercise for us.

CONCLUSION

I. Today I have described three different forms of exercise: step aerobics, jogging, and swimming.
    A. I am passing out a brochure from the university's Fitness Center that gives you information about these and other exercise activities, and gives specific information on how to use the university's facilities. I am also passing out a brochure from the "Y" that explains what it has to offer.
    B. All of us are intelligent people; we know that exercise is good for us. What I have tried to do is to suggest that there are a variety of ways to exercise and that you can find one way that is best for you when you decide to act on the phrase that all of us have said to ourselves at one time or another: "I really ought to exercise more."

SOURCES

Aldridge, Mary. "To Step or Not to Step," *Fitness Management*, May 1990: 32-36.

"An Ultimate Fitness Program for Swimming," *Esquire*, May 1985: 173.

"Better Body, Better Heart," *Science News*, November 5, 1988: 294.

Birge, Elizabeth. "There's No Excuse for One to be Out of Shape," *Post Tribune* (Gary, IN), May 26, 1992.

Burstein, Nancy. "How to Stay Healthy When You Don't Think You Have Time," *Women's Sports and Fitness*, March, 1992: 73.

Colfer, George. *Running for Fun and Fitness*. Iowa: Kendall/Hunt, 1980.

Drake, Donald. "A Little Pain, a Lot of Gain," *Philadelphia Inquirer*, November 26,1989.

Fink, Leslie. "Swim For Strong Bones," *Women's Sports and Fitness*, August 1987: 19.

Francis, Peter R. "In Step With Science," *Fitness Management*, May 1990: 37-38.

Malanka, Phyllis. "Aerobics Abound!" *Health*, March 1990: 59.

Sussman, Vic, "No Pain and Lots of Gain," *U.S. News and World Report*, May 4, 1992: 86.

Zwiefel, Jeff, "Banishing the Blues with Exercise," *Newsweek*, May 11, 1992: A26.

SAMPLE OUTLINE: PROBLEM-SOLUTION

Title: PREVENTING DATE RAPE

General Purpose: Speech to Persuade (actuate)

Specific Purpose: I want my audience to take steps to prevent date rape.

Organizational Pattern: Problem-solution

INTRODUCTION

I. College students are at risk from "date rape."

 A. Recently I read a story in *Newsweek* that told of a college freshman who went with a date to a fraternity party where she drank quite a bit (.349 blood alcohol level—enough to cause death), went to her date's room where he forced her to have sex, and then was taken to a shower room where two other men had sex with her. She was found later by police lying in a hallway at the fraternity house next door with her skirt pulled up and her pants removed. After this experience the woman left school and entered a psychiatric hospital where she tried to kill herself.

 B. This is not an isolated instance: *Public Health Reports* recently reported that 84% of the rapes committed on college campuses are committed by someone the victim knows, and approximately half occur on dates.

 C. Chances are that many of you in this audience could find yourselves in a date rape situation: The *Newsweek* article also reported that one out of nine college women had been raped—and of these eight out of ten knew their attackers; four out of five of these sexual assaults were committed by male students.

Transition: If all of us are to avoid being involved in date rape—as an aggressor or as a victim—we need to understand what date rape is, what is being done by colleges to prevent it, and what each of us can do to prevent it.

BODY

I. Rape occurs when one of the persons involved is not willing to have sexual contact.
   A. An article in *Parents Magazine* explained that if the victim says no and then sexual contact occurs, it is considered rape or some form of sexual assault.
   B. When people are on a date or with an acquaintance—no matter how well they know each other or what their relationship is—if one person forces the other to have sex, that is rape. In this instance, it would be called "date rape" or "acquaintance rape."

Transition: Since date rape so often affects college students, Aileen Adams, in *Sexual Assault on Campuses: What Colleges Can Do,* has recommended that "all colleges distribute a clear institutional policy against rape to let students know that this will not be tolerated on campus under any circumstances."

II. Making it clear that date rape is wrong is one thing that many universities are doing; furthermore, other specific steps are being taken.
   A. Universities are setting up special programs.
      1. At the University of Oregon a special educational project is aimed at men as well as women students.
      2. At Indiana University a group called "Men Against Rape" presents programs devoted to changing male attitudes toward rape, and a student group, "Peer Presenters" give presentations on date rape to students.
   B. Greek organizations have set up special projects to combat date rape.
      1. UCLA requires rape awareness workshops as a part of the rush process.
      2. SAGA (Sexual Awareness Greek Association) at the University of Florida conducts mandatory programs on sex roles and rape education at Fraternity and sorority houses.

Transition: We have seen that date rape is a serious problem for college students and that colleges and universities are taking steps to prevent it, but what each of us does individually may be the most important factor in preventing date rape.

III. Date rape can be combatted by both men and women.
   A. Men need to realize that "no" means "no" and that forcing sex on women is a crime for which they can be charged and punished.
   B. Everyone should control the consumption of alcohol.
      1. *Newsweek* reported that 50% of victims and 75% of aggressors had been drinking before the incident occurred.
   C. In the event that a woman finds herself in a threatening situation, she should take specific actions:
      1. Be very firm in saying no: a recent issue of *Health* suggested a phrase like "No, get your filthy hands off me."
      2. An article in *Nation's Business* suggested that screaming is one of the best deterrents.
      3. Attempt to resist with physical force.
         a. *Psychology Today* reports that women who screamed or physically resisted were less likely to go into long term depression after the event.
         b. The article in *Health* suggested kicking the assailant in the groin or hitting him with a closed fist in the eyes, and then running away.

Transition: No woman wants to be in a position similar to that of the college freshman I told you about in my introduction, and no man wants to be guilty of an act that is both indecent and criminal.

CONCLUSION

I. Understanding what date rape is and how to prevent it can be important to all of us.
   A. I've tried today to explain that many rapes are committed by people that know the victim.
   B. Preventing date rape is a major concern on college campuses throughout the country, many of which are taking steps to stop it.
   C. All of us, both men and women, must act responsibly to prevent rape and decisively to escape from a rape situation if it occurs.
II. It is shocking to realize that a rape occurs every six minutes—do everything you can to make sure it doesn't happen to you.

SOURCES

Adams, Aileen. *Sexual Assault on Campus: What Colleges Can Do*. Santa Monica, CA: Rape Treatment Center, Santa Monica Hospital Medical Center, 1988.

Copenhaver, Stacey and Elizabeth Grauerholz. "Sexual Victimization Among Sorority Women: Exploring the Link Between Violence and Institutional Practices," *Sex Roles* 24 (January 1991): 31-41.

Elkind, David. "Preventing Date Rape," *Parents*, April 1989: 198.

Malone, Debbie. Sexual Assault Crisis Center, Indiana University: telephone interview, February 26, 1993.

Mathews, Craig. "The Mind of the Rapist," *Newsweek*, 2 July 1990: 54-58.

Mayer, Raleigh. "Defensive Moves," *Health*, September 1989: 90-91.

Nelton, Sharon. "Learning How to Cry Rape," *Nation's Business*, January 1987: 67-68.

Parrot, A. *Coping with Date and Acquaintance Rape*. New York: Rosen, 1988.

Ricker, Scott R. "Reduction of Date Rape on a University Campus, *Public Health Reports* 107 (March-April 1992): 226-27

Smith, Pete. "Offering Resistance: How Most People Respond to Rape," *Psychology Today*, April 1989: 13.

Warchaw, Robin. *I Never Called It Rape*. New York: Harper and Row, 1988.

SAMPLE OUTLINE: CAUSE-EFFECT

Title: THE DESTRUCTION OF OUR FORESTS

General Purpose: Speech to Persuade (convince)

Specific Purpose: I want my audience to agree that the practice of "clear cutting" is wrong and produces detrimental effects to the environment.

Organizational Pattern: Cause-effect.

INTRODUCTION

I. Our forest lands are in danger of being destroyed.
    A. Many of you have been to state forests or state parks and have enjoyed the beauty of the setting and have appreciated the wildlife that lives there.
    B. One of my favorite places is the ancient forests of Washington State. Imagine a trip to the Pacific Northwest woodlands where you anticipate seeing the magnificent ancient trees that reach into the skies. But, when you arrive, what you might see are bare and empty holes that go for acres; no animals are to be seen, no birds to be heard.
    C. These wastelands are caused by a common method of logging known as "clear cutting."

II. This destruction can have grave consequences for our environment, and can be stopped.
  A. Today I want to explain the importance of the ancient forests, tell what "clear cutting" is, and describe the damaging effects of this logging method.

Transition: First, let's consider the question of why preserving the forests is so important, taking the Pacific forest as an example.

BODY

I. The Pacific forest contains some of the largest and oldest trees in the world.
  A. The Pacific forest stretches along the coast from Alaska to just north of the Golden Gate, a radius of 2000 miles.
  B. Within these forests are trees of 300 feet or higher with diameters of 50 feet.
  C. Some of these trees are 2000 years old.

II. It is important to save these trees for several reasons.
  A. The forest helps to preserve the biological diversity upon which the ecological system depends.
    1. The Pacific forest is home to a greater mass of life than even the tropical rain forests.
      a. Little known species, such as the marbled murrelet live there; the spotted owl that lives there and that we have heard so much about, is so important because it is, as a recent article in the *Economist* pointed out, an "indicator species," meaning that other forest animals are also thriving because of it.
  B. The forest helps preserve the earth's ecological balance.
    1. The destruction of trees that produce oxygen can effect the biosphere, causing drastic changes in climate and weather.
    2. Trees are of such varying ages and the wide variety of species nurtured by the forest contribute to the over-all health and balance of the system.
    3. Even dead trees are useful: the wealth of decomposing mass provides the nourishment of a rich, healthy soil that supports more living vegetation per acre than any other place in the world.
  C. The loss of biological diversity could eliminate potential medical breakthroughs.
    1. Recent experiments have shown that the Pacific yew tree has properties that have the potential to combat cancer.
    2. A story in *USA Today* last March reported that fifty percent of all medication comes from organic sources.

Transition: Now that you see how important and valuable the forests are, let me tell you about the logging method that is destroying them.

III. "Clear-cutting" is the most common and detrimental method used by the lumber industry for the past 50 years.

    A. This is the method whereby large chain saws can cut through a 200-year-old Douglas fir in seconds; when the tree falls over it is yanked out by bulldozers who clear the slash and burn the rubble. When they are finished, little remains.

    B. Simply put, "clear cutting" is the practice of cutting down every tree of a large tract of land.

    C. *The Economist* noted that when a tract had been subjected to clear cutting it is "as if a squadron of B-52s had ravaged the pristine beauty of the Wind River Mountains."

Transition: Now that you understand the importance of the forest and the clear-cutting method, you can probably infer the result; let's go through the devastating effects of this logging method.

IV. Clear-cutting has the single most devastating impact on a forest ecosystem.

    A. The canopy of trees that encloses and insulates the unique, self-contained climate and all its distinctive vegetation and wildlife is eliminated instantly.

    B. In a clear-cut, 60% of all rainfall runs off the surface, eroding nutrients and top soil.

        1. This also fouls streams with mud and silt.

        2. This has the potential to spoil local water supplies.

    C. Extensive logging destroys animal habitats, as it is destroying the breeding ground for the spotted owl in the Pacific Northwest.

    D. In eradicating the unique plants and animal species, we may be destroying the chance of finding cures for deadly diseases.

Transition: With such drastic results from clear-cutting, can we afford to allow it to continue?

CONCLUSION

I. I hope that you will agree with me that cutting down magnificent and very useful trees and bulldozing acres of forest land it dangerous to the environment and should be stopped.

    A. The famous environmentalist John Muir put it best when he wrote, "simply left alone, the natural world, and especially the wilderness areas, have a priceless and irreplaceable ecological value that science has yet to comprehend."

SOURCES

Caufield, Catherine. "A Reporter at Large: The Ancient Forest," *The New Yorker,* May 14, 1990: 50-60.

Chapman, Jeffery L. "Forests Under Siege," *USA Today,* March 1991: 17.

Fotheringham, Allen. "A Final Warning About the Last Frontier," *Maclean's,* May 28, 1990: 64.

"Messy Loggers Welcome," *The Economist,* September 1, 1990: 25.

"For the Birds," *The Economist,* March 4, 1989: 26.

CHAPTER 10

SPEAKING CONFIDENTLY WITH YOUR AUDIENCE: STYLE AND DELIVERY

After studying this chapter you should understand:

- How style can promote understanding and belief through the use of clear, interesting, and appropriate language.

- How style can affect listeners' responses.

- How making the speaking situation predictable can reduce "stage fright" and improve delivery.

- How volume, rate, clarity, and variety can affect your vocal presentation.

- What characterizes good delivery.

STYLE: PROMOTING UNDERSTANDING AND BELIEF

Style is a very difficult term to define. One reason it is so difficult to define is that we use it in so many different ways. If we refer to a person as having "style," the context of our reference will tell whether we mean that person dresses very well, sings in a unique way, or plays basketball with a special skill or flair.

When we talk about a speaker's style, we may also mean many different things. One might say that a speaker's style is the *unique or specific type of image he or she creates for the audience: an image in which the speaker's use of language, movement and gestures, movement and appearance on the platform affect the way he or she is perceived by the audience.* Of course, style in its most general sense really covers much that has been discussed in this book. For certainly a person's style is influenced by the way he or she thinks, by the way he or she puts arguments together, and by the way he or she relates to the audience. Also, what listeners have heard about a speaker, know about a speaker, or *think* they know about a speaker can create for them certain types of expectations. These expectations often lead listeners to expect that the speaker will exhibit some striking qualities that they might call "style."

All things we have been discussing thus far contribute to your personal style as a speaker, but this section will focus specifically on *language*—how to choose it and how to use it. That is to say, *for the moment we will consider style to be your use and choice of language.* This consideration will be followed by an examination of the qualities of delivery, a process that many consider also to be a part of style. In this chapter we look at style as it relates to the understanding of messages as well as it relates to persuasion.

One thing that is difficult for a speaker to appreciate is that he or she and the listeners *do not always speak exactly the same language.* All of us, for example, may speak English. But we do not use and choose language in the same ways. For one thing, we may come from different cultural backgrounds that provide us either with different words or different meanings for words, Black English for example, is often rich in linguistic patterns and usage that are different from other forms of English. Often this usage is absorbed by the rest of the culture, so that by now most speakers and listeners would at least comprehend what was meant if they were urged to "be cool," or told that one of their friends was really "bad." Yet, particular meanings are not universal and, they are known to different people at different times.

As with use of black English, regional uses of English, ethnic use of language and generational uses of language, can be confusing to those outside of the linguistic group. Sometimes, language uses are very specific and unusual. For example, at a New Jersey college what was usually called in other places "making out" or "necking" was called "grouching." People who attended that institution would know what "grouching" meant, they might even go so far as to say that someone had given them a "little grouch" when that person had given them a little kiss. No one else, however, would have the slightest idea of what such a reference meant. Indeed, the normal listener would probably assume that the term referred to someone who was very grouchy or someone who was grumbling or complaining.

Of course, language is not always or usually so specific or limited. The point, however, is that *no speaker can assume that his or her language choices will inevitably or automatically be those that are normally used by his or her listeners.* As in all other aspects of communication, the speaker needs to consider who his or her audience is. Given these basic kinds of considerations, the speaker needs to choose and use a language to promote the following characteristics.

LANGUAGE SHOULD BE CLEAR TO LISTENERS

In all aspects of the speaking situation, the speaker needs to keep in mind that a speech, being oral, is very different from a written presentation. This is especially true when it comes to the language chosen. You know that if you are reading a page and you come across words that you have never seen before, you will either figure out the meaning from the context (which might require rereading the paragraph a couple of times) or you will go and look up the words in the dictionary. Indeed, a good book will often challenge the reader and contribute to his or her own knowledge of the language. College textbooks, for example, that are written at the ninth-grade reading level deprive students of the opportunity to learn more and to expand their vocabulary. But, a speech is a somewhat different matter.

A listener can't stop the speaker and get him or her to run through a section of the oral message again, nor can the listener stop the speaker and go look up a word. The speaker needs constantly to keep in mind the types of problems that the audience might face in relation to his or her language.

One way to promote clarity is to be sure to use words with which the audience is familiar. Once the author of this textbook was giving a lecture in which he described as "pedestrian" a political speech that had recently been broadcast over television. After the lecture was over, one student came up to talk to him. The student was somewhat puzzled and frustrated at not being able to understand precisely the instructor's evaluation of the speech. "I thought a pedestrian was someone who walked across the street," the student said. "How can a speech be pedestrian?" This is an extreme example. One should be able to assume that a college student would know the meaning of "pedestrian" in this context. Nevertheless, the instructor might have said, "This was a very pedestrian speech, one that had nothing unusual, striking, or interesting about it; it was very ordinary." Such restatement would have explained the unfamiliar word and reinforced the idea.

A speaker should always remember that *technical words may be unfamiliar to an audience*. Sometimes we are so wrapped up in our own experience and interests that we forget that the terms we regularly use may be unusual to someone else. A chemistry major will have no difficulty understanding what a reagent is and an accounting major in understanding a trial balance. For someone training to be an auto mechanic, a sparkplug is an ordinary object and its use and function is readily understood. A nutritionist knows what carbohydrates are, a laboratory technician what a blood sample is, and a teacher what a lesson plan is. In other words, technical language doesn't have to be words such as "aerodynamics," "quantum mechanics," or "iambic pentameter." *Technical language is any language that has a very precise meaning within a particular field of endeavor*. It's easy, therefore, for us sometimes to forget that language we consider to be ordinary may be considered by an audience to be technical.

The same, of course, is true of technical or specialized abbreviations or substitutions for longer words or titles that are commonly used in specific contexts. The best example of this is the way in which we us letters to stand for names or titles. Anyone in an audience who is interested in broadcasting will know what is meant by the FCC, whereas others in the audience may not know that this refers to the Federal Communications Commission. Many college students will know what a GPA is, whereas their parents, friends, or others not associated with the university may not know the reference is to a grade point average. Anyone in the medical or paramedical field will know that a GP is a doctor who does not have a specialty, a general practitioner. The speaker, then, needs to be conscious of the fact that *his or her language grows out of his or her experience and knowledge and needs at times to be translated for the experience and knowledge of the listeners.* Words that are chosen for their *concreteness* and their *specificity* increase clarity. Telling an audience, for example, that they must exert increased effort or that they must be very active is not really telling them what they are expected to do. The vagueness of these words will not leave a clear impression in the minds of the audience. On the other hand, saying to an audience that they could appear at the student union building at nine o'clock in the morning to distribute handbills is saying something specific. Asking an audience to vote for a candidate because she or he is in favor of enlarging educational opportunities is vague. Asking an audience to vote for a candidate because he or she supports an increase in the federal loan program for students is specific. Describing someone as a humanitarian does not make that person's contribution clear to an audience; but describing him or her as someone who has voluntarily gone to prison in order to teach inmates how to improve their educational skills does tell the listener something.

Individual words must be chosen to promote clarity, but they must also be used together to promote clarity. This means that *words have to be put together in as straightforward a way as possible so the sentences they form are direct and easy to follow.* Clarity of oral style as opposed to clarity of written style might demand that a speaker use more repetition than a writer would use; things might have to be repeated and restated in order to be clear. Even so, the speaker aims to talk in a way that will promote the audiences' efforts to *follow,* to *remember,* and to *understand.* One device that helps promote a clearer style is the use of *transitional language* that continually points the audience in the proper direction. For example, as a speaker amplifies a particular point, he or she might say, "I've been telling you that a diet that is not properly supervised can be very dangerous for you. Let me give you an example of just how dangerous it can be by telling you about a college student named Joan." The move by the speaker from the generalization to the specific example is thus clearly delineated through the use of specific transitional language.

Probably the best advice that can be given to anyone to help that person use language clearly is to be sure that one's thinking is clear. If a speaker first understands what an idea is, then it will be much easier for him or her to convey that idea to an audience. When a speaker has not thought out an idea clearly, when she or he is vague about the concept, the result will likely be confusion for the listeners.

LANGUAGE SHOULD BE INTERESTING TO LISTENERS

Factors of attention and interest have already been discussed earlier in this book. Nevertheless, some special observations can be made regarding language. One of the things that always interests us is *action*. The way we choose language and the way we put it together can create a type of action for our listeners. We can create the illusion of action and help the listeners to understand more precisely what we have in mind in several ways. One of the best things for a speaker to keep in mind is that *simple and precise words and sentences help contribute to an active speech.*

Consider, for example, the way Winston Churchill described to the U.S. Congress events in North Africa in the early days of World War II. Things had not been going well for the British in Europe or for the Americans, who had entered the war just a few weeks before, in Asia. Churchill hoped to create a sense of forward movement and a sense of hope for success. There are no exceptional or unusual words in the passage, no particularly unique sentence construction. But here is clarity and forcefulness that gives a good picture of what is going on:

> For many months we devoted ourselves to preparing to take the offensive in Libya. The very considerable battle which has been proceeding for the last six weeks in the desert has been most fiercely fought on both sides. Owing to the difficulties of supply on the desert flank we were never able to bring numerically equal forces to bear upon the enemy. Therefore we had to rely upon a superiority in the numbers and quality of tanks and aircraft, British and American. Aided by these, for the first time we have fought the enemy with equal weapons. For the first time we have made the Hun feel the sharp edge of those tools with which he has enslaved Europe. The armed force of the enemy in Cyrenaica amounted to 150,000 men, of whom about a third were Germans. General Auchinleck set out to destroy totally that armed force—and I have every reason to believe that his aim will be fully accomplished.

Style also promotes the feeling of action when it is *lively*. Language that gives the most *realistic and vivid description* of events, people, or ideas is the most lively. To meet an assignment in a speaking class, for example, two speakers each described a teacher that they had had sometime in the past. Consider which of the following two examples is the more lively:

> When I first went into class a tall man with slightly grey hair sat at the front of the room on the desk. He smiled and handed me a card to fill out. When I gave it back to him, he smiled again and said, "Thank you," in a quiet voice. But it was a funny thing, I knew somehow that that quiet voice was a powerful one, too, one that I was going to like to listen to, one that would sort of fill the room, but not batter at your ears. He looked relaxed sitting there, but I could tell he was watching everyone that came in, studying them, sizing them up. This was a lit class, and I figured there was going to be a lot of BS about books that nobody had really read. But as I watched this guy I got a feeling that phonies were not going to get away with anything, that you had to know what you were talking about here. When he got up to talk, I actually felt excited, like something was going to happen. I was a little scared, scared that this guy would be tough, but more scared that maybe he wouldn't be, maybe I was wrong. English always bored me, but I really hoped maybe this time it would be worth it. When he started to talk he looked right at me and at everybody. He made some kind of joke. But then he started to talk to us, right to us, and I thought to myself, "My God, this might be OK after all."

> Mr. Harrison was an excellent teacher that I had in high school. He was always well prepared and tried to enlighten the class when he had the opportunity. He tried to understand student needs and the values we held and to adapt accordingly to our experiences. He was certainly a good teacher and served as such a role model for me that I decided to become a teacher, too.

The first example is clearly more real, creates more suspense, is more specific and as a whole, accordingly, more lively.

Language that is in and of itself *striking* or *impressive* can create interest for an audience and contribute to the audience's understanding of ideas. For centuries, students of rhetoric have studied what are literally called "figures of speech"; these are special ways of using language to heighten the beauty of expression or the clearness of idea. It is not important for the beginning student of public speaking to understand and identify all the technical names for the different types of figures of speech. But both the listeners and speakers should be aware of some special ways of using the language. These special ways offer some additional opportunities to increase the interest and clarity of a speech, and so could prove to be very helpful. Most of these figures of speech are often used in public speaking.

Language should be used in a special way to compare things. A direct comparison can be made between things that an audience might not see as being similar. (This kind of comparison is called a *simile*, and the word "like" or "as" always appears.) "A day in the life of the college student," one student began her speech, "is like a day at an amusement park. You have ups and downs; you can get spun around; you can do new things you've never done before; you can have a lot of fun; and you can end by throwing up."

Another kind of common comparison is the *metaphor*, in which two objects that the audience might think of as being quite dissimilar are compared. (The technical distinction between metaphor and simile is that "like" or "as" does not appear in the metaphor.) One freshman college student at the end of her first semester, facing her first set of finals, described her feelings through metaphor: "I think I understand the principles of swimming, but I'm about to find out by jumping into the deep end of the pool; I just hope I don't drown." Because these images not only arouse interest but also create feelings and moods, they can make an important contribution to the audience's total understanding of the speech.

Language can be used to make contrasts. The special device known as an *antithesis* is a way of putting two things together that have sharply contrasted meanings. This is a way in which language can reinforce an idea. By using strong contrasts in words or phrases, strong contrasts in thought can also be suggested. One student speaker, for example, argued that "Forces of life and personal sacrifices are contending with the forces of death and personal profit right here on this campus." This speech was one that attacked those who would risk the effects of pollution in order to make money. The antithetical language construction in the example pits life against death and sacrifice against profit in such a way that those who put money first are allied with death.

There are many other stylistic devices that are used to enhance ideas and thus make them more believable or understandable. Through *irony*, a speaker can imply a meaning that is really the opposite from that which is stated: "As we all know, doctors who have taken the Hippocratic Oath care a great deal about their patients and don't care anything at all about how much money they can make." Using *alliteration*, a speaker employs a repetitive pattern of sound that can hold the audience's attention and reinforce the idea: "For some, the university, instead of being a passport to plenty, is the doorway to doom." Through *personification* the speaker gives the characteristics of human beings to nonhuman forms or things: "This city can be a very hostile place. It can ignore you, it can frighten you, and it can punish you very severely if you ignore its unwritten rules." Through *eptamorthosis* a speaker modifies a statement that he or she has just made by making a type of retraction: "This is a great school; by that I mean this is a great faculty. This is a great school; no, it doesn't have the most beautiful buildings, and maybe the equipment is not as extensive or as new as we would like, but this is a great school because it has great people working in it."

There are literally dozens of other devices that could be listed, but the point is that language can have a force of its own. It can be interesting, clarifying, and persuasive for an audience when used properly. The important thing for the speaker to keep in mind is: *The language that is chosen and the way in which it is used can make a difference in the way an audience responds, so it is of primary importance to the speaker to become conscious of language and of all the possibilities that are afforded in its use.*

LANGUAGE SHOULD BE APPROPRIATE TO THE SITUATION

If you give the matter any thought, you will realize that we all use *different language in different types of situations*. One of the most dramatic examples of contrasting uses of language was demonstrated by the publication of the famous Watergate tapes. These recorded conversations illustrated the startling differences between public and private choices of language made by President Richard Nixon and many of his advisers. All of us know that we use different conventions in language for different people and contexts. We all know that the words we choose when talking to our friends tend to be vastly different than the ones we choose when talking to our parents, to employers, or to teachers. We know that a conversation in a dormitory might involve different types of language from a conversation one might have with the parents of a roommate who are visiting. One of the things in the Watergate transcripts that was terribly shocking to some people was not so much the use of specific expletives, but the fact that those words were used by the President of the United States in the Oval Office of the White House. Somehow to many people who had surely heard the language before and perhaps even used some of those expletives themselves, their use in that setting did not seem fitting.

Of course, the issue being discussed here is much greater than the issue of when does one use words that may or may not be socially acceptable or unacceptable. The real issue is much broader: *What language is best suited to the context in which the public speaking occurs?* Within this context the speaker himself or herself is an important element. The speaker must deal with the fact that the language to be used may be different from his or her normal conversational language, but it should remain true to his or her self. That is, a speaker will probably *think about and choose and use language more carefully in a public speech than he or she would in a private setting.*

Nevertheless, he or she is not going to "fake" language in order to sound like someone else. For example, it would be absurd and inappropriate for a well-educated speaker to assume poor grammatical construction or coarse language choice because he or she thought that it was called for by the nature of the audience. Such an action would probably be interpreted by the audience as being condescending and insulting rather than adaptive. It would probably be unwise for a speaker to assume slang and special cultural or technical languages of a group when such language choices do not come naturally to her or him.

Other aspects of a situation—the audience, the topic of the speech, and the occasion setting in which the speech takes place—also have an impact on language choice. For example, Martin Luther King's speech addressed to the famous rally in behalf of civil rights in Washington, D.C., on August 20, 1963, is probably the best example of language use that grows out of all the constituents of a situation. His first words in the speech itself are, "Five score years ago a great American in whose symbolic shadow we stand today signed the Emancipation Proclamation." Standing on the steps of the Lincoln Memorial, King used an opening that was the epitome of situational factors guiding language choice: it was well-calculated to vividly remind the audience of Lincoln, his Gettysburg Address, and, by extension, the entire long and bloody struggle over slavery and racial prejudice.

Most of us do not appear in public-speaking settings that are as dramatic or as overriding as the setting in which King found himself. No matter where we are, however, we need to ask ourselves what the audience knows and thinks about the topic, what level of linguistic sophistication the audience holds, how serious or how casual are the constraints of the setting, how formal or how informal the situation is, and what the physical limitations and relationships between speaker and listener are in the situation. In short, *the speaker must ask himself or herself what the audience expectations are and how they will affect his or her choice of language.*

A commencement speaker, for example, might begin her formal remarks with a greeting to all those distinguished persons on the platform, naming the president of the university, the president of the board of trustees, some other guests, the graduating class, and so on. It would be absurd in a public-speaking class for someone (someone who is not burlesquing the form) to get up in front of the audience and begin saying, "Professor Jones, chairman of the day Mr. Smith, fellow speakers, . . ." and so on. The public-speaking class is a much more informal type of situation. It calls for, among other things, different stylistic choices to be used. *The wise speaker is one who thinks carefully about what an*

Delivery must be adapted to the setting.

audience expects of him or her and adjusts to meet those expectations. In a public-speaking class, one speaker conveyed a message in this way:

> I'm planning to say something today that is very important. I hope you're going to see how important it is, but what is really vital to me is that what I'm going to say is larger than this situation we find ourselves in. What I'm going to say is of great interest and importantce not only to us but to people everywhere, and I just hope I can say it in a way that is fitting and proper.

Conveying much the same idea, a minister in a church preceding his sermon with the old prayer, "May the words of my mouth and the meditations of our hearts be always acceptable in thy sight, O Lord our strength and our redeemer." Quite obviously reversing those two openings would be inappropriate, even though the essential conception or thought might be the same.

Style, then, call make a real difference in substance. It makes a difference because the way we use language can influence the way the audience receives and perceives our public messages.

STYLE AND THE LISTENER'S RESPONSE

It should be apparent from reading the foregoing section that style can have a strong impact on listeners almost apart from the ideas that are being expressed. That is, *the way in which the ideas are expressed can be as important as the ideas themselves in forming listener reactions.*

Words, for example, have both denotative and connotative meanings. *Denotative words* are those that carry less emotional baggage with them, those that tend to be more objective and less susceptible to a wide variety of interpretative responses. *Connotative words,* on the other hand, are those that are more highly charged for the listener, those that suggest a range of subjective and emotional interpretations. It should be pointed out that the same word can be essentially denotative for one person and connotative for another. The word "cat" for many people might simply denote a four-footed, furry feline, a small animal; for those people there is hardly any reaction to the word. To another person, however, one who has been severely scratched and almost lost an eye as a child in an encounter with a cat, the word can be much more emotionally charged.

Denotative or connotative meanings are infused into language by the context in which they appear and by the perceptions of the listener. Nonetheless, in our society, some words seem to be more highly charged than others: mother, honor, free enterprise, Maoists, reactionaries, and so on. All these words are liable to conjure up a wide variety of more or less intense personal responses.

The important point to the listener is that charged language not only supports and furthers argument, it can be substituted for argument. For example, instead of pointing out the shortcomings of a plan or program, a speaker might simply say, "We should totally reject all such Marxist thinking." In this case, by labeling, by using language that is meant to connote much that the speaker sees as being evil or opposed to our American value system, the speaker rejects categorically a proposal that he or she does not like. *What the listener must do in this type of situation is ask himself or herself, "On what basis will I respond?"* In this example, is there evidence that this is a "Marxist" idea? And, if so, is there evidence that the idea is truly a bad one? If the listener finds himself or herself saying, "Well, if this is Marxist, then I don't want to have anything to do with it," without questioning the support for the assertion, then he or she may be falling prey to a stylistic substitution for argument.

There are ways other than using a specific word choice in which stylistic substitutions can occur. Consider, for example, some of the devices discussed in the preceding section, when a speaker condemns a proposal by saying, "This would make as much sense as playing tennis without a net." The listener must ask himself or herself whether or not this comparison is really a good one. Of course, tennis would be a much different game without a net, but how does that really relate to the plan or to the proposal being made? And because a speaker has two ideas as being antithetical—"democracy is based on participation; this plan is based on exclusion"—does that really prove that the plan is undemocratic?

In a preceding chapter we considered the need for supporting ideas with evidence. The same principle should be kept in mind when one is faced with persuasive language use. Here, too, the listener will be wary of accepting the speaker's word alone, even if the word is most aptly and interestingly chosen.

DELIVERY AND PREDICTABILITY

After all the preparation, thought, and work, the speaker ultimately must present himself or herself to an audience. Delivery is, after all, only a small part of this total process of speech preparation and reaction. The speaker who stands before an audience for ten minutes or so has spent hours getting ready to do that. The listeners who hear ten minutes or so of speaking bring to the situation an evaluative screen made up from years of experience and, one hopes, from careful training. Yet even so, *the actual delivery of a message is the climax and culmination of the public-speaking experience.*

Certainly, delivery is one of the most obvious aspects of public speaking, and one on which both speaker and listener tend to focus automatically at first. If, for example, one were to ask an audience as soon as they had finished listening to a student give a speech in class what they thought of that speech, the most likely kinds of answers would be something like this: "I think he had a very nice voice." "I think she should have moved around more." "I couldn't always hear him." Delivery may be a small part of the entire process, but it is a very noticeable part. And it can be a very influential part.

Most potential speakers recognize the importance of delivery, and quite often it terrifies them. The phenomenon known as *stage fright* is almost universal. ("Stage fright," although it is a term most of us are familiar with, is a somewhat old-fashioned one. Scholars who study this problem tend to refer to it as "speech anxiety" or "communication apprehension," because these terms better describe what is actually going on.) No doubt different degrees of apprehension exist, but almost every speaker feels some discomfort and anxiety before he or she speaks.

Part of these feelings come from *physiological activities.* There is more energy as more blood sugar becomes available to us; we experience the increases in blood pressure and respiration. These and other physiological influences don't usually make it impossible for the speaker to speak. On the contrary, they can often provide an extra type of stimulation that will make the speaker think faster and act in a more lively and energetic fashion.

The worst problems that a speaker faces are *psychological* activities. The speaker is entering a situation that he or she cannot confidently predict, and so some anxiety is bound to result. The less familiar a person is with a type of situation, the greater will be his or her anxiety. Part of a solution for dealing with this problem, then, lies in the area of *predictability,* that is, in *making the situation one in which the speaker understands and feels better because he or she has a good idea of what will happen.*

Unquestionably, the speaker must remember that it is quite all right to be fearful or uncomfortable: such feelings are normal. Too often speakers assume that they are so "nervous" that they will not be able to speak, as if this nervousness were somehow abnormal or unusual. Everybody feels some distress, so at least the speaker should not be anxious about the fact that he or she does, too. Given the universality of distress, how does the speaker go about reducing the problem by making the situation more predictable? That is a very important question and needs to be addressed specifically.

DEVELOPING CONFIDENCE

The answer to the question of predictability is the key to developing confidence. The more you think you know what's going to happen, the less afraid you will be of the unexpected, the more confident you will feel. Here are some ways in which a speaker can go about doing just that:

1. *A speaker can make the situation more predictable by being well prepared.* It is quite natural to worry about whether or not one will forget specific bits of information, or get mixed up in one's notes, or sound foolish, or seem not to know what one is talking about. The best way to reduce these fears is to *know as well as possible what one is talking about.* All that has gone before in these chapters has been designed to help the speaker to prepare himself or herself as fully and as completely as possible. It takes time and effort to do this, but the result can be a reduction in the fear produced by not knowing what's going to happen in the speaking situation.

2. *The situation will be more predictable as it is more often experienced.* Stated simply: speakers will find it easier to continue speaking the more they do it. The situation will become familiar, so uncertainties will be reduced. Even the most experienced speaker, like the most experienced actor, is apt to feel some degree of stage fright. Nevertheless, the intensity and feelings of alarm should decrease over time.

3. *The situation will be more predictable if the speaker has practiced extensively and appropriately.* You may have had the experience of deciding that you will say something to another person that is not entirely pleasant or that is in another way difficult. And you may have run through in your mind beforehand what you thought you would say. And then, as you actually said it, you may have discovered to your chagrin that it was much more difficult to say than you thought it would be. Very often we first play something through in our heads and then experience difficulty when we actually say it out loud. This is because we managed to deceive ourselves by filling in little words and transitions, by completing half-formed thoughts. The speaker who decides to run through his or her speech while lying in bed at night before going to sleep is going to be shocked and distressed when he or she tries to articulate that speech in front of a audience.

So, one way of making the situation more predictable is by *simulating the situation* itself, by pretending that one is in the situation. Now, of course, getting up in front of an empty room or in front of your roommate is not the same thing as getting up in front of a larger group of people. But getting up and talking is a similar kind of process in both the real and simulated situation. In both cases, you can force yourself to put your ideas into clear, straightforward language, and in both situations you can assess how well you are doing for yourself. Certainly, as you speak in front of an audience you will be getting some feedback or response that you wouldn't get when you're all by yourself or when you have a very limited audience. Nevertheless, by speaking in front of a small audience first, you can tell whether or not it is possible for you to explain an idea; you can tell whether the notes you have prepared are adequate; and you can tell whether that ten-minute speech you planned to give takes thirty-five minutes. Also, your practice sometimes can be helped if you use a recording device. By playing back your speech, you can make a judgment about whether or not you have said what you wanted to say as clearly and forcefully as you wanted to say it.

One note of caution is important here. A practicing speaker can be much too hard on himself or herself. The speaker can assume that every manifestation of nervousness or anxiety that he or she feels will be perceived and responded to negatively by the audience. That's just not the case. While audience members may be aware of some nervousness on your part, they will not be as concerned with it nor will they perceive it as being as important as you.

4. *The situation will become more predictable if the speaker has prepared adequate notes*. Some speakers try to control a situation absolutely by writing out every word that they will say. There may be situations in which the preparation and delivery of a manuscript speech is the right thing to do. But these are highly formal, highly structured, and very rare situations in the course of most public speaking. *Most of the speaking that we will do will involve careful and extensive preparation but not memorization or reading of a manuscript.* Most classroom speeches will be what is normally referred to as *extemporaneous* speeches. These speeches are like those that we have just been describing: carefully prepared and thought out but not memorized. Some classroom speeches may also be *impromptu*, which is to say *speeches that are given on the spur of the moment*.

The *extemporaneous* speech usually calls for some type of notes to be used. The speaker should prepare these notes and use them during the practice sessions. A very normal temptation for one who has things on paper is to read everything that is there. A speaker thus will be freer to interact with his or her audience if his or her notes are not too extensive. The important thing to remember is that *notes serve as an aid to memory. They do not serve as a complete outline of the speech nor as a major source of the speaker's material as he or she speaks*. They help the speaker to keep on the track, but the speaker must know the subject very well.

SPEAKING FROM A MANUSCRIPT

There are, of course, occasions when a speech should be given from a prepared manuscript Basically, the same principles of delivery apply: being well prepared, having experience, practicing, and working from a good copy are important. A written speech, however, will cause special problems.

First, the more that has to be read, the less eye contact that can be maintained with an audience. In order to overcome this problem, a speaker must *practice* extensively so that he or she knows the material well enough to look at the audience and get back to the manuscript without losing the place. A good, readable copy of the manuscript itself is, naturally, essential. It is not uncommon for speakers to discover that their own handwriting is indecipherable, and that what seemed like a good addition, made hastily in ink, becomes an embarrassing stumbling block during presentation of the speech. A clean, well-typed, adequately spaced copy of the speech is absolutely necessary.

Second, the manuscript speech gives the speaker less opportunity to move around. The speaker will be reading from a manuscript that he or she is holding or has placed on a lectern. (The speaker should know, if possible, which of these two possibilities will occur and practice accordingly.) Such restriction means that the speaker will not be able to move as freely as he or she might during an extemporaneous speech. The speaker, therefore, will need to think carefully about what movement is possible and take advantage of it. It is still possible to move from side to side or toward or away from an audience. Appropriate gestures are also possible. What the speaker should avoid is the tendency to grasp tightly the podium or the manuscript itself, and hold on as if to anchor herself or himself in the strong wind. Again, *the key to being able to develop physical rapport with the audience through bodily flexibility is to be well prepared and to have practiced extensively.*

Third, use of the voice becomes especially important in a manuscript speech. Preparation should specifically include, in the case of a manuscript speech, attention to ways in which the voice may be used to add the variety, color, and emphasis that lack of movement tends to make more difficult to achieve. Use of the voice, such an obvious part of the delivery of any speech, is wortll considering seriously. At this point, let us consider important factors in the use of the voice and how the speaker should attend to them.

USING THE VOICE EFFECTIVELY

One of the most obvious aspects of delivery is, of course, the speaker's voice. There are those who have speech problems of varying degrees of seriousness— the person who is so hoarse that he or she cannot be understood; the person who substitutes or distorts sounds so that "rabbit," for example, comes out "wabbit" or the person who stutters. These speech problems are of a type that require special attention by professionals trained to deal with the pathologies of speech. Furthermore, some people have difficulties that are not severe, but they could benefit from work designed to improve their voices.

Most beginning speakers, however, will not need such intensive, individu-alized therapy. All speakers, nevertheless, should consider seriously how best to use their voices to aid them in communicating as effectively as possible. *Since the voice itself plays such a prominent role in shaping the listener's perception of the speaker and his or her message, it cannot fail to have an impact on the ultimate successfulness of public speaking.*

Some features of the voice a speaker can modify by recognizing their importance, by monitoring their operation in his or her own speaking, and by paying special attention to them in oral practice. These features are *volume, rate, clarity,* and *variety.*

VOLUME

It should be apparent that no idea, no matter how clearly developed, will be understood, and no idea, no matter how persuasively constructed, will be motivating if the idea cannot be heard. Nor will an audience be able to concentrate on the speaker's message if the speaker is so loud that the listeners are uncomfortable.

The speaker's volume may directly influence the audience's perception of and attentiveness to the speaker. One speaker, who later reported that he wanted to be "emphatic" and "forceful," virtually shouted his speech to an audience of about twenty people in a small classroom. In discussing the speech, the listeners concentrated almost exclusively on the excessive volume, describ-ing the speaker as "obviously very nervous," "too aggressive," "too emotional," and, even, "insulting." Members of the audience could hardly reconstruct the speaker's major theme or remember the major points he made, so unnerved were they by the loud delivery. At the other extreme, speakers whose voices come out in soft whispers usually cause an audience first to strain to hear and then to lapse into bored inattention.

The degree of loudness or softness should be determined by the *setting* in which the speaking takes place. Naturally, a small room calls for use of a quieter voice than does a large lecture hall or an outdoor setting. The speaker, as he or she gains experience, will learn to consider the listeners' needs and increase or decrease volume as the situation demands. Practice is an essential element, of course, in helping the speaker to meet the situation. Standing up and giving the speech, with a volume that seems realistic for the actual presentation, will help the speaker monitor his or her own voice and begin to get the feel of speaking loudly or softly enough for the listeners to understand and be comfortable.

RATE

It is not uncommon for a beginning speaker to sit down after giving a speech, look at the clock, and be amazed to find that the planned ten-minute speech only took five minutes to give. Several miscalculations in planning could account for such a result, but frequently the problem is that the speaker has rushed through the speech far too quickly. In his or her anxiety to "get it over with" the speaker can forget that *an audience needs time to follow, to absorb, and to react.*

The needs of the listeners are paramount. *Just as they can't keep up with the too-fast speaker, so do they lose interest in and patience with the too-slow one.* Often speakers who have not practiced enough, have not prepared adequately, or have underestimated the audience's powers of comprehension drag through a speech—stumbling along with the "umm's" and "ahh's", pausing too frequently or too long, filling in gaps with the ubiquitous and irritating, "you know." In such situations the listeners may easily give up efforts to grapple with the speaker's intent and meaning.

As with every other factor in speech preparation, the rate is determined in large measure by the speaker's estimate of *the nature of the listeners' responses.* As was pointed out earlier, listening to a speech can be contrasted with reading a book. The reader can slow down or speed up as his or her needs dictate. The speaker, on the other hand, cannot be stopped and replayed, as it were, by the listener, just as the listener cannot skip ahead to the speaker's next point. The speaker must anticipate the listeners' reactions and must be prepared to adjust to the actual feedback that he or she observes. This, of course, means that the speaker's focus is on the audience and on its response to the material and not exclusively on the material being presented.

Reacting to and planning for listeners' responses, therefore, forces the speaker to *modify rate as the situation demands.* Furthermore, *the material itself will also influence the speaker's rate.* A speaker describing the last few laps of the Indianapolis 500, for example, will undoubtedly speak at a faster rate than will a speaker who is describing the feelings of someone who is going into a hypnotic trance. This is to say that, in order to increase the potential for achieving his or her desired response, the speaker will use a rate that is *appropriate to the mood of the speech* and will thus enhance the meaning.

CLARITY

To be an effective informer or persuader, the speaker must be understood. One speaker, for example, baffled an audience for some time until they finally understood that he was not making frequent references to a friend, his "buddy," but, rather, to his "body." Another speaker who was generally well prepared and well informed discovered in a discussion following the speech that many listeners interpreted his mispronunciation of key words as a sign that he didn't really know what he was talking about. To achieve clarity, and thus to further his or her communicative purpose, the speaker should aim to achieve primarily three important qualities.

First, the speaker should achieve *distinctness of articulation*. Dropping the endings of words, slurring sounds, and running words together can interfere with the meaning of a message and cause listeners to work more to understand what a speaker is saying.

Second, the speaker should achieve *accuracy of pronunciation*. Every speaker should feel confident that words he or she uses are pronounced correctly. This means going to the dictionary whenever there is the slightest doubt about the pronunciation of the word he or she will use. Especially, the speaker should take care that he or she has practiced aloud and checked the pronunciation of words used in quoted material. Mispronunciation can lead to audience misunderstanding and to negative assessment of the speaker's ability.

Third, the speaker should achieve *freedom from mannerisms*. It is pointless and distracting, for example, to keep saying "you know." One speaker, obscured the clarity of his message by concluding almost every statement with the unnecessary question, "Right?" Also, there are regional mannerisms that clutter speech and thus reduce clarity, such as the questioning "hear?" at the end of a sentence, or the unnecessary and ungrammatical "at" tacked on to such statements as, "He didn't know where I was *at*." Such mannerisms are distracting to listeners, and listeners who are distracted are less likely to receive the message clearly.

VARIETY

Some of the features of a good speaking voice do not always operate in the same fashion. The preceding discussion points to a general rule that is consistent with the basic principle of good public speaking: in its support of the ideas being communicated, *the speaker's voice is adapted to the needs of the audience, setting, and content of the speech itself.* One unvaried volume and one unvaried rate will not only affect the listeners' attention negatively, but may distort the basic meaning of the ideas being discussed.

To develop variety, as to develop all aspects of a good speaking voice, *the speaker needs to cultivate an awareness of his or her own voice.* The speaker must learn to listen to himself or herself and begin to appreciate what listeners will hear as he or she speaks. Through practice, through careful attention to one's own behavior, the speaker can produce a voice to which listeners will be pleased to listen.

A good speaking voice is an important part, but only a part, of the total process of delivery. Developing good vocal technique, along with the other suggestions for enhancing your own feeling of confidence that have been made in this chapter, should help you to make the *unpredictable situation somewhat more predictable by pointing to ways that you can prepare to meet this potentially threatening public-speaking situation.* Keeping this in mind, consider now the basic principles that govern good delivery.

THE BASIS OF GOOD DELIVERY

If you have ever gone away after hearing a public speech or a speech on television and observed to someone, "That person really has a nice voice," or "That person sounded pretty good," you would have been responding, in part, to the delivery of the speech. Sometimes we find ourselves in the uncomfortable situation of thinking that someone sounded good but not being quite sure of what he or she said. *Sometimes delivery is so striking that it takes us away from the content of the communication itself.* This may be a purposeful act on the part of the speaker or it may be an accident. But in either case *it is not good delivery.* What does characterize good delivery?

First, good delivery grows out of an audience-centered approach to public speaking. A speaker whose constant and consistent attention is on himself or herself is liable to be far more concerned with what he or she sounds or looks like, or how he or she moves, than with how the audience is reacting to what is being said. The speaker is, after all, not really putting on an "act"; the speaker is trying to get a response from a specific audience. Good delivery, therefore, reflects such a mental set. The speaker who is delivering his or her speech well, for example, focuses physically on the audience. He or she watches them, talks with them, and looks for responses from them. Such a speaker speaks loud enough to be heard by them and does not embarrass them by using extravagant gestures or excessive movement. This first characteristic, the audience-centered quality of delivery, naturally leads to the second characteristic, good delivery.

Second, good delivery does not call attention to itself. The best delivery is one that the audience doesn't notice at all. It is the type that the audience will not respond to by obliterating content or meaning because of a physical action on the part of the speaker. This means that the speaker should want to exhibit behaviors that are appropriate to the situation, such as using a conversational type of voice when speaking to an audience of fifteen or twenty people sitting close to him or her. It means avoiding distracting types of mannerisms as one speaks. One instructor, for example, was notorious for his unique ability to balance a piece of chalk on the end of his finger. This fascinating skill always drew the attention of the students in his class; most of the time the attention was so complete as to distract students entirely from the content of the lecture.

Speakers sometimes exhibit verbal mannerisms as well, and these can also distract from the message. Remember that the speaker who says, "like" with great frequency or who punctuates his sentences with great numbers of "um's" or "ah's" will divert the audience's attention from the message itself.

Third, good delivery is that which best promotes the listener's belief and understanding. Delivery must be consistent with the rest of the speech. The speaker's body, voice, and gesture must be in tune with the mood and nature of the message. It is not always easy for a speaker to judge in advance the best way to integrate his or her delivery into a speech situation. Delivery probably is best improved through practice and through the critical response of a trained observer. But the speaker should not allow himself or herself to forget that *what is happening in front of that audience is all that the audience really knows about the speaker and the topic at that particular moment.* The speaker may have some very good and compelling reasons for urging an audience to take an action, but, if that speaker, through a dull and lifeless delivery, doesn't seem to care at all, the content of the message may be canceled out.

"SOUNDING GOOD" AND BEING "SOUND"

The fact that what the audience sees is for them the total communication experience sometimes puts an undue emphasis on and gives unwarranted influence to delivery. Quite often beginning students of public speaking will sit in a classroom and listen to a speaker who is poised, who has a good voice, who seems not to be at any loss for words, who is confident, and who is friendly. Often, because most people feel so insecure themselves, or because they are so sure they would be much more nervous and much less articulate, they greatly admire the ability of such a speaker. They tend, in fact, to judge the speaker almost solely on this demonstrated ability to be at ease with a group of listeners. Sometimes, however, such a speaker is merely *facile.* He or she can *speak easily, but might not be saying very much.* One thing that this book has been designed to do is to prepare you to distinguish between a speaker who is sound and a speaker who just sounds good.

A speaker who is sound will be the one whose *ideas pass the rigorous tests that grow out of the theory embodied in the preceding chapters.* As much as we might admire the ease and grace with which someone can address an audience, we need to be on our guard constantly against the slick, superficial person who is out to sell himself or herself and not to grapple with important ideas. One of the chief distinctions between the academic or school approach to public speaking and the popular type that promises you instant success is this: the former is designed to help you expand your intellectual and communicative powers in order to deal rationally and sensibly with listeners and to prepare listeners to be discriminating critics of what they hear; the latter is designed to help you give merely a good impression of yourself and your personality. *The educated person, then, is one who looks beyond the outward facade and hopes to test the firmness of the foundation.*

PRINCIPLES INTO PRACTICE: A SUMMARY

HOW TO DEVELOP GOOD STYLE AND DELIVERY

Delivery, the culmination of the public communication process for the speaker and for the listener, is also the culmination of our consideration of the public-speaking process. All that has gone before this chapter has been designed to help participants in the process design and evaluate a meaningful message. This chapter has attempted to clarify the role that style and delivery play in the final presentation of a message. To improve his or her style and delivery, the speaker should:

1. Use language to clarify ideas for the audience.
2. Use language that is interesting to the listener.
3. Use language that reflects the communication situation.
4. Reduce the unpredictability of the speaking situation by preparing extensively and by gaining as much experience as possible.
5. Reduce the unpredictability of the speaking situation by practicing carefully.
6. Prepare and practice using a good set of notes.
7. When practicing, keep in mind that good delivery is that which is audience centered, that which does not call attention to itself, and that which best promotes the listeners' belief and understanding.

Throughout this book we have discusses the way a speaker prepares himself or herself to speak. In doing so, the listener's special role has often been mentioned. In the next chapter we will turn to the listener exclusively and try to sum up the major observations on listening that have been implied already.

CHAPTER 11

LISTENING CRITICALLY: THE INFORMED RESPONSE

After studying this chapter you should understand:

- Why and how listening is an active process.

- How to develop and employ a strategy for listening that considers:
  - The listener's identity
  - The listener's purpose
  - The influence of setting
  - The speaker's target
  - The listener's knowledge of the speaker
  - The speaker's purpose

- How to listen defensively.

EFFECTIVE LISTENING

The best and most comprehensive advice that can be given to a listener is to be sure to know what's going on. That, of course, sounds very simple, but it is not simple at all. Very few of us know what's going on all the time during a speech. Most of us would not like to admit how often we are persuaded to do things without being aware of just how the persuasion has occurred. And then there a few of us who almost never know what's going on.

A major portion of this book has been devoted to helping you know what's going on. As you become a more effective speaker, you should also become a more effective listener. And this is very important, because *you will find yourself consuming a lot more communication than you will produce.* In this book, a lot has already been written about you as a listener. In this chapter we will discuss a fundamental principle of listening that should have been obvious from what has already been said and then suggest the outlines of a *strategy for listening* that should contribute to making you more effective in that role.

LISTENING AS AN ACTIVE PROCESS

The principle that should determine your approach to listening is simple: *listening is an active process.* We often tend to forget that when we are not talking, we are still very much a part of the communication process. We can forget this especially in a public-speaking setting where constant recognizable feedback is not called for and where overt interaction is minimal. Many students in a public-speaking class, for example, think that it is not very important to be in class when someone else is speaking except perhaps as a courtesy—so that there will be an audience to listen. *But, listening to speeches ought to be as important as giving them.* The dismissal of the listening process as being unimportant is reflected by the type of comment that some students make (students who have not considered the effects of such comments on their ethos) when they ask instructors, "Did we do anything important when I was absent on Tuesday?" The implication is that if no assignments were given, if no tests were taken, or if no material was handed out, then the instructor only talked, so nothing important happened. But how students responded to that lecture might have been, or could be, vitally important to each listener.

The point, of course, is not so much that one is present as that one does something—not just that one hears, but that one listens actively and critically. Being active means that you have to move. You have to keep your mind going, and going on the same track as the speaker, and not let it stop and float about, aimlessly drifting from topic to topic until the sound to which you are not really listening finally stops. *Listening critically means that you assess what you hear.* You try to make what you hear relevant to what you need to know. You weigh it carefully before you decide whether to act or not to act. There is a type of relentless skepticism about the good listener who worries about an idea the way a dog does a bone, devoting full attention to it, not letting it get away until all the juice is long sucked out of it, and rejecting a brittle, and even dangerous chicken bone for a good, substantial T-bone.

Since a speech is designed to get a response from you, you ought to ask yourself what it is doing to and for you as you listen. *The search for the answer to such questions can never be a passive one.* You can be a productive listener only to the extent that you pursue a careful and complete strategy aimed at getting the most for yourself out of listening to a speech. Let us now lay out the tactics, most of which we have alluded to in the preceding pages, that should form your listening strategy.

A STRATEGY FOR LISTENING

1. *Think about your own identity.* Perhaps that sounds strange to you. Yet it must not be forgotten that we all have many facets to our lives. The topic, the setting, and the general situation in which public speaking takes place will influence the roles we play as listeners. If you can approach a speaking situation aware of its relationship to you in your personal and social attributes and in the roles you play and the memberships you hold, you will begin to uncover your own initial positions on topics and your own predispositions and biases. No one can totally eliminate bias, nor can one be purely objective. But you can, through a self-analysis, at least indicate to yourself what some of the forces are that are at work. Your aim is to face the situation realistically and honestly so that you know what you bring to a speaking situation and who you are in relation to it.

2. *Listen with a purpose.* The speaker has a purpose in getting up to talk and each audience member ought to have one as he or she sits and listens. Do you hope to learn something? Can you relate the topic to your life and decide what

Good listening requires active concentration.

aspect of it will be useful to you? If so, you can aim to identify the practical aspects of the speech as it pertains to you. You can't, of course, be certain of your own purpose before you begin to listen to a speech, although the topic will give you an indication of what's happening, as will the resolution of other issues (issues that will be raised as this discussion goes on). The point is that you can provide your own focus in the situation. You can take from and respond to the message on your own terms. This is not to say that you should ignore the speaker and his or her function. The speaker may want to tell you about something that you initially may find to be meaningless but about which you may eventually be very happy to have heard. All that is being urged here is that you try before and during a speech to relate yourself personally to what is happening and try to understand the relationship of the speech to you.

3. *Understand the setting.* As we pointed out earlier, the setting in which communication takes place imposes restrictions and expectations on a speaker. A political candidate who has bought thirty seconds of radio time is very limited in what he or she can say. A speaker in an outdoor rally and one in a classroom will be working under different restraints. The listener will need to be aware of the handicaps and the advantages afforded to a speaker by the immediate surroundings if that listener is going to evaluate accurately what the speaker is doing and can do.

4. *Try to understand to whom the speaker is talking.* Before a listener can appreciate and understand the choices made by a speaker, the speaker must identify his or her target audience. Given the topic and the context out of which the speaking event has arisen, the listener can determine who the audience being immediately addressed is—that is, who is listening to and sitting in front of the speaker—and, also, who the larger audience might be. The President of the United States, for example, might give a speech to the American Legion or a national labor convention. In both cases, the subject matter and specific material would be strongly influenced by those groups. Nevertheless, the President would be aware of television and newspaper coverage and of the mass audience beyond the immediate one. The types of appeals a speaker makes, the types of arguments he or she uses, and even the topic selected may be puzzling to a listener who does not understand that public communication may have wide ramifications. Although it is unlikely that this would be so in a public-speaking class, a speech may be directed at an audience unseen by the listener, and the serious listener will be aware of such a possibility.

5. *Examine your assessment of and knowledge about the listener.* The listener ought to get his or her perception of the ethos of the speaker out in the open. The ways in which ethos will influence you ought to be made explicit so that you can determine whether or not they are really sensible. If, for example, you know the speaker is someone you don't like, then face up to that fact. You could fool yourself into believing that you won't take the desired action because

it is too expensive, because it isn't logical, or because you are too busy but the real reason would be that you just don't want to give the speaker the satisfaction or pleasure by doing what he wants you to do. If the matter is not of vital importance, then it may not make any difference whether or not you follow the course of action recommended. But suppose it is a very serious matter that will affect your health or well-being. Can you afford to base your decision on purely personal grounds? If you fool yourself, you will never even question whether or not you should act solely on the basis of the ethos of the source. Thus, you may lose the opportunity to listen effectively and, consequently, to act effectively.

You should be realistic in your assessment of the speaker. Gossip, half remembered impressions, and second-hand accounts of the actions of others that you hear can influence a speaker's ethos significantly. The listener who hopes to be as effective as possible will be as skeptical in assessing the speaker's reputation as he would be in other things. In most cases, it is unwise to assume that any speaker's life is an open book to the listener. To be too confident of who and what a speaker is can lead the listener to overestimate and underestimate the ability or integrity of a speaker. This is not to say that all a person has said and done in the past can or should be ignored. In a sense, we all stand on our records. The listener should satisfy himself or herself that the speaker's record is as straight as it can be.

6. *Consider the speaker's purpose*. The listener who knows what the speaker is trying to do is better prepared to respond effectively. Speakers may sometimes be unclear or they may intend to mislead an audience. It will not always be easy to identify the speaker's purpose. However, what the listener knows about the setting, the speaker, and the general nature of the topic should provide clues to be used to pinpoint the goal of the speaker. Sometimes a speaker's purpose is completely compatible with the listener's, as in the typical classroom situation in which the lecturer hopes to gain understanding and the listeners really want to learn something. In such a case, the listeners will want to know the speaker's purpose in order to cooperate actively with her achievement.

7. *Listen defensively*. If a speaker is really trying to communicate, he or she is attempting to get the listener to *do* something. This "something" can be a direct action, such as voting in a certain way, or a less overt action such as agreeing that more money should be spent on higher education. It could be in your best interest to respond as the speaker wished or it could *not* be in your

best interest to respond as the speaker wished. As a listener, your major responsibility to yourself is to respond as intelligently as possible. This means that you cannot jump to conclusions. Instead, you must suspend judgment until you are convinced that you are making the best choice for you. To do that, you must defend yourself against the appeals and pressures put on you by the communication event.

Defending does not necessarily mean rejecting. You might, in the end, accept a speaker's arguments and respond as he or she would wish. You might be skeptical of a television message, for example, and end up finally buying the product or voting for the candidate. *Being defensive means that the listener works to uncover and evaluate the basis of his or her own responses.* When the ways ideas explained and advocated in public speaking were discussed in previous chapters of this book, an attempt was made to provide listeners with specific tests to help them evaluate messages. All these suggestions were directed toward the general stipulation that a listener should understand *why* he or she is reacting in a certain way to a speech and then ask himself or herself if that is a sensible thing to do. For example, if you have decided to buy aftershave lotion because Pete Rose thinks it smells terrific, you should be aware that his

Active listeners attempt to understand and evaluate the content of messages.

ethos has convinced you. You need to ask yourself if that really is proof of the superiority of one product over another. If you tend to feel silly because you're acting as you do, you should then reevaluate your decision.

In examining your own motives you should try to uncover the extent to which you are acting on the basis of the image or reputation of the source. Furthermore, you have to determine how you are responding to the ideas in the speech, asking yourself how clear they are and how well assertions are supported by hard evidence. Certainly you should consider the extent to which you are responding on the basis of your feelings—that is, because you feel sympathetic, frightened, hostile, or loving. The speaker, considering the case at hand, must ask himself or herself: How *appropriate* are those feelings? But, as the listener you must ask if they are the ones that you believe you ought to have in that situation? Has the speaker identified with strong (but, in your case irrelevant) feelings you have, as, for example, by associating your feelings of independence and self-esteem with a brand of cigarette?

PRINCIPLES INTO PRACTICE: A SUMMARY

HOW TO LISTEN CRITICALLY

The tools of defensive listening go hand-in-hand with the techniques of successful speaking. When both the speaker and the listener are equipped to make intelligent and effective decisions, then the communication process itself is improved. To be most effective, the listener should:

1. Be sure of his or her own identity in the context of the speaking situation.
2. Listen with a purpose.
3. Understand the setting for the speech.
4. Understand to whom the speaker is talking.
5. Examine her or his own assessment of the speaker.
6. Consider what the speaker's purpose is.
7. Listen defensively by understanding the basis for his or her own responses.

PART III

BECOMING AN EFFECTIVE SPEAKER AND LISTENER: A PLAN FOR ACTION

CHAPTER 12

HOW TO BECOME AN EFFECTIVE SPEAKER

Studying this review chapter will help you to pull together all that you have learned so far about speaking. It will also be helpful to you as a reminder and guide in speaking situations that you will someday face, and it could be used as a reference in the future

Following are the actions that you will need to take to become an effective speaker. What you have learned in your public-speaking course, by studying this book, and by practical experience can be summarized in the outline of the strategy that follows. Consider these principles and the ways they are put into practice each time you speak.

1. *Carefully consider your audience.*
   - Know the special characteristics of your audience and how they might relate to your topic.
   - Know the circumstances under which listeners will be attending to your message.
   - Determine as accurately as possible how much listeners know about your topic.
   - Determine as accurately as possible how your listeners stand on the issue that you are discussing with them.
   - Assess how your audience feels about you and your relationship to your topic.

- Have as clear a conception as possible of the needs and value of your listeners and how they relate to your topic.

2. *Have a clearly stated specific purpose.*

- The purpose should reflect the overall response called for informative, persuasive, or entertaining.
- The purpose is a statement of the response that you want from the listeners.
- The purpose is one that can be realistically achieved in the communicative setting.
- The purpose is clear and unambiguous.

3. *Develop ideas designed to further the purpose.*

- Ideas should be stated in clear, complete, and precise sentences.
- Ideas should be simple enough to be undrestood and followed by your listeners.
- Ideas must be appropriate to the listeners and the context in which they are listening.
- Ideas are ones that make sense to the audience.

4. *Organize ideas clearly and appropriately.*

- Ideas are arranged in a pattern that helps make them more understandable or believable, whether it be a chronological, spatial, topical, problem-solution, or causal one.
- The total structure of the speech should be one that will promote clarity of ideas.
- The form of the speech should suggest the persuasive ends of the speech.

5. *Gather and arrange enough supporting material to make the ideas understandable and believable to an audience.*

- Carefully and systematically search through printed material for information relevant to your topic and directly related to your purpose.
- Search for and interview or write to people who can provide significant information on the topic.
- Search for the statements and opinions of experts on the topic and use their testimony to support appropriate ideas.

- Find and use as support adequate statistical information.
- Use specific examples to make ideas more understandable or believable.
- Unusual or new ideas or objects should be brought within the experience of the audience through comparison with the more familiar.

6. *Plan communicative methods appropriate to the ideas in the speech.*

   - Plan clear transitions from one idea to another.
   - Plan to repeat and restate difficult and important ideas to help an audience follow and remember them.
   - Develop visual or audio aids that will clarify and heighten the impact of ideas.

7. *Test the soundness of your argument.*

   - The relationship between the evidence presented and the conclusion reached must be clear.
   - The evidence used must be sufficient to support generalizations reached.
   - The speaker must distinguish, both for himself or herself and for the audience, between those reasons that may be given publicly for the support of an idea and those reasons that may lie beneath the rationalizations.

8. *Involve listeners in the speech.*

   - Demonstrate for the audience the ways in which the speech bears directly on their lives and experiences.
   - Devise ways to arouse listeners' curiosity about the speech.
   - Associate the ideas in the speech with listeners' needs.
   - Associate the ideas in the speech with listeners' values.
   - Introduce the speech by stimulating audience interest in what is to come.
   - Conclude the speech with a final statement that reinforces the mood and message of the speech and points the audience to appropriate action.

9. *Prepare a fully developed outline.*

- The outline must show clearly the relationship of the ideas to the purpose.
- The ideas themselves should be stated as complete sentences.
- The material included must support (that is, make more understandable or believable) the ideas that it is supposed to support.
- The introduction and conclusion must fit into the total scheme of the outline and be carefully prepared.

10. *Use language carefully and appropriately.*

- Use language that will be clear and persuasive to listeners.
- Use language to heighten interest.
- Use language that is appropriate to the total situation.

11. *Plan and practice the delivery of the speech carefully.*

- The speaker must be as well-prepared as possible.
- Practice the speech out loud, with some listeners if possible.
- Prepare and practice using adequate notes.
- As the speech is delivered, the speaker must focus on the listeners and their responses to the ideas presented.

CHAPTER 13

HOW TO BECOME AN EFFECTIVE LISTENER

Studying this review chapter will help you to pull together all that you have learned about listening. It will also be helpful to you as a reminder and guide in communication situations that you will someday face, and it could be used as a reference in the future.

The listener, unlike the speaker, has less conscious preparation for the public-speaking situation, although the listener can and should do some preplanning and thinking. Most of what the listener must do in order to participate effectively in the process, however, should be done while he or she is receiving the message. Consider the following principles as directions for critical listening in the public-speaking setting.

1. *Prepare beforehand for the speech.*

- If possible, determine the topic and try to consider the ways in which it relates to you.
- Think about what you bring to the event in the form of opinions you have already formed, conceptions you have already developed, or biases you already hold.
- Come to the event prepared to concentrate and to try to further successful communication.

2. *Formulate a purpose for yourself.*

- As the speech unfolds, the listener should ask, "What should I be getting out of this?"
- The listener should ask himself or herself, "Can what the speaker says affect in any way what I do in my daily life?"

3. *Consider the setting of the speech and its impact on both the speaker and the listener.*

- Try to understand the limitations that time imposes on the message being presented.
- Try to understand how the environment in which the speech is produced helps or hinders the successful completion of communication.
- Assess the impact of the surroundings on you and your reactions to the speech.

4. *Understand to whom the speaker is talking.*

- Look for evidence that the speaker has analyzed his or her audience.
- Try to understand the ways in which the speaker tries to reach listeners who might be different from you.
- Try to discover whether or not the speaker seems to be talking to an audience beyond the immediate one.

5. *Uncover the basis of your own assessment of the speaker.*

- Identify any preconceptions you might have about the speaker.
- Be aware of the ways in which your perception of the speaker may influence the way you listen to the speech.
- Constantly check your preconception with what you are hearing.
- Be aware of the extent to which you are relying on your own image of the speaker in responding positively or negatively to the speech.

6. *Determine the speaker's specific purpose.*

- Understand what the speaker is trying to get you to do.
- Compare the response that you think the speaker hopes to get with your own goals for the communication interaction.

As you listen to the speech, try to determine the quality of that speech by searching for the answers to a series of questions about the ideas and their development:

7. *Assess the quality of the ideas presented in the speech.*

- Are the ideas distinct and readily identified as separate ideas?
- Are the ideas clearly stated?
- Are the ideas simple enough to follow without getting confused?
- Do the ideas seem to fit into the speech and the setting for the speech?
- Do the ideas make sense to you as you think about them?

8. *Assess the organizational pattern of the speech.*

- Can you determine a clear sequencing of ideas?
- Does the sequence of ideas seem a good one for the topic?
- Does the way the ideas are put together help you to understand better what the speaker wants you to understand?
- Does the way the ideas are patterned suggest that the speaker is trying to get a specific response from you?

9. *Judge the adequacy of the evidence presented.*

- Does the speaker support ideas with concrete evidence that makes the ideas more believable or understandable?
- Does it seem that the speaker has enough evidence to support ideas?
- Does the speaker seem to have taken the trouble to gather as much information as possible?
- Does the quantity and quality of the evidence lead you to believe that the speaker knows what he or she is talking about?
- Are the examples used typical, accurate, and important?
- Are the sources and methods of gathering statistics used mentioned, and do they allow for the possibility of bias or inaccuracy?
- Is the testimony by relevant authority, timely, and consistent with the context?
- If ideas, events, and people are compared, are they being compared alike in essential ways to make the comparison valid?

10. *Judge the quality of the overall argument.*

- Is the relationship between the evidence and the conclusion on which the evidence is based a clear and direct one?
- Are the generalizations offered in the message warranted by what the speaker has told the audience or by what you know and have experienced?
- Does the argument get to the real issues involved in the topic?
- Do you believe the argument as it is being presented, or are you willing to accept it as a convenient rationalization?

11. *Assess the ways in which the speaker tries to involve you in the topic.*

- Does the speaker realistically relate the topic to your life?
- Does the speaker arouse your curiosity?
- How does the speaker relate his or her ideas to your needs and values?
- Do the relationships made by the speaker fit your needs and values?
- Does the speaker make an effort to gain your attention and interest?
- Does what interests you distract you from what the speaker is trying to do?

12. *Be aware of the way the speaker uses language.*

- Is the speaker using language that you can understand and follow?
- Does the speaker's choice of language help) to make the ideas more understandable or believable?
- Does the language chosen seem to be appropriate to the setting in which the speech occurs?
- Does the language suggest conclusions, generalizations, attitudes, or values that the speaker hopes to further?
- Does the language ever function to reinforce, or even substitute, for argument?
- To what extent are you reacting to people or ideas because of the labels used to describe them?

13. *Put the delivery of the speech in the proper perspective.*

- Is the speaker's message made clearer or more convincing by the way he or she says it?

- Are you doing your best to avoid being distracted by what you see and hear, and are you trying to concentrate on ideas?
- Do you know what the speaker is saying as well as how he or she is saying it?
- Do you find yourself dismissing the speaker's ideas because you don't like the way he or she sounds or looks?
- Do you find yourself agreeing with a speaker because you like the way he or she sounds and looks?

EPILOGUE

SPEAKER AND LISTENER AS CONFEDERATES

Students often get together to study for tests. In these study sessions there may be one specific point that one student understands better than his or her friend. In such a case, the knowledgeable student will explain the idea or provide additional information or interpretation for the friend. Both the speaker and the listener want communication to be successful.

Much communication is like that; *both the source of the message and the receiver of the message hope that the goals will be accomplished.* If someone wants to sell you a motorcycle and hopes to persuade you that it is a good one, and if you want to buy a good motorcycle, you will want to be persuaded of its quality. If you saw a good movie and want to convince someone you like to go to that movie, and if your friend wants and enjoys the pleasurable experience of going to an entertaining film, successful persuasion would then be a mutual goal.

In many situations, then, communication is a cooperative effort. Public speaking often demands that all parties concerned in the process work actively to bring about the type of response that will benefit all. Both speakers and listeners will be searching for the meaning of their relationship: speakers to understand audience motivations and relate messages to listeners' needs and values, listeners to understand and make applicable the ways in which the speaker's message has the potential for influencing or enhancing their lives.

When an idea is a difficult or a complicated one, the best speaker makes every effort to develop to the full the strategies, tactics, and techniques discussed in this book in order to promote the listener's understanding and belief. For his or her part, the best listener aids the speaker by seeking actively to understand relationships among ideas and by concentrating on the evidence presented and its relation to the purpose the speaker seems to want to accomplish. The speaker who says, "I'm going to say what I want to and it's up to them whether they get it," or the listener who says, "Okay, I'm here; see if you can do anything to me," are both failing to meet their obligations to further the public-speaking process and will probably both be losers for it.

Of course, if you have been reading this book carefully, you know that the speaker and the listener do not and should not accept each other's ideas, assertions, and prejudices without question. There are times when the speaker and the listener must assume an adversarial relationship.

THE SPEAKER AND LISTENER AS ADVERSARIES

The speaker cannot always say what the audience wants to hear any more than the listener can always accept what the speaker says without question. Although public speaking is essentially a cooperative venture, it is not always without conflict between the participants. A speaker may know very well the values of an audience, but he or she may wish to reject those values. A speaker who truly hopes to communicate will adapt to his or her listeners, but that speaker is not expected to adopt wholesale ideas that are repugnant to him or her. The listener should try to fill in gaps and seek structure and unity in a speech, but he or she can't be expected to imagine evidence or relationships that just aren't there. And as we all know and have experienced, there are times when purposes just are not compatible; we listeners may want to spend as little money as possible, and the speaker may be urging us to spend as much as we have.

The fact that speaker and listener are often in conflict however, does not mean that their relations should be hostile or antagonistic. In a world of message sending and receiving, we must recognize that we depend on public communication for much of our information, instruction, and inspiration. And we switch roles from speaker to listener as the occasion and situation demands.

What is needed is *a healthy critical stance on both sides,* an awareness that all the participants in public speaking will not always be hoping for the same outcomes, and an attitude of friendly, but hardheaded, skepticism that demands that messages be examined very carefully and dispassionately before judgment is reached. All that has been said in this book has been directed toward helping you develop for yourself such a critical stance, and toward helping you devise ways of improving your participation in the process of public speaking.

THE LAST WORD

Speakers and listeners who can conscientiously carry out all the practical principles that are enumerated in the two final chapters of the book should feel quite confident that they are ready for whatever public-speaking situation in which they find themselves. Of course, it will take time and experience in applying principles to develop a well-grounded appreciation for and skill in public speaking. This book has laid out for the student the basic principles, what you must be able to understand and put to use to make communication work. Over time, you will learn much more about the complicated human process of relating to one another in the special way that we call communication. This book, and, more importantly, the personal instruction you have received and the experience you have gained in your study of public speaking should point you clearly in the right direction. This book may also continue to be helpful to you as a reference as you go on developing your expertness as a speaker and as a consumer of communication.

In the end, of course, your success depends on you. If you want to communicate in an effective way, and if you have the understanding and skills to do it, you will, indeed, be a more effective public speaker. And, as a consequence, you may be a more effective person in all you do.

APPENDIX

SAMPLE SPEECHES FOR ANALYSIS

As you read these speeches, look for ways in which the speaker has employed the basic principles of good public speaking. Consider the following questions as guides for analysis:

- In what ways does the speaker use himself or herself as a resoure for the speech?

- What do you read in the speech that demonstrates the speaker's awareness of his or her audience? What special efforts are made to involve the audience in the speech?

- Does the speaker appear to make use of the situation in which the speech is given?

- How would you state the speaker's purpose in this speech?

- How well does the speaker use material designed to achieve his or her purpose?

- Can you identify the speaker's arguments? How well are they supported in the speech?

- Is the speech structured clearly? Does it follow a specific pattern?

- In what ways is the speech introduced and concluded? Do these seem to be effective?

- How do you think you would have responded to the speech as a listener?

STUDENT SPEECHES

The following speeches were given by students in a beginning public-speaking class. They were delivered as part of the *Raymond G. Smith Public Speaking Contest* which is held annually at Indiana University for students in the freshman public-speaking class.

DOING WHAT COMES NATURALLY
David Brown

Although I may appear rather normal to you at first, barring a few abnormalities, there is something quite unique about me. This uniqueness is so special that only 1 percent of the population ages twenty-twenty-nine can put themselves in the same group as myself. This 1 percent can further be divided into three subcategories: The veges, the lactos, and the lacto-ovos which I consider myself.

Before I confuse you anymore, let me explain to you what I am and give you the many options open to you with the hopes that you will join me. I am a vegetarian. That's right; I don't eat meat. I don't eat Big Macs. I don't eat Quarter Pounders.

People are vegetarians for quite a few different reasons. For some, like the Seventh-Day Adventists and the orthodox Hindus, they're vegetarians for religious reasons. While some are vegetarians for health reasons. They cannot tolerate the saturated fats and cholesterol found in red meat. While others are vegetarians for ecological reasons. They think it's far less wasteful to eat the crops directly after harvest than to give the crops to the animals and then feed on the animals. And for some, vegetarianism is a way to control or to lose weight.

But, a meatless diet is far more than giving up a Big Mac and substituting a butterfinger instead. This should become clear when I explain to you the three different categories of vegetarians and discuss the reasons for becoming a vegetarian.

The first kind of vegetarian is the *vega* or the *vegen*. These are very strict vegetarians who will only eat food from a single plant source—plant sources such as vegetables, fruit, and grains. While the *lacto* vegetarian includes milk and milk products in his diet, the *lacto-ovo* vegetarian, the kind of vegetarian I am, will include eggs in addition to milk and milk products in his diet.

As I said before, there are quite a few different reasons why I want you to join one of these groups of vegetarians.

The first, is health reasons. Although most of us are young right now, twenty to thirty years down the line we will wish we had thought more about our health when we were young. The number-one health problem directly linked to meat consumption is heart disease. When you eat meat, saturated fat forms cholesterols along the arterial wall leading to the heart, and this constricts the flow of blood. This means that your heart has to pump harder, therefore, increasing your risk of getting a heart attack. Heart attacks are the number-one killers among Americans today. Statistics indicate that in countries where meat consumption is high, for example the United States, Canada, and Australia, the mortality rate linked to heart disease is equally high. And that in highly developed countries that do not consume a lot of meat, for example Japan and Italy, the mortality rate linked to meat consumption is very low.

Another disease linked to meat consumption is cancer. Cancer is commonly and routinely found in animals that are produced for food that we eat. For example, inspectors routinely cut out cancerous tumors in cows that go to market, right before they go to market. So, therefore, cancer can be found, traces of cancer can be found, in our food supply. There is also a common and certain form of cancer found in chickens that cannot easily be detected without the investment of a lot of money and without taking a lot of time, so it is often passed over. The food that we eat every day, then, could easily have cancerous material in it. That increases our own chances of getting cancer also.

Another major health risk involved with meat consumption is harmful bacteria. We all know that meat is a dead corpse. Accordingly, it has a high amount of harmful bacteria in it. Researchers studied thirty-two brands of hot dogs in various supermarkets across the country. From these thirty-two brands they used a base level which said rotting begins when the hot dog has a bacteria level of ten million per gram. Of these thirty-two, 40 percent had already begun to spoil and one particular brand had a bacteria count of 140 million per gram. I'm not going to mention the brand, but I'll give you a hint: it has a first name.

I not only want you to think of the health reasons involved, but also to think of ecological reasons. There is an increasing ecological dilemma, and this has to do with our decreasing supply of land. It has been found that the land will support far more human beings per acre if this land would be devoted to the growing of crops for human consumption rather than the growing of crops for animal consumption, which, in turn, we would feed upon. Isaac Asimov, noted biochemist at Boston University, stated that in each step of the feeding process there is considerable waste, so that only 10 percent of the living material of the creature fed upon is converted into living material of the creature who is feeding. If we were to stop eating animals, this would increase the food supply of the world ten times. Wouldn't that put a dent in the world hunger problem as we see it now?

Although all of these very good things would result if we all gave up eating meat, the vast majority of you won't and I can understand why. But the reason you will give me is "Well, ah, ah, I'd lose nutrients and vitamins." But, this is only partially true. The only vitamins and nutrients you will lose if you convert from a meat diet to a vegetarian diet are vitamin B12 and iron. But vitamin B12 can easily be picked up in animal products such as milk, and eggs, so if you're a lacto or lacto-ovo vegetarian you will have no problem. And the iron can be picked up in iron supplements. So that's not a real problem.

Furthermore, the Food and Nutrition Board stated that vegetarians will get along well nutritionally if they have a large variety in their diet. A problem arises when vegetarians rely on a single plant source for their food.

Finally, studies have shown that the human being is not naturally suited to digesting and eliminating fleshy foods. Natural carnivores—wolves, bears, cats, dogs—have a digestive tract that is about proportionally one-fourth as long as the digestive tract of vegetarian animals, including humans. The long, intricate winding digestive tract of the human being is ill-suited for digesting and elimi-nating fleshy foods. Along with sharp claws, all natural carnivores have long, sharp fangs that they use for spearing and tearing at the flesh that they kill. When you go home tonight, look in the mirror. Look at your teeth. And look down at your fingernails. Can these, by any stretch of the imagination, be said to be the equivalent of a bear's claws used for tearing at his prey? Or could these little teeth up there be said to be the equivalent of a long, sharp fang of a tiger used to kill its prey? I think not.

The many dissimilarities between natural carnivores and human beings are obvious. For example, all natural carnivores kill their own prey. Except for vultures, they kill it and they eat it in a raw, bloody stage. Most of us would be sickened if we had to watch our meat being slaughtered for us, or even more sickened if we had to go outside Woodburn Hall and kill a cow along Indiana Street and then sit down and eat it right there with our fingers.

So do yourself a healthy favor. Do the whole world a great favor. Do what honestly comes natural to the human being and become a vegetarian.

TAKING CONTROL!
PRINCIPLES OF TIME MANAGEMENT
Renata Burke

There's a story about a farmer with whom I think we can all sympathize. One morning he announced to his wife that he was going out to put oil in the tractor. He knew that the oil was low, so he left a little early to do that. He found out, though, that the oil was lower than he thought, so he decided to go to the shop to get more. On the way there he noticed that the pigs looked a little hungry, so he decided to go to the corn crib to get some more feed for them. Seeing the sacks of feed, he was reminded that probably, by now, the potatoes were rotting, so he went to the potato pit. On the way to the potato pit he was reminded that his wife had specifically said that she wanted wood in the house that morning. On the way to the house with an armload of wood he had stopped to cut, he saw that the gate to the pasture was open and the horses were out on the road. He dropped the wood and ran for the horses. That night the farmer sat down tired and frustrated. He had never made it to the tractor much less to the field.

Do you ever feel, like the farmer, that you've had a busy, exhausting day but haven't accomplished what you wanted to? Well, today there are dozens of books on the market to help us accomplish what we set out to do. How to control your time and your life, making the most of your mind, managing yourself, how to become a one-minute manager. All of these are written to show us how we can squeeze all we want to do out of a day, those twenty-four hours which cannot be stopped, stored or stretched. What I would like to propose to you today is a means of gaining back control of your time so that you can use it in the wisest manner to accomplish what you set out to do.

First of all, I'd like to explain the principles of time management. Second, I'd like to apply those principles to show you how to come up with a workable schedule. And, third, I'd like to give you some reminders so you can keep your schedule on track.

First, in considering the principles of time management you should know that there are several benefits involved. The first of those benefits is learning to make decisions. We have to decide what to do and how to do it. Time management forces us to make logical, conscientious decisions that we believe yield satisfying results. Practice in making those decisions will make those decisions in the future not nearly so ominous. Second, and closely linked with learning to make decisions, is the developing purpose and direction in our lives. Because our lives are made up of time, time well spent and well managed will give us a kind of map of our lives and we won't be caught drifting through life. Third, we will gain free time. Now, I know some of you may be saying, "I can't remember the last time I had any free time," or "I feel guilty when I relax." Yet, you'll find in choosing to manage your time that you'll have free time you never knew you had. Fourth, and finally, you'll be able to balance work with three essentials: eating, sleeping, and exercising. Those three areas are essential for you to remain alert and healthy. Once those areas are out of balance then, too, every other area of your life will go out of balance. Yet, if you choose to keep those in balance, then, too, every other area will benefit.

So, if you want to learn to make decisions, develop purpose and direction in your life, gain free time, and remain alert and healthy, you will choose to manage your time well. Now that we've considered the first principle, time management will produce direct benefits for you, let us consider the second principle by considering what you want out of life.

The second principle is that, to get the most out of life, you need to have clear objectives. We need to consider two objectives: long-range objectives and short-range objectives. Now, the long-range objectives are those which give you an overall direction to your life. Those are the things that you would most like to see happen in your lifetime. The short-range objectives are those that you extract out of that long-range objective list. Those are the things that you would like to work on now during the next six to twelve months. Once you choose an objective, then go ahead and choose a program to actually accomplish that objective.

For example, let's say that I want to make exercise a regular part of my activity. Once I choose that objective, then I need to choose the best program— whether it's running, swimming, aerobics, or any number of physical activities. I need to choose that program so that I'll be able to accomplish my objective. Well, that brings us up to our third principle of time management, and that's to have a specific goal.

All of us have set goals of some kind or another. Yet, I wonder how many of us have actually accomplished them. Maybe not very many. As a result, many of us just choose to throw them out the window because we can't reach them. Yet, if you don't set those goals, you'll have no way of knowing if your life is heading in the desired direction. Therefore, we need to set goals which are attainable and measurable.

Let's go on with the example that I gave you about exercise. I set a goal of running the ten-kilometer race within six months. Therefore, I need immediately to begin planning how far I want to run each week, so I'll be able to do what I intend to do, run ten kilometers at the end of six months. Maybe the first week I want to run three kilometers, the second week six kilometers, and so on until, following my definite plan, in six months I'll be able to run that ten kilometers.

Have you ever heard anyone say, "Well, I'm so busy, I don't have time to manage my time." You will find, though, according to Sam Osterlow, who is on staff with a campus organization here, that thirty minutes of planning can actually save you thirty hours of wasted time in a week. Let's turn now from the principles of time management, to the actual planning of time management which is outlined in the book *Managing Yourself* by Steve Douglas.

Douglas says that the first thing to do is to list your activities. List those things that you think you'll be involved in during the next week. Then you'll be able to see just exactly what is expected of you and, too, you'll be able to clear your mind so that you won't be desperately trying to remember what you have to do.

Second, Douglas suggests that you should consider whether any of those activities can be delegated to someone else. Now, that is not a means of dodging responsibility. Rather, it's a means of freeing your own personal schedule of those things that could be done better or more appropriately by someone else.

Third, assess your priorities. What you need to do is consider how important each activity is and then, too, how quickly it has to be accomplished. Let's look at this transparency I've prepared as an example of what I would do to plan my time and we'll have a comprehensive list for my next week.

T	Study for math test	(4 hours)
L	Hem grey skirt	(1/2 hour)
H	Read novel for English class	(5 hours)
M	Write minutes for dorm meeting	(1/2 hour)
M	Letter to Betty	(1 hour)
H	Think about topic for next speech	(1-1/2 hours)
T	Aerobics class	(1-1/2 hours)
M	Contact film committee for meeting time	(Ask John to do)
L	Go to see *Out of Africa*	(3 hours)

You can see, by looking at the left column, that I consider some things top priority: that's what "T" is. "H" is high priority, "M" is medium priority, and "L" is low priority. On the right I've listed the time I believe it will take me to accomplish those activities. Now we're ready to schedule.

Scheduling is nothing more than doing the right thing at the right time. It just doesn't make sense to make up a schedule and then file it away. What you need to do is to keep that schedule handy so that you'll be able to consult it through the day. One thing that helps some people is to color code priorities: for example, put the top priorities and the high priorities in blue, the medium priorities in green, and the low priorities, as well as the delegated activities, in brown. To sum all this up, I want to leave you with three reminders that would help keep you on track as you go ahead and effectively manage your time.

First, do not become preoccupied with time. I am not here to convince you to become a clock watcher. Those type of people are constantly making lists, updating lists, and losing lists. Rather, I'm here to encourage you to manage your time so that you'll experience greater freedom.

Second, retain motivation. Keeping that desire fresh is going to energize you to keep making that schedule and stick to it. Ask someone to keep you accountable so that you will keep up with that. Keep making it and keep sticking with it.

Third, discipline yourself. Time management is hard work and there's no way to get around it. But reward yourself when you do a good job, and if you blow it, don't give up. Resolve to do better the next time.

Today, I've given you some principles of time management and shown you an application of time management as well as some reminders to keep you on course. The choice is now yours. But, remember, according to Steve Douglas, a goal minus a plan minus an action is but a dream. However, a goal plus a plan plus action is a reality.

THE CASE AGAINST TV VIOLENCE
Kristin Dodd

A kitchen knife, a rolling pin, a planter, and an ashtray. These are common, useful items found in the average home. Useful, yes. Did you ever consider that they might be useful to a potential killer who has just seen them employed as deadly weapons on television?—television, the main source of entertainment in most American homes today.

I'm sure you have all heard the saying, "monkey see, monkey do." Well, let us examine the evidence to show how this old adage may be working today as violence on television inspires imitation.

The case against TV violence has been around for some time. But little, however, has been done to curb the violence that enters our homes everyday, posing as "entertainment." I feel the harmful effects of TV violence is an issue worth further investigation, for it is a factor which affects all of us in this room today and the condition of the world we live in. Because its so important to us, we must oppose the television violence that leads to antisocial behavior that we're all aware of.

Let's take a look at a prime example of how violence on television has led to horrifying actualities. On September 30, 1973, the Sunday Night Movie was a film called *Fuzz*, depicting thrill-seeking delinquents who doused waterfront tramps with gasoline and then set them on fire. Two days later twenty-five-year-old Evelyn Wagler ran out of gas while driving through a Boston slum. She was on her way back to her car with a 2-gallon can of gas, when six young men surrounded her and dragged her to a vacant lot. They then poured gasoline over her and set her ablaze and left her. A human torch rolling frantically in the dirt. Four hours later Evelyn Wagler died. Boston Mayor, Kevin White, has this to say about the incident: "I saw the movie *Fuzz*, and I think there was a definite relationship." The *New York Times* agreed. The dreadful coincidence cannot be ignored.

If the point needed more emphasis, Miami provided it three weeks later. There, four twelve and thirteen-year-olds stole some lighter fluid. They doused three winos sleeping behind a vacant building, ignited a match, and laughed hilariously as the men awoke, running and screaming trying to beat the flames. One man died of his burns. All four boys had seen the movie *Fuzz*. "Monkey see, monkey do."

The evidence is overwhelming that excessive violence on television is a cause of aggressive behavior. A survey released December 17 by the United States Conference of Mayors, reported that guns, knives, and other deadly weapons appear on television an average of nine times an hour. The study involved seventy-three hours of prime-time action. During these seventy-three hours, 648 weapons were seen, 36 deaths and 41 injuries occurred, 346 bullets were fired. And, even more shocking, as many as forty-three weapons, including guns, knives, three spear guns, bottles, wrenches, four rocks, brass knuckles, a fireplace poker, an ashtray, and even a rolling pin were flashed across the screen in just one hour's viewing time.

With all these weapons seen nightly, it's no wonder the United States has one of the highest crime rates. Just look at the kinds of things that are happening in our country:

A fourteen-year-old boy laced his family dinner with ground glass after seeing it done on one of his favorite crime shows. On September 10, 1974, NBC aired *Born Innocent,* a television drama about a female juvenile detention home where six young girls surrounded a girl in the shower and raped her with the handle of a plunger. Four days later, near San Francisco, four children ages nine through fifteen seized two eight-year-old girls on a public beach and replayed the scene with beer bottles. Three of the four perpetrators told police that they had seen the movie *Born Innocent.*

To bring it a little closer to home, in the town of Mooresville, Indiana, not a half an hour away from here, a boy confessed to the brutal, senseless shooting of a woman, stating that he had been watching television one night, saw a murder, got up from the couch, grabbed his shotgun, walked out the front door and shot dead the first person he saw. Who else to blame, but television for this murder?

Now, if you're still not convinced that TV violence is harmful to your health, take note of the following: On March 8, 1973, CBS broadcast the movie, *The Marcus-Nelson Murders,* the show that *Kojak* was patterned after. On March 29, a young woman was found raped, her skull smashed and her throat slit. Homicide detective W. F. Perkins stated that the scene looked exactly like the one in the movie. A seventeen-year-old boy later confessed to the crime, saying that he had reenacted the entire movie. That's "monkey see, monkey do" with a vengeance.

The evidence undoubtedly supports the contention that television violence contributes to antisocial behavior. We do not have to accept this reign of violence. Sustained, well-aimed action can help clean up the public airways. Here's how you can help.

If you see a show that you find offensive, write the station's manager who is legally responsible for programming in the public interest. Ask him for the name and address of the president of every company whose advertising appeared before, during, and after the program. Write them. Let them know that you're not happy with the shows they're sponsoring. I feel that this is the best solution for this horrifying situation, because now more and more advertisers are realizing that they no longer wish to be associated with violent programs. Sponsors want to be popular; therefore, if enough people complain, they will take action. In fact, according to the Miracle White president, after Boston's Evelyn Wagler incident, he stated that they would no longer sponsor any crime shows. So this proves that advertisers will listen to you.

The bottom line is that you have a duty to take an active interest in the television service which networks provide and which, undoubtedly, affects all of us here. If results are not achieved quickly, what will become of TV? What new, demented acts of violence will be seen and be carried out on an unsuspecting victim? You could very well have been Evelyn Wagler who ran out of gas, found yourself surrounded, and facing your death. Or in the *Born Innocent* tragedy, one of those innocent girls could have been your daughter, sexually raped and mentally scarred for life. All due to television violence. Can you just sit by and let this happen? If action is taken now against showing violence on television, you may be able to save the life of an innocent victim. So write the local stations, write the advertisers, and write the interest groups. Your voice will be heard. With its burning, stabbings, and shootings, television pumps a steady stream of pollution into our homes daily causing immeasurable damage.

The evidence is clear, a child's mind can become polluted and corrupted just as easily as life can become contaminated by the pollutants in the environment. As William Shakespeare once said, "We but teach bloody instruction which, being taught, returns to plague the revengeful." Let's do something to stop the old adage "monkey see, monkey do" from being acted out with terrible consequences.

CONTEMPORARY PUBLIC SPEECHES

The following speeches were given by people in various professions to a variety of audiences.

LIFE'S FORCED DECISIONS
(Duet. 30:15-20; James 4:13-17)
C. Mac Hamon, Pastor
St. Marks United Methodist Church
Bloomington, Indiana

Religious confusion and uncertainty is nothing new. Moses was speaking to the people of Israel at Moab concerning a convenant with God. It seems that they had not been serving God with joy by reason of their abundant possessions. Moses urged them to choose good or evil, life or death, God or not God, but choose! Again, under the leadership of Joshua the people were confused as to which god they would serve. Their lives indicated service to another. Joshua's words to them at Shechem, "Choose today whom you will serve."

The rapid discovery of science, the abundant possessions, the proliferation of religions, and the growing number of people who claim a special revelation has only served to accentuate our modem bewilderment. Multitudes of people do not know what they think. The issues are varied and ever more significant and the winds of doctrine are gusty and variable. In this congregation there must be many of us who even when faced with basic matters of religious faith—God, Christ, the Bible, prayer or immortality—ask ourselves in our own private thinking what our opinion is. To approach this from another perspective, let us raise another question. James, in a different setting asked, "What is your life?" Not what is your opinion, whom do you choose in this religious matter or that, but what is your life?

There is a clear contrast which confronts us in the raising of these two questions, what is our opinion on this or that and what is our life? We can postpone answering the question of opinion or making the choice about whom we shall serve. We may play with the idea a bit, try this answer or that, conclude that it is extremely difficult to answer, and lay it aside for the moment. That is a familiar experience, and the result is agnosticism—not dogmatic atheism but reverent agnosticism. We find that every argument has a counter argument. So if you ask someone what they think about God, the soul, and immortality, they say they do not know. While we can avoid answering the question "whom we shall serve or what is our opinion?" For the fact is that while we can avoid making up our minds, we cannot avoid making our lives.

We can hold our opinions in suspense, but we cannot hold our living in suspense.

Some of you undoubtedly wrestled with the question of whether or not you should go to college or go directly from high school into other work. That is a debatable question. If one stays out of college, choosing to do other work, one might have more money for college later and thus be able to go less into debt. Or postponing college might enable one to discover a vocation which is more suitable. On the other hand, one might go directly to college, earn the degree sooner, and enter the job market at a higher level. You may have been unable to make up your mind, but you have made up your life. You discovered that life will not stop for any inconclusive debate, and soon or late, at the fork of the road, willy-nilly, you went one way or the other, either to college or not to college. If opinion does not force decision, life will.

Consider the debate over abortion. On the one hand one confronts the reality of abortions performed without proper counsel, as a convenient way of avoiding a difficult relationship, or a means parents use to maintain social acceptability. On the other, abortion can be life saving, physically and emotionally for a woman who cannot cope; it can help the victim of rape and incest; legalized conditions can be monitored and butchers put out of business; and it can prevent unwanted children whose parents would not give them up for adoption but use them as a source of economic aid. One way or the other, even avoiding opinions, our life will force us to decide. If we choose a simplistic, easy way out, we have closed possibilities for others and perhaps for ourselves.

Our proposition is that religion is a forced decision. Intimate, vital, personal faith, the total reaction of a personality to the whole meaning of life—that is a forced issue. Whether or not this universe is aimless or whether there is a purpose; whether Christ is a revelation of something deep at the heart of reality or a psychological spark; and whether the end of it all is a coffin and an ash heap or an open sepulcher and a hope—we have to live one way or the other. "What a person believes," said George Bernard Shaw, "may be ascertained, not from their greed, but from the assumptions on which they habitually act." Watch your life. Watch any other person's life. They may never have thought they had achieved a definite opinion. But they could not help making up their life. That was a forced issue.

What is your life with reference to faith in God? In one sense God is not a matter of faith at all, but a matter of fact. We here deal with God as a creative power. God is the power to whom many of us attribute this amazing universe. We are struck on the one hand by its order. The sun rises and sets, the stars are out at night, the clouds bring the rain, and the flowers bloom. We are also struck by the cosmic drains through which travel entire stars in to a nothingness we know not. It is difficult to react to all of this as merely accidental. Some react to the declaration of faith that God created it all as magic. Yet, of all the systems of magic ever offered to the credulity of humankind, there never was a system of magic so incredible as the proposition that a number of physical particles fortuitously moving in an empty void could arrange themselves into planets, sunsets, mothers, fathers, children, music, art, science, poetry, Christ.

Do you say this morning that you have no opinion, that you are an agnostic, that you are neutral? Well, the decision between God and no-God, between an aimless and purposeful universe, is not forced by your opinion, but your life. And what is your life? It is being made up one way or the other.

Again, what is your life with reference to faith in humankind? Are we machines, determined by genes and patterns beyond our control, with some interesting mental and spiritual by-products? That idea presents serious difficulties for me. We human beings are not only driven from behind, but are lured by ideals ahead of us, enticed by chosen goals and purposes. And we human beings repent—sometimes with heartbreaking remorse—for wrongs done, and penitently seek pardon and make restitution. No machine ever did that. And we human beings look to another beyond ourselves, however, we may describe the values we reverence; with selfless dedication. Picture a machine doing that! If I should ask you what your opinion is, you might say you have no opinion, but we are asking a deeper question today: What is your life? For, soon or late, assumptions do appear in your life with reference to human value and destiny, on which we habitually act. What is our life?

Once more, this same truth holds about faith in the future, about hope and hopelessness. It may be that death ends all, that this generation is a bonfire to warm the hand of the next generation and so on, and that the end of this whole human conflagration on the planet will burn itself out and end in an ash heap. That might be. Or it might be that the Creative Power at the heart of all things being spiritual cannot permit it to end in an ash heap; that every Calvary will have its Easter day and every winter its spring, that this corruptible must put on in corruption and this mortal put on immortality, and what eye has not seen nor ear heard is laid up as a consummation for the spiritual life and that after this flesh has thus been destroyed we shall see God. That might be true. We cannot work the argument out to absolute finality. And so, because it is so difficult to get an assured answer, people think that they will reserve their opinions and not make up their minds. But what is your life? What does it say? For, my friends, hope and hopelessness are not simply theories. They are ways of living.

For example some historians look at life in the world the way it is and suggest that we are doomed to repeat our mistakes. We are nearing the end of a millennium and a century and last time we did this the Crusades spread death and destruction. This is living without hope. Another points to what this millennium has afforded us. Rediscovery of Aristotelian works, the Renaissance, closer communication, antibiotics, dreaded diseases eradicated, the Dead Sea Scrolls. These live with lives pointing to the next millennium with hope and Godly expectation.

What is your life? It is being made up one way or the other. Neutrality is a figment of the imagination on any basic issue of life. To live as though this were a Godless, purposeless universe, as though human life were a combat between jackals and jackasses, a combat whose end is to be a coffin and an ash heap, that is hell. But to live as though God were the kind of being whom Christ revealed ultimately, as though humankind, God's child had boundless possibilities worth working for, and as though in the end,

> "All we have willed or hoped or dreamed of Good shall exist, Not its
> semblance, but itself,"

that is the kingdom of heaven in our midst. What shall we choose? Whom shall we serve? What does our life say we have already decided?

LEADERS, VALUES AND SOCIETAL CHANGE:
PHI BETA KAPPA INITIATION ADDRESS,
GAMMA OF INDIANA CHAPTER

James R. Wood
Professor of Sociology and Acting Dean
College of Arts and Sciences
Indiana University

When I was inducted into Phi Beta Kappa at Vanderbilt University in 1954 the speaker said, "This achievement will be mentioned every time you are introduced—make certain that this will not be your only achievement." In context, he was thinking of vocational achievement. I will address my remarks primarily toward your roles as citizens and participants in the voluntary sector of society, but for many of you they may also be relevant to your vocational choices.

Exploring the interrelationship of leaders, values and societal change, I will begin with a bumper sticker and end by quoting the first person to win two Nobel prizes. In between I will discuss what I have learned about leaders as I researched churches and other voluntary associations, briefly apply that knowledge to the roles of national leaders, and challenge a prominent social scientist's position on science and values.

I still see occasionally a bumper sticker from the 1960s: "Question Authority!" Those words evoke ambiguous feelings in me. The societal changes that have seemed necessary to me as a citizen and lately seem imperative if civilization is to survive, have always required the challenge of some authority whether corporate executive, bishop, or president. But as a scientist much of my work has sought to understand how organizational leaders may legitimately withstand challenges to their authority and lead us in directions we are reluctant to go. My feelings are mixed at the slogan "question authority" but they are not mixed when, as often happened in the 1960s, a four-letter verb is substituted for "question" in that slogan. Leadership is an indispensable element of a viable society.

What is the crucial function of leadership? Under what circumstances is it legitimate for leaders to override majority will? Do voluntary association leaders play a unique role in effecting societal change?

The coordination of efforts toward common purposes requires some authority that stands over against individual wills. Authority restrains the self-interested pursuits of individuals and social groups, thereby allowing the pursuit of the larger society's goals.

Sometimes for the good of society we must give up something we truly value. On the other hand, at times we act in ways that at other times we ourselves will acknowledge betray our own highest values. A dramatic example is acted out repeatedly in movie and TV westerns. A crime is committed, some evidence or rumor points at a particular individual and the community is swept up in emotion carrying the individual, rope around his neck, to the nearest tree. Just in time the authorities step in to preserve values of law, order, and justice that most members of the community, on sober second thought truly cherish. The authorities have intervened against the momentary will of the majority in order to uphold the long-range will of the majority. In a less dramatic way leaders can save us from our greed, racism, chauvinism, insensitivity to poverty, and other sources of that behavior which we ourselves recognize as less than our best.

Leaders devise and manage social arrangements that allow us to implement our highest values. Gunnar Myrdal (1944) observes that organizations often channel people toward their universalistic values rather than toward their particularistic ones. When ordinary people act through their orderly collective bodies they act more as Americans, as Christians, and as humanitarians than if they were acting independently. Referring specifically to racial prejudice, Myrdal argues that people act differently in organizations than when following their personal prejudices because they have placed their highest ideals in their organizations.

From its outset the United States has been a society of organizations. Observing the unique importance of organizations in American life, the Frenchman Alexis de Tocqueville wrote the following description in 1833:

> Americans of all ages, all stations in life, and all types of disposition are forever forming associations. There are not only commercial and industrial associations in which all take part, but others of a thousand different types—religious, moral, serious, futile, very general and very limited, immensely large and very minute.

Tocqueville was amazed at the way Americans banded together for every purpose. As important as this union for common purposes is, a byproduct of such association may be even more important. Associations in which people of differing backgrounds come together for a common purpose often create what

James Coleman called cross-cutting social attachments—that is, they create situations in which persons in one social group—let us say laborers or Catholics or whites or the rich—associate with those in other social groups—let us say managers or Protestants or blacks or the poor. Coleman discusses the effect on community controversy of social attachments which create cross pressures on individuals and hence break the cycle of polarization that so often runs out of control in controversies. One of the worst aspects of this polarization is the fact that rational discussion is precluded. Responses are made in extreme forms that leave no room for compromise. According to Coleman:

> Individuals have many . . . attachments to groups and individuals. If these attachments are spread throughout the community as a whole, then the individual has . . . internalized many different elements in the community. . . . When a controversy arises in a community . . . the individual who has attachments to many elements in the community is very often . . . pulled in opposing directions as the controversy broadens. One group of people to whom he [or she] feels close is on one side; others . . . equally close are on the other. Unable to commit himself or herself] fully to one side or the other, [the individual] either withdraws from the dispute, or, taking sides, is still beset by doubts and fears, unable to go 'all out' against the enemy. (1957:22)

Coleman stresses the way in which cross-pressured individuals absorb some of the conflict rather than letting it all come out at the community level. Equally important is the fact that cross-pressured persons can be more objective, more able to see all sides of an issue. Put another way, cross-cutting social attachments democratize both individuals and societies.

But a number of social changes have decreased the opportunity to form cross-cutting social ties—especially ties across economic lines. Among the principal changes are the urbanization and then the suburbanization of America. Where before rich and poor, employed and unemployed lived in close proximity, now we tend to be sorted out into homogeneous neighborhoods. And lately even the public opportunities for experiencing cross pressures have diminished.

According to Parker Palmer, "In public we remember that the world consists of more than self and family and friends. We belong to a human community; we are supported by it and must support it; in this world 'no man (or woman) is an island'" (1981:35). He sees the giant regional shopping mall as symbolic of the shrinking sphere of public life. Palmer's commentary on shopping malls also brings to mind private academies, exclusive clubs, and some forms of residential zoning.

> The typical shopping mall tends to repress rather than evoke public experience. The strangers one encounters on the city streets are, for the most part, fellow citizens of the local community, and the public life is enhanced by this sense of geographic relatedness. But the mall . . . is not identified with any local community, but strives to create a fantasy environment conducive only to shopping, not to the cultivation of public relatedness . . . the mall offers a center for commercial, not civic, interaction, devoid of any public purpose . . . on the public streets, the interaction of strangers always has the potential of flowering into more explicit forms of public life—such as leafletting, soliciting signatures for petitions, soap-box oratory, rallies, marches, and the like. But the mall . . . unlike the streets, is private property and thus not available for public activities—especially if those activities have political overtones. In many places people who have tried to demonstrate in malls have simply been evicted. . . .

Contrast Palmer's picture of the mall with that in an inner-city church I studied which in one year allowed 60 community organizations to use the church building for a total of almost 3000 hours—more than six times the number of hours that the building was in use for church activities (Wood, 1981). A variety of groups, ranging from musical groups to those for transcendental mediation, took advantage of the policy. Social action groups included two racial justice groups, an Appalachian seminar, a peace organization, an urban affairs group, and a welfare task force. The presence of these organizations in the church building not only make it easier for church members to participate in them, it potentially raised all church members' awareness of such organizations and their objectives. As the following statement shows, this church viewed the sharing of its building with community organizations as a major part of its ministry.

> In opening our Church doors and sharing our physical property with "non-members" and "non-church organizations" we seek to symbolize the opening of our lives as Christians to all persons and groups regardless of their needs, backgrounds, creedal positions or economic status. We offer not our facilities only but our friendship and our corporate

resources in the hope of aiding them in finding meaning and fulfillment in their own relationships and responsibilities as individual citizens, as members of their organizations, and of the larger society of mankind.

In our present society such organizations are necessary to ensure that cross-cutting attachments occur. Yet such organizations do not occur by accident but by design and often because of courageous leadership. I do not know the details of the transformation of this church but I suspect that it was similar to that of another church I studied, a church in a racially changing neighborhood. Most members wanted their church to remain all white. Calling to mind the central values of the church—thus illustrating what I call value based leadership—the minister spoke these words to his official board:

> Will we welcome people of other racial groups? This question cannot be answered today, but I do want to indicate additional questions raised by this one: (1) What does the New Testament say about Christian faith expressed in race relationships? (2) How would Jesus answer the matter of racial attitudes and race relationships? (3) Is the church in the first place 'Christ's church,' or, do we consider it as 'our church' primarily? As your pastor, I present these questions to which I hope you will give serious thought, study, and prayer.

That church would not yet decide to become racially inclusive, but this act of value-based leadership set it on course toward that decision.

I will spell out in more detail the process of value-based leadership. I find Milton Rokeach's (1973) notion of a hierarchy of values helpful. Each of us holds many values arranged loosely and more or less flexibly in a hierarchy. These values are anchored in social experience and the arrangement of the hierarchy at any given moment is largely determined by the salience of particular networks of social interaction. For most of us most of the time our more selfish values are near the top of our value hierarchies. When I polled a large sample of mainline church members about their wishes for church action on racial and poverty issues, the majority of them responded on the basis of what they were hearing in their family, neighborhood, business associations, and country club. Remarkably their own local churches were often quite involved in activities these members told me they opposed. In setting social action policy, church leaders were able to raise in their members' value hierarchies the more universalistic values they held just as genuinely as the selfish ones. Members faced up to their own inconsistencies of behavior and were willing to accept as right some actions that they disliked. Just as every day we perform some socially useful obligations that we fully recognize as right yet would prefer not to perform, church members have accepted and even supported policies that they personally disliked and would never have framed by themselves.

Churches and synagogues are important contexts for such leadership, but they are by no means the only ones. A dramatic event illustrates that voluntary organizations can draw on the Declaration of Independence, the federal Constitution, and other public documents—to enunciate values that can serve as bases of drawing members from a personal to a more democratic view of public policy.

In 1978 the American Civil Liberties Union defended a Nazi organization's right to hold a rally in Skokie, Illinois. The case was intensely emotional because of the presence in Skokie of a large number of concentration camp survivors. Thousands of ACLU members resigned, and income dropped so severely that a layoff of office staff became necessary. (A situation quite parallel to that of the mainline churches during their fight for the 1964 civil rights act.) During this crisis David Goldberger, the ACLU lawyer who argued the Skokie case, authored a widely circulated appeal for support. The appeal was cast in terms of the central values of the ACLU and mentioned "freedom of speech," "the First Amendment," "the Bill of Rights," "civil liberties," and "human rights." The heart of the appeal was a distinction between personal attitudes toward a Nazi rally and belief in the fundamental democratic values championed by the ACLU: "The Nazis asked us to defend their right to hold the rally, and to challenge one of the laws prohibiting it. Though I detested their beliefs, I went into court to defend the First Amendment."

The rapidity with which the organization regained lost support suggests that many members on sober second thought were convinced by this argument. The result of this courageous leadership is that ACLU continues to hold within it a wide variety of persons who place fundamental human values above their personal feelings.

Local chapters of such organizations provide opportunities for persons to discuss their differences face to face in a context of broader personal relationships. Rokeach argues that value change is intimately tied to the maintenance and enhancement of one's total conception of oneself. Carl Rogers (1969) believes that persons given affirmation and acceptance of self worth can understand that seeking self security they often accepted uncritically the views and the expectations of others. This recognition helps free them to choose values more intentionally. Rokeach's and Rogers' insights imply that in the context of an accepting community individuals can become free of their more particularistic social constraints and affirm values that are less closely tied to their social and economic position.

Peter Berger's concept of plausibility structure helps us understand sociologically what takes place when people change selfish values for more democratic values through participation in organizations that allow them to form attachments with persons from different backgrounds. People continue to find their attitudes and behaviors plausible so long as the people they talk with find them plausible. Berger speaks of the conversational fabric that underlies social behavior. If our ideas go unchallenged in conversation they continue to seem plausible. If they are challenged we may not change them but we will examine them more carefully and we will better understand the complexity of issues and become more tolerant of opposing points of view. For example, polls show that most Americans believe that poverty is due largely to the lack of effort on the part of the poor. If you talk only with people who hold that belief, you may never learn that more than half of the poor are too young or too old to work. You may never learn that about half of the poor families in the United States are headed by a worker, nor that in 20 percent of the poor families that the head works full time but still does not earn enough money to bring the family even above the official poverty level. Clearly poverty is more related to the availability of jobs and job training than to the efforts of the poor. But many Americans are enmeshed in a conversational fabric that prevents their comprehending basic facts necessary for decisions affecting not only the quality of life but the very survival of our unique form of democratic society. If we do not regularly have serious conversations with persons with a different perspective we are missing some of the richness of life. But if most Americans are not regularly having such conversations, then our democracy is in trouble. Leaders of voluntary associations play a vital role in weaving those conversational fabrics that make democracy possible.

Knowledge gained from research in organizational leadership has implications for the roles of national leaders. When we turn from the local to the national scene, we once more have the tension between questioning authority and needing authority. Support for questioning the highest national authority can be found in the Declaration of Independence which sets forth the right of the governed to overthrow authority. Note, however, that the same declaration sets up a new authority. There must be authority; it must be questioned by the people. It must rest on the consent of the governed. On what basis are the people to judge authority? Authority is to be judged by certain values—foremost the equal worth of each human being and each individual's right to life, liberty and the pursuit of happiness. What if the will of the people is manipulated to serve a particular group's vested interest in ideology, money, or power? This question is especially important in a day of computer generated direct mailing and mass media campaigns.

Voluntary associations in which individuals are subject to cross pressures provide a bulwark against such manipulation. Amitai Etzioni (1968) argues for an active society—a society engaged in realizing values responsible to basic human needs. Contrasted with the mass society in which people are manipulated from the top, the active society creates ways for the highest values of its membership to be expressed. Etzioni pays special attention to the process of consensus-formation—the process by which perspectives of society's members are conveyed upward to the national leadership. In contrast to the mass society in which a strong leader may have direct sway over individual citizens, a healthy society is one in which the relationship between citizens and national leaders is mediated by a large network of groups and organizations. It is in these groups and organizations that the multiple perspectives are reduced toward consensus. And the effect of any direct appeal by national leaders to individual citizens is determined largely by the multiple membership of the citizens in groups and organizations. This mediation protects against mass emotional manipulation. In this view the national leader would serve partly as facilitator and moderator of this vast consensus-formation process but would also be charged with instituting those societal changes that best reflect the informed, value-based societal consensus.

Two restraints on national leadership are implied in this description of the active society. First, national policy starts with the citizens who are encouraged to express their values at a level where they can engage in face-to face debate with those who may have differing views. These debates tend to reduce differences and move toward consensus or at least a narrowed set of alternatives as they are conveyed to national leaders. Second, though it is the duty of national leaders to form policy based on the consensus or narrowed alternatives—the same network of groups and interpersonal relationships that shaped the consensus on the way up will influence the acceptance of leaders' policies as they seek grass roots support.

The study of how religious organizations and other voluntary associations fit into the consensus formation process is crucial to our understanding of national politics and policy.

One promising research project would be to trace the formation and execution of President Johnson's Vietnam policy and President Reagan's Central American policy in the light of Etzioni's model of an active society. In the first case, had Johnson been more attuned to the people would the anti-war movement have been unnecessary? What does the role of voluntary associations (including churches) in the anti-war debate imply about their ability to contribute to an active society? Can we identify the factors that kept the churches from living up to the potential I have implied earlier?

Such a study of Vietnam policy would provide a good background for the study of current U.S. policies in Central America. Two *Washington Post* writers (Cannon and Williams, 1983) last year reported on the Reagan administration's "public-diplomacy" campaign "designed to circumvent the media and church leaders by mobilizing grass-roots organizations and their internal communications systems." The campaign attempts to "line up conservative, business, labor, ethnic and veterans' groups behind Reagan's Central American policy." Officials directing the campaign listed "34 specific undertakings on Central America originated or encouraged by the administration, including a supportive editorial in the *American Legion Magazine,* mobilization of chambers of commerce in Latin America, advertisements in major newspapers placed by the Conservative Caucus and a conference on 'Democracy for Nicaragua' sponsored by the Institute of Religion and Democracy." "Representatives of 150 organizations have participated in weekly 'outreach' meetings in the Executive Office Building in which prominent administration officials, including the president, have been featured speakers."

The article implies not only that the Reagan administration is pushing a point of view rather than trying to determine the state of consensus among the American people, but also that the organizations invited to the Reagan "outreach" meetings do not represent the cross section of the American people represented by the churches and other organizations the administration is publicly combatting. As my reference to President Johnson should make clear, the point is not that Republican presidents need to be watched more carefully than Democratic ones. My point is that presidents are mandated to implement the values of the constitution and the Declaration of Independence while allowing for societal change in an orderly fashion. And that they are most likely to approach that goal when they listen to the leaders of those organizations in which cross-cutting attachments create a context where issues can be debated on their merits rather than given automatic ideological response.

To summarize my argument: Some values are more conducive to the survival of what is noblest in human civilization. Those values are more likely to win where social arrangements cause us to rise above our selfishness. The best social arrangements for this purpose may be face to face organizations where we can associate with persons of various backgrounds and perspectives, where there is an environment in which various points of view are fairly contested, where there are leaders mandated to implement public values, and where we are secure enough to re-order our values.

The society that has numerous organizations in which different views are weighed and in which consensus formation percolates upward is the healthiest society. It is imperative that public policy be formed in an arena that allows concrete discussion going beyond ideologies, and that it tends to implement the more universalistic values in our value repertoires.

This argument has important implications for any job you might choose, but I hope that many of you will go into the social sciences and humanities— convinced that there is no more important task than to develop the theoretical and practical knowledge necessary for devising the social arrangements that allow us to implement our highest values.

But should not science or any form of scholarship be value free? Now that you have heard me speak, my answer will not surprise you. Not only is it impossible to be value free, in a world of powerful, well-funded advocates of selfish values, it is dangerous.

I do not agree with Jeffrey Hadden's statement in his 1979 presidential address to the Association for the Sociology of Religion.

> In our role as social scientists, let us not forget that it is not our business
> to care who wins, but to understand how the game is played.

Certainly the understanding of social arrangements is the vital contribution social scientists can make to appropriate societal change. But do scientists as scientists not care whether those values and social arrangements that foster science win or lose? Do scientists with their devotion to objectivity not prefer that universalistic values win? Do scientists with their devotion to empiricism not care about the survival of the empirical world? We become whole people when our roles as scholars and as citizens join in the search for those social arrangements that can pull us toward our best values yet themselves be subject to judgment by those values; the search for an authority that at the same time it bids us follow, develops our capacities to question authority: Such arrangements are a necessary precondition for a world at peace. As scholars and as citizens we must direct our efforts toward their creation.

When a discouraged Pierre Curie chided his wife for persisting at the seemingly impossible task of reducing tons of pitchblend into a test tube of the newly discovered element radium, Marie Curie answered, "If it takes a hundred years twill be a pity, I will do what I can in my life time."

I hope all of you will have that spirit as you face the future. But, precisely because of developments begun with the Curie's discovery of radioactivity, we are under a new imperative. We are running out of time. If we cannot devise social arrangements that implement the values of peace and justice, humanity will not survive another hundred years.

HALLMARKS OF EXCELLENCE:
GUIDES FOR CHOOSING A COMPANY TO GROW WITH
William A. Andres
Chairman of the Board, Dayton Hudson Corporation
Delivered to the Harvard Business School of Marketing Club
January 26, 1984

When I approached the Marketing Club's invitation to speak, I asked myself, "What are the most pressing questions facing the students at the Harvard Business School?—or at any other business school, for that matter?"

The answers were not long in coming. What job do I want? What career do I want? What company or firm should I choose? In other words, where's my best future? Where's my best chance for success and fulfillment?

Quite frankly, these are ongoing questions. I found myself asking these very same questions at various stages throughout my own career—both at "upbeat" times, when new opportunities came my way, and at "down" times as well, when I re-examined where I was and where I wanted to be.

What may interest you is that my thinking on the answers to some of these questions has changed over time as I gained more perspective. "Lifestyle" is a good example of a factor I gave too much weight when I was getting started in my own career. It's tempting to think that the "lifestyle" you grew up with, or the one you now have is what you want forever. What I found is that other factors are simply more important. So give yourself credit for being able to adjust to new and different "lifestyles." You may just find them more interesting and stimulating than you think.

In the end, I "lucked out." But it took a mid-course correction or two, so perhaps you can benefit from my experience. I recognize, of course, that no one company—and no one industry—is right for everyone. Still, the question remains: Are there ways to identify the best companies—the ones with the best opportunities for personal growth and advancement? To pose the question another way: Are there organization criteria that bright, able young men and women such as yourselves should look for in deciding what careers to choose, and what companies to work for?

In my personal opinion, the answer to that question is, yes, there are criteria to look for. There are clues and signals you can pick up that will serve your own career interests in the long run. With "20-20 hindsight," I can see some of those criteria much more clearly today, and I would like to share some of my observations with you now.

With due credit to Tom Peters and Bob Waterman, and to their best seller, *In Search of Excellence,* I have decided to frame my observations within a similar context. I call them "Hallmarks of Excellence." You might prefer to call them "Guides for Choosing a Company to Grow With."

Before I begin, however, I must acknowledge, up front, that many of these "hallmarks" borrow heavily from our experiences within the retail industry. My own career in retailing has been both satisfying and rewarding, and it would be unusual, to say the least, if I did not recommend that industry to you.

However, despite that bias, these "hallmarks" do reflect a consuming interest in the broader world of business, of which retailing is only a part. While Dayton Hudson doesn't measure up as well as we'd like on every score, these "hallmarks" represent the standard we would like to live up to. So, with that, let's begin.

From my perspective, the first "hallmark" that you should look for in deciding what job offer to accept is this: A demonstrated ability to manage change. In this rapidly changing world of ours, only the companies that can manage change will offer you the kind of growth opportunities I believe you're looking for.

There is ample evidence that the rate of change is accelerating. Demographic changes are profoundly affecting our society. Technology is advancing faster than ever before in our history. Satellite communications have made this literally one world instead of several. Political trends now sweep the globe, instead of the nation. Foreign competition is challenging both our markets and our management concepts.

In retailing, for example, we find that fashion trends that once took months to run their course now come and go in a matter of weeks. With change such a predictable part of our world, and growing in importance all the time, what does that mean for us here in this room?

What it means is this: A major challenge for all business, and for all businessmen and women, is to manage change—to anticipate change, to analyze, to understand, to adapt to change, and to thrive on the momentum of change. Ultimately, the company with a track record of capitalizing on change is the one that I believe will grow and prosper over the long haul, and will thus offer you the best opportunities for personal growth and advancement, over time.

If I were in your shoes—out interviewing, ready to enter or re-enter the job market—I'd take a close look at the company's track record on managing change. Did they change their business, strategically, "in sync" with the times, ahead of the trend? Or were they dragged, kicking and screaming, as it were, into each new era?

For retailers, that overall question might be posed in several ways: Did they see the population shift to the suburbs, back in the 50s, only after the competition had the choice locations? Did they see the discount trend, back in the 60s, only after there were Kmart stores on every corner? Did they see the customer's growing value-orientation, back in the early 70s? Do they understand that it's here to stay, in the 80s, and for the foreseeable future?

To put it yet another way: Is every executive in the company responsible for keeping up with the trends in his or her area of expertise? Is the entire management team trend-conscious, and change-oriented? Do they practice trend management throughout the organization? Do they allocate their limited resources on the basis of what is becoming more important and what is becoming less important?

These are only a few of the questions you might ask yourself about the firm you're considering. They are, in my judgment, important questions, because only if the answers are in the affirmative will that company offer you a truly excellent opportunity.

The second "hallmark" of excellence is what I call a strategic planning bias. How can strategic planning be a mark of excellence? Good question. After all, virtually all companies do strategic planning, or give "lip service" to it.

But, ask yourself, what is the evidence that strategic planning is given real importance at the company you're considering? How much time does management give to strategic planning? Is it a once-a-year exercise run by a handful of corporate strategic planners? Is it a numbers game where gross margins and projected profits are added up at each stage of the process? Is strategic planning a strictly quantitative process with little room for innovation and creativity? Or is it a more qualitative process—one that pervades the organization? Does the end result represent an equal partnership between the financial side of the business and the creative side? (I'm sure we can all think of examples where one side has overwhelmed the other, with disastrous results.)

The "bottom line" question to ask is this: Is strategic thinking thoroughly integrated into the day-to-day operation of this business? The strategic orientation of the firm you're considering is critical because, as we have learned, with the right strategy, even poor management can be successful; but with the wrong strategy, even the best management can fail. That's why I urge you, when you're interviewing for that job, to look for evidence of strategic planning bias.

The third "hallmark" is one that should be familiar to anyone who has read *In Search of Excellence*. It is keeping close to the customer—or, as I choose to call it, having a customer focus. Either way, it is a point with which I couldn't agree more.

Retailers, quite naturally, are very customer-oriented. Our job is, after all, to be the "customer's purchasing agent." Our mission in business is to know our customers, to understand them, anticipate them, woo them, win them, serve them, and, ultimately, to please them every step of the way.

But my point is: Is that not true of most other businesses? Others may talk in terms of clients, or buyers, or students, or patients, or constituents. But in the end, we're all talking about the same thing. We're all talking about customers.

There is considerable evidence that the very best businesses focus—almost single-mindedly—on serving the customer. Pleasing customers is an obsession. Service is an obsession. Quality is an obsession. Dependability is an obsession. Attention to detail is an obsession.

Look at the leading businesses of this country, and you will see businesses that are, almost without exception, thoroughly imbued with the philosophy of serving the customer. Several companies come almost immediately to mind: IBM, Frito-Lay, Johnson & Johnson, McDonald's, and Hewlett Packard, to name just a few.

My point is this: No matter what the company or the product, there is a growing awareness of the important relationship between a company's customer focus and outstanding "bottom line" performance. From my vantage point, it seems we have entered an age where the customer focus is becoming even more important for an ever increasing number of businesses and professions.

In times past, many companies were able to function quite successfully without a significant focus on customers. All that is rapidly changing. Now, because of increased competition and government de-regulation, more and more companies (AT&T and the airlines are two recent examples) are certainly discovering that serving customers is the key to their future. And that same realization is now hitting home in the health care professions, where hospitals, doctors and dentists are finding increased competition for patients.

It's a trend that affects virtually everyone. So, in considering your own future, I urge you to develop a customer focus, no matter what career you choose. Of all the habits you can acquire early in your career, a customer focus is one that will stand you in good stead. You may just find, as I did, that it is every bit as important to your success as any technical skill you can develop.

In judging any potential employer, I urge you to look for signs of whether the customer is the driving force or a necessary nuisance to be tolerated. Ask yourself these questions: Does concern for the customer permeate the organization? Does this customer focus apply to everyone? To people in finance, control and other areas of the company?

I say that because in this new, rapidly changing, highly competitive, service oriented era I believe that an organization with a customer focus will offer significantly greater growth opportunities for its people.

The fourth "hallmark" to look for in choosing a company to grow with is a spirit of employee partnership. My experience has been (and research certainly certainly bears this out) that young people today simply don't respond well to the old top-down, authoritarian management style.

Young people today (in fact, increasingly all people today) want to contribute to the decision-making process. They want to be recognized for their contributions. They want to agree, rather than obey. They want to participate. They want to be partners in the process of meeting the organization's challenges.

Not only is this consensus approach a more satisfying approach, there is ample evidence it is a much more effective approach. The Japanese have certainly demonstrated that fact, and so have many American companies, such as Hewlett-Packard and Delta Airlines, and others.

It is extremely important, then, to your own job satisfaction and to your own future, to investigate the company's track record on partnership with employees. Does the company care enough about people to invest in training and development? At all levels? Do they care enough to mentor and coach their people? Do they promote from within the organization? Do they value employee ideas? Is there a meaningful process for sharing those ideas? Does that process permit—even encourage—participation at all levels?

What is the evidence that the people who are closest to the problems are consulted and involved in solving those problems? In retailing, we believe that the people who are closest to the customer can see the problems (and the opportunities) better than top management, sitting in their Ivory Towers.

We've seen how effective an employee partnership approach is, for instance, at Mervyn's, our California-based operating company. In fact, one consultant told us, "Mervyn's employees are so gung-ho about that company, they think God put them on earth just to work for Mervyn's!"

Much the same is true here in the Boston area, at Lechmere, our hardlines specialty retailer. Employees at all levels have made important contributions to the very exciting turnaround in the fortunes of that company. Today, the enthusiasm of Lechmere's management team is downright contagious! And I think that spirit is carried through their organization.

Throughout Dayton Hudson—at Target, B. Dalton, Dayton's, Hudson's, and all our operating companies—we are equally committed to building this spirit of employee partnership. We realize we're far from perfect, but we are very aware this is the management style of the future. And for us, the future is now.

In my opinion, ladies and gentlemen, that fact holds true for you, as well. This is a very formative period for you. It is quite likely that the management style of your first company, even of your first boss, will significantly influence your own management style in the future. So, I urge you to examine that management style very closely.

Is there an open atmosphere? Can you make a mistake and live to tell about it? Is your would-be boss candid and accessible? Are people treated fairly and equitably, including women and minorities? Indeed, is there respect for each and every individual in the organization?

In my judgment, these questions are every bit as critical to your success and to your sense of personal fulfillment as your starting salary, and the job description itself. Job descriptions and compensation packages change over time. In all likelihood, the company's management style won't. Make sure it's a good one, and a good fit for you.

The fifth "hallmark" I believe you should look for is an obvious one where the pursuit of excellence is the objective. It is a challenging culture. In choosing

Harvard, obviously you have opted for a challenging educational experience. You weren't satisfied to pick up "just any" MBA. You decided to aim for the best. You made a conscious decision to study with some of the country's best minds, and to compete with some of the country's best students.

My point is this: When you select a company, choose one that also aims high—and pushes its people to aim high, as well. Choose a company that sets challenging performance standards, a company that isn't satisfied with being just "good," or even "excellent," a company that pushes itself to be all it can be.

Choose a company that challenges itself to be, in a word, premier. A premier retailer (or manufacturer, or banker or whatever), a premier employer, a premier investment, a premier citizen in the communities where it operates. Choose a company that says, up front, "We want to be the best there is." Or, as Jack Welch, the CEO of General Electric, puts it, "to be better than the best." That is, after all, the essence of excellence.

If that's the goal, what do you look for? What clues can you pick up to help you identify a challenging culture? Here are a few questions that you might ask: Does the company have a philosophy of striving to be the best? Is everyone in the organization challenged to be thoroughly professional, no matter what their job? Are the company's performance standards clearly spelled out? Are they aggressive? Does the CEO's letter in the annual report speak—in glowing platitudes—only of the company's successes? Or does it deal candidly with failures and "near-misses," as well? Is there a climate for innovation and risk-taking?

For additional clues, ask yourself: Is there diversity on the management team? Are young people represented in the ranks of top management? Or do you have to wait until your "seniority number" comes up? Is there a mix of personalities, or is the management team a succession of clones?

That's a good clue to look for, in my opinion. Because a diverse management team is an important sign that the company is results-oriented. That it is a performance company. That it has a challenging culture—the kind of culture that would challenge you in your business career, as you have been challenged in your academic career.

The sixth and final "hallmark" is one that serves as a base for all the others: It is an ethical foundation. Without an ethical foundation, I submit, there is no excellence. So it becomes, in a sense, the ultimate "hallmark" of an excellent company.

What is an ethical foundation? How do you define it? How do you look for it? What are the clues? Try these: What is the company's overall business philosophy? Is the "bottom line," as Vince Lombardi used to say about winning, not only the most important thing, but the *only* thing? Or, is profit seen in a broader perspective?

Does management understand, as Warren Phillips, the CEO of Dow Jones puts it, that, "profit is not the No. 1 goal—the No. 1 goal is serving the public."

In other words, does management see profit as the company's reward for serving society? Is "service" a shared value? Service not only to customers, but to society at large? Is that "spirit of partnership" we talked about earlier extended to the community? Is community involvement considered an essential part of the personal and professional development of the management team?

Does the company recognize that community involvement broadens the vision of a management team? That it heightens our awareness of how society is changing, and thus makes us more effective managers of change?

To sum up, ladies and gentlemen, I urge you to look for a firm that has learned, as we have learned at Dayton Hudson, that a strong ethical foundation pays off where it counts: in the health of our communities, in our strategies, in the effectiveness and satisfaction of our people—in short, on the "bottom line."

I am convinced that today's young people want more than just a job, or a career. They want the opportunity to serve people in the broadest sense of the word. If you pick a company with a strong ethical foundation, a philosophy of serving society, I am equally convinced you can do as much good in a business career as you can in government, education, the ministry, law or medicine! But you have to pick right, in my judgment.

These, then, are my candidates for the "hallmarks" of an excellent company—your "Guides for Choosing a Company to Grow With":

- A demonstrated ability to manage change.
- A strategic planning bias.
- A customer focus.
- A spirit of employee partnership.
- A challenging culture.
- And an ethical foundation.

At this point I have a confession to make: This list of hallmarks reflects more than just my personal judgment. It represents more than one man's opinion, and one person's experiences. The list I have just outlined represents the collective wisdom of my management colleagues at Dayton Hudson, who participated with me in fine-tuning the list.

All in all, we found it a useful exercise to stake out and define for ourselves what we believe to be the Hallmarks of Excellence. I commend the process to you.

Take this list as a starting point. Or, if your prefer, make your own. Measure any company you are considering against the criteria you consider important. More importantly, measure yourself against them, as we did.

Measure yourself against carefully defined high standards, and don't be discouraged when you don't "measure up" 100%. In other words, I urge you to dedicate yourself—now and throughout your career—to the pursuit of excellence. That kind of dedication pays off

If I were to offer any parting "words of wisdom," it would be these: Choose a career in a field of business that you truly like. Join a company and a management team you can be proud of and enthusiastic about.

If you are truly committed, you will go beyond the 8-hour day, or the 40-hour week. You'll read the trade journals. You'll keep up with the trends in your field. You'll dedicate yourself fully to the pursuit of excellence, no matter what your job. That kind of dedication I believe, is as important to your success as the technical and conceptual training you've received here at Harvard.

You have an exciting future ahead of you and I wish you well. Thank you very much.

EDUCATION: A CAPITAL INVESTMENT

Mary Hatwood Futrell
President, National Education Association
Delivered to the Cleveland City Club, Cleveland, Ohio
April 13, 1984

I relish the opportunity to be here with you today. I can think of no more important time for us to speak frankly to each other about a topic of vital interest to us both—public education.

I'm sure you're well aware that there has been a new surge of interest in education recently. Over the past 12 months, we've all seen a veritable torrent of national reports on education.

But there's something about all these national reports that you may not know—something that I think you'll be happy to learn. Every single one of the national panels on education that has so far reported has included among its members—or carefully consulted with—one or more prominent business leaders.

One of the first panels to report was the task force on education for economic growth established by the education commission of the states.

This panel's 41 members included 13 state governors and 13 business executives, and it produced a report that touts the many benefits of closer working relationships between school and business.

Another example: the education report published last year by the National Science Board. That report culminated a 17-month study that involved discussions with hundreds of educators, scientists, government officials, technologists, and industrialists.

The report that emerged from all those discussions mapped out a program to make our nation's science and math teaching the finest in the world by 1995.

The surge of education reports at the national level has spawned a slew of equally important state-level studies on education. Business executives are serving on these panels, too.

Business, in other words, has picked up the ball on education reform. The prestigious Committee on Economic Development, a prominent national organization of corporate CEOs, is turning its attention to education for the first time in 15 years. The committee is looking at how our schools might benefit from the expertise of the nation's business leaders.

Corporate America—just like the rest of America—is reawakening to the importance of educational excellence.

The reason is clear. America's future lies in our ability to stay on top of advanced technology, our ability to maintain a competitive edge in the international marketplace.

And to keep that edge we need, above all, a skilled and well-educated labor force.

Just how important is education to the economy?

The Brookings Institution credits education as the major engine of economic growth in the U.S. since 1930. Between 1948 and 1973, we saw an extraordinary increase in public investment in our nation's educational system. During that same period, we also saw unprecedented economic growth. Improved education, the economists tell us, accounted for two-thirds of that remarkable growth.

Studies prepared for Congress have reported that every dollar spent on education returns six dollars to our gross national product.

As a business teacher myself, that statistic doesn't surprise me. I don't think it surprises most business people either. We all know how crucial education is because we share common economic concerns.

You want to recruit employees who know how to work, who know how to get along with others, and who know how to communicate and solve problems.

Those of us who work in the schools want to prepare students to enter the job market—and to succeed.

Public schools are the key to developing skillful and productive employees. That's been true for a long time. But today I think there are even more compelling reasons why you as business leaders cannot afford to be passive when it comes to education.

Our country is in the midst of a great transition. The old industrial giants—coal, steel, autos, and the like—can no longer conduct business as usual. America stands on a brink of a new age—the information age—and no business can ignore what that means—and hope to survive.

Futurists tell us that information and data—basic knowledge—will become the raw materials for whole new industries.

In electronics, the futurists' tomorrow is today. Information is already the raw material of the electronics industry. Computers, satellites, and telephone lines are merely the means to transmit that material. Information retrieval—less than 10 years old—is already a $1.5 billion a year business.

The demand for information is growing so rapidly that the communications industry is expected to be the growth industry of this decade.

As city and state planners debate how to attract these new industries—or keep old ones vital—one fact is certain: the industries of the information age are in no way dependent on strategic location near markets or resources.

With today's communications technology, information age businesses can prosper virtually anywhere.

So what's going to convince a company to locate or expand here in Cleveland?

I'll tell you what: education.

Communities that develop quality educational systems at every level—kindergarten through higher education—will attract and retain quality information age businesses.

Communities that neglect their education infrastructure will fail. It's as simple as that.

In the information age, industry will go to those communities that can offer a pool of intelligent, resourceful employees, communities that can help retrain today's employees for tomorrow's jobs. It is these education conscious communities that will emerge as the winners in the race for economic growth and stability.

The American Society of Engineers says that in the next two decades we're going to have to retrain half the blue-collar workers now employed in our factories.

But we have to do more than retrain. We need to change the way we think about work and careers.

In tomorrow's economy, a worker prepared for one career will be a worker programmed for obsolescence. Our economy is changing too fast for anyone to succeed in a single lane. We need to start preparing people for two and three careers in a lifetime.

How can we give our students that preparation? How can we best create the quality school systems we need for tomorrow? How can we be sure that our students get the education they need to prosper in our rapidly changing society?

There can be no more fundamental questions for us to ask—and I mean all of us. It is time we brought all sectors of American society together to explore education. It is time to get serious about promoting closer relationships between the business and school communities.

We need to find some answers about education, and we need to find them together.

We need to build cooperation—and understanding—between business leaders and educators.

The effort to build that cooperation, I am happy to say, has started, and it's started in a big way right here in Ohio.

Last fall, NEA's affiliate—the Ohio Education Association—joined with the Ohio Chamber of Commerce and the Ohio Manufacturer's Association to set up a Business Education Roundtable.

This Roundtable held its first meeting last September, outside Columbus, and that meeting was a huge success.

The Roundable tackled some pretty tough questions:

- How can education help rebuild the economy?
- What can education do to respond to the productivity needs of business?
- What can we do to boost community support for the schools and counter the negative picture painted by the news media?
- How can we reduce the educational system's overhead and make the most efficient use of our tax dollars?

I personally liked many of the ideas that came out of the Roundtable's discussions.

I like the idea of having bankers and retailers help students learn to manage their personal financial affairs.

I like the idea of exposing more of our teachers to the business world.

I like the idea of programs that can encourage local firms to get more involved in school bond and village elections.

We need more projects like these, more projects that help our schools develop a real-world perspective for our students. Our classrooms can easily become too isolated. Business can help our schools open windows to the larger world.

Let me just give you some examples of the cooperation that's already taking place all over the United States.

In the school district next door to where I teach—Fairfax County, Virginia—a business-school partnership is helping teachers understand the high-tech world—so they can better identify the skills needed for a changing work force.

A hospital in St. Louis has developed a curriculum for that city's middle schools on drug abuse and other health-related subjects.

In Florida, the Suncoast Chamber of Commerce set up a partnership with the Pinellas County Public Schools to create an economics education program called "Educational Excellence: A Shared Commitment."

Several San Francisco teachers have received paid internships in the business community under the "Corporate Action in Public Schools" program.

I believe that these examples make one point abundantly clear. There is no one form school-business cooperation should take.

The only limits are your imagination—and ours. You can set up a project on whatever scale is feasible for your company. You don't have to be a huge corporation or conglomerate to help the schools. You don't have to take on some enormous and costly task.

You can help one student. You can help a dozen. The numbers don't matter. What matters is the positive difference that you and we can make for our young people.

Let me make one point clear. I believe school-business cooperation can work wonders for our schools. But I don't believe that school-business cooperation is a panacea for all of education's ills. It's not. And it's not a substitute for public support of education either.

We can't have excellence in education if local school districts repeatedly vote down local tax levies.

We can't have excellence if state governments turn their backs on what the schools need.

And we can't have excellence if the federal government ignores its obligations to education.

Education is a national resource. And that means every level of government must do its part.

Unfortunately, that hasn't been happening. Too many politicians—on local school boards, in state capitals, even in the White House—mouth the rhetoric of school reform, then don't back up the rhetoric with resources.

I've been a teacher for 20 years, and I know rhetoric won't buy smaller classes or time for more individual instruction.

Rhetoric won't put more aides in our classrooms to help with all those necessary but time-consuming tasks that steal teachers' time from teaching.

Rhetoric won't raise teachers' salaries to a level high enough to attract the brightest students into teaching or halt the flight of quality teachers to higher paying jobs in the private sector.

Today's teachers' average annual salary is $20,530—after 10 years of earning a master's degree. That's $40 less than the average construction worker earned three years ago! And that's why I say that the salaries paid to teachers today are scandalous.

But don't take my word for it. Listen to William Missimer Jr., a top executive for the Pratt & Whitney Aircraft Group of United Technologies. "Salaries for teachers are a national disgrace," Missimer tells us. "Teachers are now among the nation's lowest paid professionals," he continues. "Many jobs in industry which do not require a college education pay better."

Retired Admiral Hyman Rickover, a virulent critic of the schools, agrees that teachers are grossly underpaid. And he sees boosting salaries dramatically as a prerequisite to drawing more top talent into the profession. ". . . in this country we're operating under a capitalist system," he says, "(which means) the talent goes to where the money is. Today, the money is so relatively low in teaching that we're not getting good people."

It's a fact that the average public school teacher earns 28 percent less than professionals in jobs requiring similar educational preparation.

Our research shows that the average teacher works 46 hours a week for 37 weeks at an hourly rate of $12.04. The Bureau of Labor Statistics has data showing that accountants, auditors, buyers, computer programmers earn $15.43 per hour.

And look at the salaries paid in occupations that don't even require a college degree or years of experience:

Airline reservation agents can make $20,000 easily within two years on the job.

Legal assistants, mail carriers, telephone repairers—even pest control technicians—can all top $20,000 within three years of employment.

And for you sports fans, did you know a relief pitcher can earn a beginning teacher's salary for one year in one inning of play?

That's right. I read recently that San Diego is paying Goose Gossage what amounts to $12,500 an inning this season.

I believe we must raise teachers' salaries—and raise them substantially.

I believe starting salaries for public school teachers should be in the $20,000-25,000 range.

Clearly, we need better resources and higher salaries to draw top talent into our classrooms. But those resources won't be available to all of our public school students until we have the political will to make them available.

Political will—I've seen it here in Ohio. I saw it here last November.

I want to congratulate all of you who helped defeat State Issues two and three last fall.

The committee for Ohio—the coalition that helped voters understand what issues two and three would mean for education—received much-needed funds from the business community here in Cleveland. You should feel proud of your victory. You've shown the rest of the country that Ohioans are willing to invest in their future.

And our future, our collective future, is why it's up to all of us to support public education.

Our schools can improve—and they will improve.

Our students can excel—and they will excel.

But it's up to us, up to us to make sure that a significant proportion of our people care about public education here in Cleveland, here in Ohio, and here in our nation.

Thank you.

THE UNDERCOVER AGENT: SERVING THE ENDS OF JUSTICE

William H. Webster
Director, Federal Bureau of Investigation
Delivered before the Police Foundation, London, England
June 5, 1984

It is a great pleasure for me to be here today and to have the honor of delivering the second annual address to the Police Foundation. In the past several years I have twice been privileged to come to England as a member of our Anglo-American Exchange. On the first occasion our team, headed by our Chief Justice, studied Appellate practices. Later in 1980, we studied the criminal justice process. The English teams, headed by Lord Diplock returned our visits, and in the process we tried to learn from each other's experiences. In subtle but important ways these exchanges have brought us closer together toward our common heritage—the pursuit of justice.

Justice according to Daniel Webster, is the great interest of man on earth. Sometimes within our concept of justice there are competing values, each of undeniable worth. Those who enforce our laws are often caught between these values. If the law enforcement officer listens to one set of voices, he may hear the words "leave us alone." If in other times he listens to another set of voices, he may hear the words "do something about it." The voices of those concerned about individual liberties and personal privacy and the voices of a society collectively demanding to be kept safe and free advance and recede as with the tide; yet, both sets of voices speak of values deeply treasured by us all. The law enforcement officer, however, must chart his course as best he can by the navigational aids laid out for him—case by case, statute by statute—by lawyers, judges and legislators. It is not an easy task. The ultimate challenge for those of us involved in the administration of justice is to strike the balance true.

Today I speak to you, not from the vantage point of a judge, but as one whose agency stands at the threshold of our criminal justice system, and who knows that if we fail in our efforts or violate the law's commands in the name of protecting the law, no prosecutor and no judge can rectify our error.

As I see it, our goal today in Federal law enforcement—in the United States—is not to be content with the arrests of street criminals. But instead, with the limited resources available to us, we must reach beyond the streets and into the upper echelons of criminal enterprises that infect our Nation with espionage, terrorism, drug trafficking and public corruption. The degree of sophistication and insulation associated with modern criminal enterprise has shown the futility of depending entirely upon traditional investigative methods; in such cases we have found it necessary and fruitful, to turn to arguably, more intrusive, more sensitive, but legally sanctioned investigative techniques, including the informant court-authorized electronic surveillance, and the undercover agent.

All law enforcement is, to some extent, a matter of intrusion. No investigation can be conducted without talking to people, looking into records, making telephone calls, examining forensic evidence. Most of us willingly accept some degree of intrusion as both necessary and permissible. Few would argue that the security measures we undergo at airports should be eliminated. The procedures are intrusive, but they protect us in flight. Of course, some techniques used in law enforcement are more intrusive than others and raise important issues that must be carefully considered. One of the more controversial techniques has been the use of our own Agents acting undercover to ferret out criminal activity.

The undercover technique has been the subject of debate in both our countries. There are valid arguments on both sides of the controversy—a controversy that must ultimately be resolved within the context of our legal systems. My purpose tonight is to share some of our experiences and thinking on this subject, to give you a better understanding of why we use this technique, ways in which we use it and how we manage its proper role in law enforcement.

The use of undercover Agents in property "sting" cases has been a recognized technique in law enforcement for many years. Law enforcement officers posed as fences, and thieves hoping to sell their loot came willingly into the traps that had been set for them. Similarly, police officers posed as likely victims in parks and deserted streets while other officers waited to arrest the mugger who attempted the assault.

The FBI began adapting this technique to its major Federal programs in the mid-70's. Stolen art treasures formed the basis for a burgeoning industry on both sides of the Atlantic and the undercover Agent became an effective way of penetrating sophisticated enterprises. The individual car thief has given way to sophisticated car theft rings, utilizing thieves, computerized marketing techniques and chop shops to disassemble and dispose of auto parts with great speed. Copyrighted films and tapes were being pirated on a grand scale. Charge cards were being counterfeited and used fraudulently by rings that reached across the United States. In these and similar criminal activities the undercover Agent proved to be a useful and generally acceptable technique for identifying and taking our entire enterprises rather than settling for the bottom man on the street.

During this period the FBI began to focus its attention and resources upon some of the most invidious activity ever to inflict our society: the La Cosa Nostra traditional organized crime families; nontraditional organized groups such as the outlaw motorcycle gangs; the activities of domestic and international terrorists; drug cartels and traffickers operating on a mammoth scale; and significant white-collar crime cases involving fraud and embezzlement. Many of these activities involved corrupt public officials whose cooperation was essential to the success of the criminal enterprise.

To attack a major criminal enterprise requires staying power. We had always used informants to provide leads and occasionally function as cooperating witnesses acting under a predesigned scenario. We soon found that the cooperating witness, often with a criminal background, was not sufficiently disciplined or trustworthy to carry out the demanding responsibilities—often with large sources of money—that such an investigation required. Increasingly, we turned to our own undercover Agents to pursue the investigation once their credibility had been established by the cooperating witness.

Although we currently budget less than one percent of our field resources to undercover work, and use it only when most traditional methods have been unsuccessful, it has been extraordinarily cost effective. Since October 1,1983, investigations using the technique have produced more than 550 arrests, almost 500 convictions, over $52 million in recoveries and fines of $1.1 million.

It was not until our undercover leads took us to corrupt political activity that the full dimensions of the controversy developed. Charges of agent provocateur, entrapment, and Government misconduct became part of the criminal defense arsenal and continue to this day, although such forms of counter attack have been singularly unsuccessful in the courts, rejected in the main by both juries and judges.

One of the more publicized applications of this technique to the problem of political corruption involved our investigation of certain members of Congress in an operation codenamed ABSCAM. This case demonstrates how an undercover operation can provide a dynamic and flexible approach to investigating crime, while accommodating a reasonable sensitivity to individual rights and liberties.

ABSCAM began early in 1978 in New York State as an operation to recover stolen artwork and securities. Our Agents were working with a convicted swindler who agreed to cooperate with the Government in the hope of receiving a lenient sentence. The scenario was simple. After hearing street talk that foreign money was available to purchase stolen art, we formed a company, Abdul Enterprises Limited. We spread the word around the network of con men that wealthy foreign operators had money available for questionable transactions. Our undercover Agents posed as representatives of these operators. In this manner, we recovered about $1 million worth of stolen art.

During this period our Agents were introduced to a number of "con" men. Several months later, a group that had sold our Agents phony certificates of deposit raised the prospect of investing in casino gambling in Atlantic City, New Jersey. They told us that the mayor of Camden, New Jersey, who also was a member of the state legislature, could obtain a casino license—for a price. Later, during a meeting with our undercover operatives (whom he believed were criminals), the mayor explained that only with his help could we acquire the license and that a cash payment would be necessary to obtain his assistance. With the concurrence of Federal prosecutors, a $25,000 bribe payment was authorized. We directed our Agents to document this payment, as well as others in ABSCAM, on video and audio tape.

After receiving this initial bribe payment, the mayor introduced us to an official of the state casino control commission. Later, with this state official at his side, the mayor accepted a $100,000 bribe.

During subsequent discussions of the casino transaction, an FBI Agent, posing as the right-hand man of some Arab sheiks, remarked that they might have to flee their country and seek asylum in the United States. The mayor and his law partner began to identify congressmen who, in return for cash, would take actions to guarantee asylum for the fictitious sheiks.

In the following months, the mayor and his associates identified, and in some cases brought to us, congressmen they claimed would assist the foreigners for cash. During the course of the investigation we made $50,000 payments to five congressmen and a $25,000 payment to another. An important point is that not one member of Congress was ever suggested by one of our Agents or informants. All the names were suggested by corrupt influence peddlers, such as the mayor, who were unaware they were dealing with the FBI.

The objectives of ABSCAM were the same as those of every criminal investigation. We pursued allegations of criminality and developed evidence of criminal activity. On the basis of the evidence presented, the Department of Justice decided to prosecute those who were indicted.

The ABSCAM cases were tried before ten separate juries who returned guilty verdicts against all 20 defendants including six congressmen and one senator. Each conviction has been upheld on appeal, including 16 denials of certiorari by our Supreme Court. I believe our efforts to identify and root out public corruption has had enormous support from the American people. The videotaped spectacle of a United States Congressman stuffing his pockets with currency and asking "Does it show," or others boasting of their own corruptibility did not sit well with our citizens and the messages we received in overwhelming numbers was the same: "We're glad there is an agency in Government which will not look the other way; don't stop."

ABSCAM is but one of the problems which involves political corruption. Some have resulted in legislation reforms long overdue; others have caused local leaders to take needed action to clean their houses. It has been healthy.

As I indicated, the ABSCAM investigation, and its application of the undercover operation to political corruption, received a great deal of public attention. However, we should not lose sight of the fact that undercover operations have proven to be extremely useful in a wide variety of investigative situations. Narcotics investigations such as the ones conducted in operation BANCOSHARES, are a good example.

In that case, our undercover agents posed as brokers willing to launder illicit drug money through a fictitious corporation. Transactions of over $1 million per day were videotaped. The primary services offered by the undercover corporation were the conversion of small bills to large bills; the conversion of U.S. currency to cashier's checks; the maintenance of large quantities of U.S. currency in bank accounts of the undercover corporation; and the depositing of "clients" U.S. currency in Miami area banks to protect them from being identified as the source of funds.

When we terminated the covert stage of this investigation in August, 1981, over 60 arrest warrants were issued, and over 30 subjects were arrested. Property and cash recovered, seized, or frozen as a result of this operation included numerous airplanes and vehicles, large quantities of cocaine, a 4,600 acre ranch with an estimated value in excess of $4 million, three residences and $18 million in cash and bank accounts.

We have also used the undercover technique to conduct successful investigations of groups classified as criminal enterprises by our RICO— Racketeer Influenced and Corrupt Organizations—statute. RICO outlaws certain criminal enterprises that affect commerce. Its penalties include prison terms of up to 20 years and the forfeiture of all assets obtained by violating the statute. It has been a fruitful investigative tool against the criminal enterprise.

In our UNIRAC case we sought to determine the extent to which our maritime industry—including unions and the service, shipping and trucking companies—was influenced and controlled by organized crime members and labor racketeers. Many of these people had eluded detection by threatening potential witnesses with violence and economic ruin. Our investigation ultimately involved 20 of our 59 field offices and over a hundred Special Agents, some in undercover roles. Informants and court-authorized electronic surveillance were also used.

This investigation resulted in over 110 convictions including that of Anthony Scotto, the most prominent docking labor official on our east coast who was also a capo in the Gambino organized crime family. In three years he had accepted over $300,000 dollars to ensure labor peace and control fraudulent insurance claims. Although we have not eliminated crime on our docks, we know this case has had an impact on a pervasive scheme of corruption on the waterfronts from New York to Miami.

We also have successfully used undercover operations in terrorism investigations. Terrorists enterprises are often difficult to penetrate because they operate in small, cellular groups. In three separate undercover operations, we identified a number of people responsible for the illegal transportation of arms and weapons from the United States to the Irish Republican Army to support terrorist activities. Our efforts led to the disruption of their operation and the seizure of ammunition and military supplies. Six individuals were convicted of various firearms and explosives charges, one of which involved a conspiracy to purchase a heat-seeking missile for use in Northern Ireland.

All of these cases were, from our point of view, very successful operations. But the success of an investigative technique must never be the sole determinant for its use. The traditional role of law enforcement is to apprehend criminals and prevent crime, not manufacture it. Our mission is to uphold the law.

Nonetheless the Government does owe a duty to its citizens to effectively enforce the criminal statutes. And we have found that the simple truth of the matter is that the only practicable means of detecting and prosecuting some forms of criminal behavior is through infiltration and the appearance of partici-pation in the unlawful activities in order to collect evidence for prosecution. It is important to understand, however, that this is done subject to judicial oversight. The courts ultimately define permissible and impermissible police conduct largely by how they rule on a defendant's assertion of one of two defenses: entrapment and due process.

I recognize that our legal systems may deal with these issues in different ways. In the United States, entrapment is an affirmative defense. It requires dismissal of criminal charges if the Government induced or encouraged an individual to engage in illegal activity that he would not be disposed to commit. The defense derives from the principle that otherwise innocent people should not be convicted if they were enticed by the Government into violating the law.

The test for entrapment in the American Federal system is a subjective one. If based upon the facts the jury determines that the defendant had a preexisting willingness to violate the law, the entrapment defense will fail. The rationale for this approach is that it is not desirable for the law, in effect, to grant immunity from prosecution to a defendant who planned to commit a crime, and then committed it, simply because Government undercover Agents provided induce-ments that might have persuaded a hypothetical individual not so predisposed. It is important, as the Supreme Court has said, that "A line . . . be drawn between the trap for the unwary innocent and the trap for the unwary criminal."

Unlike the entrapment defense, which examines the defendant's state of mind, the focus of the due process defense is on the conduct of the Govern-ment. It is based on constitutional provisions prohibiting the Government from depriving individuals of life, liberty or property without due process of law. In the criminal law context, it essentially means fairness. Although our Constitution affords our Government wide latitude to enforce the laws, courts do recognize that police conduct may be so outrageous and overreaching as to render prosecution of a defendant fundamentally unfair.

In ruling on a defendant's due process claim the courts consider a variety of factors. One of these is the difficulty of detecting the crime under investigation. The courts may also inquire into whether Government Agents or informants instigated the crime or merely infiltrated an ongoing criminal enterprise; whether the Government directed or controlled the criminal activity or merely followed the defendant's directions; and whether the Government supplied the criminal enterprise with a substantial amount of essential resources and technical expertise to enable the suspects to commit the offense.

Clearly, Government infiltration may be outrageous in some but acceptable in others. It would, for example, be impermissible to instigate robberies or physical violence to gather evidence to convict members of an outlaw gang. And I think we recognize the dangers inherent in any investigation that threatens the exercise of basic human rights such as free speech and assembly.

In response to these concerns, we have taken steps to ensure that our undercover operations receive close scrutiny and constant supervision at all stages of the investigation. Undercover subjects that originate in our field offices are designed to investigate a particular crime problem or groups of individuals suspected of participating in illegal activity. Once a field office develops a concept for an undercover project, and before its submission to FBI Headquarters, the proposal is reviewed by field office managers as well as FBI lawyers and Federal prosecutors. The review includes an examination of legal and ethical considerations including an assessment of whether planned investigative tactics pose a danger of entrapment or violations of due process. Many projects are rejected during this initial review process.

If approved by the field office, the proposal is forwarded to FBI headquarters in Washington where it is further evaluated by the Criminal Undercover Operations Review Committee. I established this committee in 1978, and it includes operational program managers and lawyers from both the FBI and the Department of Justice who evaluate proposals, identify potential problems and give operational guidance. If the committee is satisfied that the proposal merits approval after considering the legal, ethical and operational aspects of the plan, it will make such a recommendation to the head of the Criminal Investigative Division, or where particularly sensitive circumstances are involved, directly to me. No operation is approved for more than six months and time extensions are granted only upon committee approval.

Once in place, undercover operations are monitored closely to ensure compliance with legal requirements and guidelines promulgated by the Attorney General. For example, ABSCAM was reviewed on a daily basis by Federal prosecutors in New York and monitored in Washington by Justice Department attorneys who made recommendations on numerous investigative steps. Prosecutors personally monitored on closed-circuit television many of the transactions as they took place. One purpose for this on-line monitoring was to guard against conduct amounting to entrapment. The attorneys could pick up a telephone and call into the meeting room. The undercover Agent would answer as if he was receiving a business call and obtain instructions necessary to ensure that all legal requirements were being followed.

Such safeguards as these help us maintain the delicate balance of competing values as we use more sensitive and intrusive techniques to combat sophisticated criminal enterprises and crimes not easily detected by normal investigative means.

The management of investigative techniques such as I have discussed today is a small but important part of the pursuit of justice. It illustrates the endless balancing process by which our methods are accommodated to emerging standards of law and decency and yet may still be utilized effectively to deal with increasingly sophisticated criminality.

In your long and our much shorter history, our great nations have developed legal systems that are at once sensitive to the rights of the individual, the needs of society and the victims of crime. This is an ongoing task and one that I dare say is too important to be left entirely to judges, lawyers, and law enforcement officers. Justice belongs to all our citizens. We must work at it, work to keep the machinery functioning, work to keep our societal standards decent and high, work to instill in our children a clearer vision of justice—a system of justice that functions both for individuals and for society because it is fair. We in law enforcement and indeed all those who serve and revere the law must strike the balance true, because in our ability to keep the scales in balance lies the future of that ordered liberty which has been our rich heritage and is now entrusted to our care.

There are no finer professional law enforcement agencies in the world than those that serve the British Commonwealth and the United States. The forensic advances in the past decade have been without parallel. Cooperation between our agencies is at an all time high. I pledge you the full cooperation of the FBI as we work together, increase our skills together, and together serve the ends of justice under law.

HISTORIC SPEECHES

The following speeches were given by political leaders and spokespersons for great causes in our country's history. These speeches may require a different approach to reading and understanding them. The speaker, the speaker's audience, and the situation in which the speech was given are all quite different from those we might encounter today. All the speeches were given in response to very real and very important events, but they are events long past, events that will certainly not be remembered by readers of this book and can be understood only by those who have studied our history.

If a student knows or can learn about the context within which the speech was given, then the same set of questions about how the speech works—the questions that appear on the first page of this appendix—apply.

Following the speeches are a few suggested readings for students who want to understand the biographical and historical context, and thus appreciate the persuasive power of the speech more fully.

GIVE ME LIBERTY

Patrick Henry
Delivered to the Virginia Convention,
March 23, 1775

Mr. President: No man thinks more highly than I do of the patriotism, as well as abilities of the very worthy gentlemen who have just addressed the House. But different men often see the same subjects in different lights; and, therefore, I hope that it will not be thought disrespectful to those gentlemen, if, entertaining as I do, opinions of a character very opposite to theirs, I shall speak forth my sentiments freely and without reserve. This is no time for ceremony. The question before the House is one of awful moment to this country. For my own part I consider it as nothing less than a question of freedom or slavery; and in proportion to the magnitude of the subject ought to be the freedom of the debate. It is only in this way we can hope to arrive at truth, and fulfill the great responsibility which we hold to God and our country. Should I keep back my opinions at such a time, through fear of giving offense, I should consider myself as guilty of treason toward my country, and of an act of disloyalty toward the majesty of heaven, which I revere above all earthly kings.

Mr. President, it is natural to man to indulge in the illusions of hope. We are apt to shut our eyes against a painful truth, and listen to the song of that siren, till she transforms us into beasts. Is this the part of wise men, engaged in a great and arduous struggle for liberty? Are we disposed to be of the number of those who, having eyes, see not, and having ears, hear not, the things which so nearly concern their temporal salvation? For my part, whatever anguish of spirit it may cost, I am willing to know the whole truth; to know the worst and to provide for it.

I have but one lamp by which my feet are guided; and that is the lamp of experience. I know of no way of judging of the future but by the past. And judging by the past, I wish to know what there has been in the conduct of the British ministry for the last ten years to justify those hopes with which gentlemen have been pleased to solace themselves and the House? It is the insidious smile with which our petition has been lately received? Trust it not, sire; it will prove a snare to your feet. Suffer not yourselves to be betrayed with a kiss. Ask yourselves how this gracious reception of our petition comports with these warlike preparations which cover our waters and darken our land. Are fleets and armies necessary to a work of love and reconciliation? Have we shown ourselves too unwilling to be reconciled, that force must be called in to win back our love? Let us not deceive ourselves, sir. These are the implements of war and subjugation; the last arguments to which kings resort. I ask gentlemen, sir, what means this martial array, if its purpose be not to force us to submission? Can gentlemen assign any other possible motives for it? Has Great Britain any enemy, in this quarter of the world, to call for all this accumulation of navies and armies? No, sir, she has none. They are meant for us; they can be meant for no other. They are sent over to bind and rivet upon us those chains which the British ministry have been so long forging. And what have we to oppose to them? Shall we try argument? Sir, we have been trying that for the last ten years. Have we anything new to offer on the subject? Nothing. We have held the subject up in every light of which it is capable; but it has been all in vain. Shall we resort to entreaty and humble supplication? What terms shall we find which have not been already exhausted? Let us not, I beseech you, sir, deceive ourselves longer. Sir, we have done everything that could be done to avert the storm which is now coming on. We have petitioned; we have demonstrated; we have supplicated; we have prostrated ourselves before the tyrannical hands of the ministry and parliament. Our petitions have been slighted; our remonstrances have produced additional violence and insult; our supplications have been disregarded and we have been spurned, with contempt, from the foot of the throne. In vain, after these things, may we indulge the fond hope of peace and reconciliation. There is no longer any room for hope. If we wish to be free— if we mean to preserve inviolate those inestimable privileges for which we have been so long contending—if we mean not basely to abandon the noble struggle in which we have been so long engaged, and which we have pledged ourselves never to abandon until the glorious object of our contest shall be obtained, we must fight! I repeat it, sir, we must fight! An appeal to arms and to the God of Hosts is all that is left us!

They tell us, sir, that we are weak; unable to cope with so formidable an adversary. But when shall we be stronger? Will it be the next week, or the next year? Will it be when we are totally disarmed, and when a British guard shall be stationed in every house? Shall we gather strength by irresolution and inaction? Shall we acquire the means of effectual resistance by lying supinely on our backs, and hugging the delusive phantom of hope, until our enemies shall have bound us hand and foot? Sir, we are not weak, if we make a proper use of the means which the God of nature hath placed in our power. Three millions of people, armed in the holy cause of liberty, and in such a country as that which we possess, are invincible by any force which our enemy can send against us. Besides, sir, we shall not fight our battles alone. There is a just God who presides over the destinies of nations; and who will raise friends to fight our battles for us. The battle, sir, is not to the strong alone; it is to the vigilant, the active, the brave. Besides, sir, we have no election. If we were base enough to desire it, it is now too late to retire from the contest. There is no retreat but in submission and slavery! Our chains are forged! Their clanking may be heard on the plains of Boston! The war is inevitable—and let it come! I repeat it, sir, let it come.

It is vain, sir, to extenuate the matter. Gentlemen may cry peace, peace—but there is no peace. The war is actually begun! The next gale that sweeps from the North will bring to our ears the clash of resounding arms! Our brethren are already in the field! Why stand we here idle? What is it that gentlemen wish? What would they have? Is life so dear, or peace so sweet, as to be purchased at the price of chains and slavery? Forbid it, Almighty God! I know not what course others may take; but as for me, give me liberty, or give me death!

SPEECH TO THE ANTISLAVERY SOCIETY

Angelina Grimke
Pennsylvania Hall, Philadelphia,
May 16, 1838

Men, brethren and fathers—mothers, daughters and sisters, what came ye out for to see? A reed shaken with the wind? Is it curiosity merely, or a deep sympathy with the perishing slave, that has brought this large audience together? [A yell from the mob without the building.] Those voices without ought to awaken and call out our warmest sympathies. Deluded beings! "They know not what they do." They know not that they are undermining their own rights and their own happiness, temporal and eternal. Do you ask, "what has the North to do with slavery?" hear it—hear it. Those voices without tell us that the spirit of slavery is here, and has been roused to wrath by our abolition speeches and conventions: for surely liberty would not foam and tear herself with rage, because her friends are multiplied daily, and meetings are held in quick succession to set forth her virtues and extend her peaceful kingdom. This opposition shows that slavery has done its deadliest work in the hearts of our citizens. Do you ask, then, "what has the North to do?" I answer, cast out first the spirit of slavery from your own hearts, and then lend your aid to convert the South. Each one present has a work to do, be his or her situation what it may, however limited their means, or insignificant their supposed influence. The great men of this country will not do this work; the church will never do it. A desire to please the world, to keep the favor of all parties and of all conditions, makes them dumb on this and every other unpopular subject. They have become worldly-wise, and therefore God, in his wisdom, employees them not to carry on his plans of reformation and salvation. He hath chosen the foolish things of the world to confound the wise, and the weak to overcome the might.

As a Southerner I feel that it is my duty to stand up here tonight and bear testimony against slavery. I have seen it—I have seen it. I know it has horrors that can never be described. I was brought up under its wing: I witnessed for many years its demoralizing influences, and its destructiveness to human happiness. It is admitted by some that the slave is not happy under the worst forms of slavery. But I have never seen a happy slave. I have seen him dance in his chains, it is true; but he is not happy. There is a wide difference between happiness and mirth. Man cannot enjoy the former while his manhood is destroyed, and that part of the being which is necessary to the making, and to the enjoyment of happiness, is completely blotted out. The slaves, however, may be, and sometimes are, mirthful. When hope is extinguished, they say, "let us eat and drink, for tomorrow we die." [Just then stones were thrown at the windows,—a great noise without, and commotion within] What is a mob? What would the breaking of every window be? What would the leveling of this Hall be? Any evidence that we are wrong, or that slavery is a good and wholesome institution? What if the mob should now burst in upon us, break up our meeting and commit violence upon our persons—would this be anything compared with what the slaves endure? No, no: and we do not remember them "as bound with them," if we shrink in the time of peril, or feel unwilling to sacrifice ourselves, if need be, for their sake. [Great Noise.] I thank the Lord that there is yet left life enough to feel the truth, even though it rages at it—that conscience is not so completely seared as to be unmoved by the truth of the living God.

Many persons go to the South for a season, and are hospitably entertained in the parlor and at the table of the slaveholder. They never enter the huts of the slaves; they know nothing of the dark side of the picture, and they return home with praises on their lips of the generous character of those with whom they had tarried. Or if they have witnessed the cruelties of slavery, by remaining silent spectators they have naturally become callous—an insensibility has ensued which prepares them to apologize even for barbarity. Nothing but the corrupting influence of slavery on the hearts of the Northern people can induce them to apologize for it; and much will have been done for the destruction of Southern slavery when we have so reformed the North that no one here will be willing to risk his reputation by advocating or even excusing the holding of men as property. The South know it, and acknowledge that as fast as our principles prevail, the hold of the master must be relaxed. [Another outbreak of mobocratic spirit, and some confusion in the house.]

How wonderfully constituted is the human mind! How it resists, as long as it can, all efforts made to reclaim from error! I feel that all this disturbance is but an evidence that our efforts are the best that could have been adopted, or else the friends of slavery, would not care for what we say and do. The South know what we do. I am thankful that they are reached by our efforts. Many times have I wept in the land of my birth over the system of slavery. I knew of none who sympathized in my feelings—I was unaware that any efforts were made to deliver the oppressed—no voice in the wilderness was heard calling on the people to repent and do works meet for repentance—and my heart sickened within me. Oh, how should I have rejoiced to know that such efforts as these were being made. I only wonder that I had such feelings. I wonder when I reflect under what influence I was brought up, that my heart is not harder than the nether millstone. But in the midst of temptation I was preserved, and my sympathy grew warmer, and my hatred of slavery more inveterate, until at last I have exiled myself from my native land because I could no longer endure to hear the wailing of the slave. I fled to the land of Penn; from her, thought I, sympathy for the slave will surely be found. But I found it not. The people were kind and hospitable, but the slave had no place in their thoughts. Whenever questions were put to me as to his condition, I felt that they were dictated by an idle curiosity, rather than by that deep feeling which would lead to effort for his rescue. I therefore shut up my grief in my own heart. I remembered that I was a Carolinian, from a state which framed this iniquity by law. I knew that throughout her territory was continued suffering, on the one part, and continual brutality and sin on the other. Every Southern breeze wafted to me the discordant tones of weeping and wailing, shrieks and groans, mingled with prayers and blasphemous curses. I thought there was no hope; that the wicked would go on in his wickedness, until he had destroyed both himself and his country. My heart sunk within me at the abominations in the midst of which I had been born and educated. What will it avail, cried I in bitterness of spirit, to expose to the gaze of strangers the horrors and pollutions of slavery, when there is no ear to hear nor heart to feel and pray for the slave. The language of my soul was, "Oh tell it not in Gath, publish it not in the streets of Askelon." But how different do I feel now! Animated with hope, nay, with an assurance of the triumph of liberty and good will to man, I will lift up my voice like a trumpet, and show this people their transgression, their sins of omission towards the slave, and what they can do towards affecting Southern mind, and overthrowing Southern oppression.

We may talk of occupying neutral ground, but on this subject, in its present attitude, there is no such thing as neutral ground. He that is not for us is against us, and he that gathereth not with us, scattereth abroad. If you are on what you suppose to be neutral ground, the South look upon you as on the side of the oppressor. And is there one who loves his country willing to give his influence, even indirectly, in favor of slavery—that curse of nations? God swept Egypt with the besom of destruction, and punished Judea also with a sore punishment, because of slavery. And have we any reason to believe that he is less just now?—or that he will be more favorable to us than to his own "peculiar people?" [Shoutings, stones thrown against the windows, etc.]

There is nothing to be feared from those who would stop our mouths, but they themselves should fear and tremble. The current is even now setting fast against them. If the arm of the North had not caused the Bastille of slavery to totter to its foundation, you would not hear those cries. A few years ago, the South felt secure, and with a contemptuous sneer asked, "Who are the abolitionists? The abolitionists are nothing?"—Ay, in one sense they were nothing, and they are nothing still. But in this we rejoice, that "God has chosen things that are not to bring to nought things that are." [Mob again disturbed the meeting.]

We often hear the question asked, "What shall we do?" Here is an opportunity for doing something now. Every man and every woman present may do something by showing that we fear not a job, and, in the midst of threatenings and revilings, by opening our mouths for the dumb and pleading the cause of those who are ready to perish.

To work as we should in this cause, we must know what Slavery is. Let me urge you then to buy the books which have been written on this subject and read them, and then lend them to your neighbors. Give your money no longer for things which pander to pride and lust, but aid in scattering "the living coals of truth" upon the naked heart of this nation—in circulating appeals to the sympathies of Christians in behalf of the outraged and suffering slave. But, it is said by some, our "books and papers do not speak the truth." Why, then, do they not contradict what we say? They cannot. Moreover the South has entreated, nay commanded us to be silent; and what greater evidence of the truth of our publications could be desired?

Women of Philadelphia! allow me as a Southern woman, with much attachment to the land of my birth, to entreat you to come up to this work. Especially let me urge you to petition. Men may settle this and other questions at the ballot-box, but you have no such right; it is only through petitions that you can reach the Legislature. It is therefore peculiarly your duty to petition. Do you say, "It does no good?" Then South already turns pale at the number sent. They have read the reports of the proceedings of Congress, and there have seen that among other petitions were very many from the women of the North on the subject of slavery. This fact has called the attention of the South to the subject. How could we expect to have done more as yet? Men who hold the rod over slaves, rule in the councils of the nation: and they deny our right to petition and to remonstrate against abuses of our sex and of our kind. We have these rights, however, from our God. Only let us exercise them: and though often turned away unanswered, let us remember the influence of importunity upon the unjust judge, and act accordingly. The fact that the South look with jealousy upon our measures shows that they are effectual. There is, therefore, no cause for doubting or despair, but rather for rejoicing.

It was remarked in England that women did much to abolish Slavery in her colonies. Nor are they now idle. Numerous petitions from them have recently been presented to the Queen, to abolish the apprenticeship with its cruelties nearly equal to those of the system whose place it supplies. One petition two miles and a quarter long has been presented.

And do you think these labors will be in vain? Let the history of the past answer. When the women of these States send up to Congress such a petition, our legislators will arise as did those of England, and say, "When all the maids and matrons of the land are knocking at our doors we must legislate." Let the zeal and love, faith and works of our English sisters quicken ours—that while the slaves continue to suffer, and when they shout deliverance, we may feel the satisfaction of having done what we could.

THE GETTYSBURG ADDRESS

Abraham Lincoln
Delivered at the dedication of the cemetary at
Gettysburg, Pennsylvania,
November 19, 1863

Four score and seven years ago our fathers brought forth on this continent, a new nation, conceived in Liberty, and dedicated to the proposition that all men are created equal.

Now we are engaged in a great civil war, testing whether that nation or any nation so conceived and so dedicated, can long endure. We are met on a great battle-field of that war. We have come to dedicate a portion of that field, as a final resting place for those who here gave their lives that that nation might live. It is altogether fitting and proper that we should do this.

But, in a larger sense, we can not dedicate—we can not consecrate—we can not hallow—this ground. The brave men, living and dead, who struggled here, have consecrated it, far above our poor power to add or detract. The world will little note, nor long remember what we say here, but it can never forget what they did here. It is for us the living, rather, to be dedicated to the great task remaining before us—that from these honored dead we take increased devotion to that cause for which we gave the last full measure of devotion— that were here highly resolve that these dead shall not have died in vain—that this nation, under God, shall have a new birth of freedom and that government of the people, by the people, and for the people, shall not perish from the earth.

FIRST INAUGURAL ADDRESS

Franklin Delano Roosevelt
Washington, D.C.,
March 4, 1933

President Hoover, Mr. Chief Justice, My Friends: This is a day of national consecration, and I am certain that my fellow-Americans expect that on my induction into the Presidency I will address them with a candor and a decision which the present situation of our nation impels.

This is pre-eminently the time to speak the truth, the whole truth, frankly and boldly. Nor need we shrink from honestly facing conditions in our country today. This great nation will endure as it has endured, will revive and will prosper.

So first of all let me assert my firm belief that the only thing we have to fear is fear itself—nameless, unreasoning, unjustified terror which paralyzes needed efforts to convert retreat into advance.

In every dark hour of our national life a leadership of frankness and vigor has met with that understanding and support of the people themselves which is essential to victory. I am convinced that you will again give that support to leadership in these critical days.

In such a spirit on my part and on yours we face our common difficulties. They concern, thank God, only material things. Values have shrunken to fantastic levels; taxes have risen; our ability to pay has fallen; government of all kinds is faced by serious curtailment of income; the means of exchange are frozen in the currents of trade; the withered leaves of industrial enterprise lie on every side; farmers find no markets for their produce; the savings of many years in thousands of families are gone.

More important, a host of unemployed citizens face the grim problem of existence, and an equally great number toil with little return. Only a foolish optimist can deny the dark realities of the moment.

Yet our distress comes from no failure of substance. We are stricken by no plague of locusts. Compared with the perils which our forefathers conquered because they believed and were not afraid, we have still much to be thankful for. Nature still offers her bounty and human efforts have multiplied it. Plenty is at our doorstep, but a generous use of it languishes in the very sight of the supply.

Primarily, this is because the rulers of the exchange of mankind's goods have failed through their own stubbornness and their own incompetence, have admitted their failure and abdicated. Practices of the unscrupulous money changers stand indicted in the court of public opinion, rejected by the hearts and minds of men.

True, they have tried, but their efforts have been cast in the pattern of an outworn tradition. Faced by failure of credit, they have proposed only the lending of more money.

Stripped of the lure of profit by which to induce our people to follow their false leadership, they have resorted to exhortations, pleading tearfully for restored confidence. They know only the rules of a generation of self-seekers.

They have no vision, and when there is no vision the people perish.

The money changers have fled from their high seats in the temple of our civilization. We may now restore that temple to the ancient truths.

The measure of the restoration lies in the extent to which we apply social values more noble than mere monetary profit.

Happiness lies not in the mere possession of money; it lies in the joy of achievement, in the thrill of creative effort.

The joy and moral stimulation of work no longer must be forgotten in the mad chase of evanescent profits. These dark days will be worth all they cost us if they teach us that our true destiny is not to be ministered unto but to minister to ourselves and to our fellow-men.

Recognition of the falsity of material wealth as the standard of success goes hand in hand with the abandonment of the false belief that public office and high political position are to be valued only by the standards of pride of place and personal profit; and there must be an end to a conduct in banking and in business which too often has given to a sacred trust the likeness of callous and selfish wrongdoing.

Small wonder that confidence languishes, for it thrives only on honesty, on honor, on the sacredness of obligations, on faithful protection, on unselfish performance. Without them it cannot live.

Restoration calls, however, not for changes in ethics alone. This nation asks for action, and action now.

Our greatest primary task is to put people to work. This is no unsolvable problem if we face it wisely and courageously.

It can be accomplished in part by direct recruiting by the government itself, treating the task as we would treat the emergency of a war, but at the same time, through this employment, accomplishing greatly needed projects to stimulate and reorganize the use of our natural resources.

Hand in hand with this, we must frankly recognize the over-balance of population in our industrial centers and, by engaging on a national scale in a redistribution, endeavor to provide a better use of the land for those best fitted for the land.

The task can be helped by definite efforts to raise the values of agricultural products and with this the power to purchase the output of our cities.

It can be helped by insistence that the Federal, State and local governments act forthwith on the demand that their cost be drastically reduced.

It can be helped by the unifying of relief activities which today are often scattered, uneconomical and unequal. It can be helped by national planning for supervision of all forms of transportation and of communications and other utilities which have a definite public character.

There are many ways in which it can be helped, but it can never be helped merely by talking about it. We must act, and act quickly.

Finally, in our progress toward a resumption of work we require two safeguards against a return of the evils of the old order; there must be a strict supervision of all banking and credits and investments; there must be an end to speculation with other people's money, and there must be provision for an adequate but sound currency.

There are the lines of attack. I shall presently urge upon a new Congress in special session detailed measures for their fulfillment, and I shall seek the immediate assistance of the several States.

Through this program of action we address ourselves to putting our own national house in order and making income balance outgo.

Our international trade relations, though vastly important, are, in point of time and necessity, secondary to the establishment of a sound national economy.

I favor as a practical policy the putting of first things first. I shall spare no effort to restore world trade by international economic readjustment, but the emergency at home cannot wait on that accomplishment.

The basic thought that guides these specific means of national recovery is not narrowly nationalistic.

It is the insistence, as a first consideration, upon the interdependence of the various elements in, and parts of, the United States—a recognition of the old and permanently important manifestation of the American spirit of the pioneer.

It is the recovery. It is the immediate way. It is the strongest assurance that the recovery will endure.

In the field of world policy I would dedicate this nation to the policy of the good neighbor—the neighbor who resolutely respects himself and, because he does so, respects the rights of others—the neighbor who respects his obligations and respects the sanctity of his agreements in and with a world of neighbors.

If I read the temper of our people correctly, we now realize as we have never before, our interdependence on each other; that we cannot merely take, but we must give as well; that if we are to go forward we must move as a trained and loyal army willing to sacrifice for the good of a common discipline, because, without such discipline, no progress is made, no leadership becomes effective.

We are, I know, ready and willing to submit our lives and property to such discipline because it makes possible a leadership which aims at a larger good.

This I propose to offer, pledging that the larger purposes will bind upon us all as a sacred obligation with a unity of duty hitherto evoked only in time of armed strife.

With this pledge taken, I assume unhesitatingly the leadership of this great army of our people, dedicated to a disciplined attack upon our common problems.

Action in this image and to this end is feasible under the form of government which we have inherited from our ancestors.

Our Constitution is so simple and practical that it is possible always to meet extraordinary needs by changes in emphasis and arrangement without loss of essential form.

That is why our constitutional system has proved itself the most superbly enduring political mechanism the modern world has produced. It has met every stress of vast expansion of territory, of foreign wars, of bitter internal strife, of world relations.

It is to be hoped that the normal balance of executive and legislative authority may be wholly adequate to meet the unprecedented task before us. But it may be that an unprecedented demand and need for undelayed action may call for temporary departure from that normal balance of public procedure.

I am prepared under my constitutional duty to recommend the measures that a stricken nation in the midst of a stricken world may require.

These measures, or such other measures as the Congress may build out of its experience and wisdom, I shall seek, within my constitutional authority, to bring to speedy adoption.

But in the event that the Congress shall fail to take one of these two courses, and in the event that the national emergency is still critical, I shall not evade the clear course of duty that will then confront me.

I shall ask the Congress for the one remaining instrument to meet the crisis—broad executive power to wage a war against the emergency as great as the power that would be given me if we were in fact invaded by a foreign foe.

For the trust reposed in me I will return the courage and the devotion that befit the time. I can do no less.

We face the arduous days that lie before us in the warm courage of national unity; with the clear consciousness of seeking old and precious moral values; with the clean satisfaction that comes from the stern performance of duty by old and young alike.

We aim at the assurance of a rounded and permanent national life.

We do not distrust the future of essential democracy. The people of the United States have not failed. In their need they have registered a mandate that they want direct, vigorous action.

They have asked for discipline and direction under leadership. They have made me the present instrument of their wishes. In the spirit of the gift I take it.

In this dedication of a nation we humbly ask the blessing of God. May He protect each and every one of us! May He guide me in the days to come!

INAUGURAL ADDRESS

John F. Kennedy
Washington, D.C.,
January 20, 1961

Mr. Chief Justice, President Eisenhower, Vice President Nixon, President Truman, reverend clergy, fellow citizens, we observe today not a victory of party, but a celebration of freedom—symbolizing an end, as well as a beginning—signifying renewal, as well as change. For I have sworn before you and Almighty God the same solemn oath our forebears prescribed nearly a century and three-quarters ago.

The world is very different now. For man holds in his mortal hands the power to abolish all forms of human poverty and all forms of human life. And yet the same revolutionary beliefs for which our forebears fought are still at issue around the globe—the belief that the rights of man come not from the generosity of the state, but from the hand of God.

We dare not forget today that we are the heirs of that first revolution. Let the word go forth from this time and place, to friend and foe alike, that the torch has been passed to a new generation of Americans—born in this century, tempered by war, disciplined by a hard and bitter peace, proud of our ancient heritage—and unwilling to witness or permit the slow undoing of those human rights to which this nation has always been committed, and to which we are committed today at home and around the world.

Let every nation know, whether it wishes us well or ill, that we shall pay any price, bear any burden, meet any hardship, support any friend, oppose any foe, in order to assure the survival and the success of liberty.

This much we pledge—and more.

To those old allies whose cultural and spiritual origins we share, we pledge the loyalty of faithful friends. United, there is little we cannot do in a host of cooperative ventures. Divided, there is little we can do—for we dare not meet a powerful challenge at odds and split asunder.

To those new states whom we welcome to the ranks of the free, we pledge our words that one form of colonial control shall not have passed away merely to be replaced by a far greater iron tyranny. We shall not always expect to find them supporting our view. But we shall always hope to find them strongly supporting their own freedom—and to remember that, in the past, those who foolishly sought power by riding the back of the tiger ended up inside.

To those peoples in the huts and villages across the globe struggling to break the bonds of mass misery, we pledge our best efforts to help them help themselves, for whatever period is required—not because the Communists may be doing it, not because we seek their votes, but because it is right. If a free society cannot help the many who are poor, it cannot save the few who are rich.

To our sister republics south of our border, we offer a special pledge—to convert our good words into good deeds, in a new alliance for progress, to assist free men and free governments in casting off the chains of poverty. But this peaceful revolution of hope cannot become the prey of hostile powers. Let all our neighbors know that we shall join with them to oppose aggression or subversion anywhere in the Americas. And let every other power know that this hemisphere intends to remain the master of its own house.

To that world assembly of sovereign states, the United Nations, our last best hope in an age where the instruments of war have far outpaced the instruments of peace, we renew our pledge of support—to prevent it from becoming merely a forum for invective—to strengthen its shield of the new and the weak—and to enlarge the area in which its writ may run.

Finally, to those nations who would make themselves our adversary, we offer not a pledge but a request: that both sides begin anew the quest for peace, before the dark powers of destruction unleashed by science engulf all humanity in planned or accidental self destruction.

We dare not tempt them with weakness. For only when our arms are sufficient beyond doubt can we be certain beyond doubt that they will never be employed.

But neither can two great and powerful groups of nations take comfort from our present course—both sides overburdened by the cost of modern weapons, both rightly alarmed by the steady spread of the deadly atom, yet both racing to alter that uncertain balance of terror that stays the hand of mankind's final war.

So let us begin anew—remembering on both sides that civility is not a sign of weakness, and sincerity is always subject to proof. Let us never negotiate out of fear. But let us never fear to negotiate.

Let both sides explore what problems unite us instead of laboring those problems which divide us.

Let both sides, for the first time, formulate serious and precise proposals for the inspection and control of arms—and bring the absolute power to destroy other nations under the absolute control of all nations.

Let both sides seek to invoke the wonders of science instead of its terrors. Together let us explore the star, conquer the deserts, eradicate disease, tap the ocean depths, and encourage the arts and commerce.

Let both sides unite to heed in all corners of the earth the command of Isaiah —to "undo the heavy burdens and to let the oppressed go free."

And if a beachhead of cooperation may push back the jungle of suspicion, let both sides join in creating a new endeavor, not a new balance of power, but a new world of law, where the strong are just and the weak secure and the peace preserved.

All this will not be finished in the first hundred days. Nor will it be finished in the first thousand days, nor in the life of this administration, nor even perhaps in our lifetime on this planet. But let us begin.

In your hands, my fellow citizens, more than in mine, will rest the final success or failure of our course. Since this country was founded, each generation of Americans has been summoned to give testimony to its national loyalty. The graves of young Americans who answered the call to service are found around the globe.

Now the trumpet summons us again—not as a call to bear arms, though arms we need; not as a call to battle, thought embattled we are; but a call to bear the burden of a long twilight struggle, year in, and year out, "rejoicing in hope, patient in tribulation"—a struggle against the common enemies of man: tyranny, poverty, disease, and war itself.

Can we forge against these enemies a grand and global alliance, north and south, east and west, that can assure a more fruitful life for all mankind? Will you join in that historic effort?

In the long history of the world, only a few generations have been granted the role of defending freedom in its hour of maximum danger. I do not shrink from this responsibility—I welcome it. I do not believe that any of us would exchange places with any other people or any other generation. The energy, the faith, the devotion which we bring to this endeavor will light our country and all who serve it—and the glow from that fire can truly light the world.

And so, my fellow Americans, ask not what your country can do for you: Ask what you can do for your country.

My fellow citizens of the world: Ask not what America will do for you, but what together we can do for the freedom of man.

Finally, whether you are citizens of America or citizens of the world, ask of us the same high standards of strength and sacrifice which we ask of you. With a good conscience our only sure reward, with history the final judge of our deeds, let us go forth to lead the land we love, asking His blessing and His help, but knowing that here on earth God's work must truly be our own.

SUGGESTED READINGS

Following are sources that will give you more information on the speakers and the settings for the speeches included in this section on historical speeches.

PATRICK HENRY

Richard Beeman, *Patrick Henry*. New York: 1974.

Thomas J. Wertenbaker, Give Me Liberty: *The Struggle for Self-Government in Virginia*. Philadelphia: 1958.

ANGELINA GRIMKE

Richard Curry, *The Abolitionists*. New York: 1965.

Gerda Lerner, *The Gremke Sisters from South Carolina: Rebels Against Slavery*. Boston: 1967.

Lillian O'Connor, *Pioneer Women Orators*. New York: 1954

ABRAHAM LINCOLN

Carl Sandberg, *Abraham Lincoln: The Prairie Years*, 2 vols. New York: 1926.

_____, *Abraham Lincoln: The War Years*, 4 vols. New York: 1931.

Benjamin P. Thomas, *Abraham Lincoln*. New York: 1952.

FRANKLIN DELANO ROOSEVELT

Denis W. Brogan, *The Era of Franklin D. Roosevelt: A Chronicle of the New Deal and Global War*. New Haven: 1950.

James MacGregor Burns, *Roosevelt: The Lion and the Fox*. New York: 1956.

Arthur M. Schlesinger, *The Age of Roosevelt*, 3 vols. Boston: 1957,1959,1960.

JOHN F. KENNEDY

James MacGregor Burns, *John Kennedy: A Political Profile*. New York: 1961.

High Sidey, *John F. Kennedy: President*. New York: 1963.

Theodore C. Sorenson, *Kennedy*. New York: 1965.

INDEX

Argument, defined, 140
    determining quality of, 133
    structure of, 136
    See also Reasoning
Arrangement, *See* Organization
Attention and interest, 157–159
Audience, 13–15; 19–20; 46–63
    adaptation to, 63–68
    analysis of, 46–63
    common ground, 159–161
    situational influence on, 68–72
    values and beliefs of, 149–152
    See also Listeners
Communication, as process, 4–7
    effectiveness, 4–5
Conclusions, 164–166
Delivery, 21–22; 240–250
    basis of, 248–250
    extemporaneous, 243
    improvement of, 241–243
    manuscript speaking, 243–244
    preparation for, 241–243
    voice in, 244–248
Emotional proof, 19–20; 152–157
Entertaining speeches, 93–95
Ethical proof, *See* Ethos
Ethos, defined, 12
    and ethics, 35–37
    and situation, 38–39

creation of, 39–40
    influence of, 35–38
    listeners' assessment of, 35–36
Evidence, 116–126
    comparison, 125–126
    example, 116–120
    statistics, 120–122
    testimony, 122–125
Extemporaneous speaking, *See* Delivery
Image, 34–35; *See also* Ethos
Informative speaking, 84–86
Interviewing, 107–109
Introductions, 161–164
Language, and clarity, 229–232
    appropriate, 235–238
    interesting, 232–235
Listeners, attitudes and beliefs, 149–152
    and speakers as adversaries, 276–277
    characteristics of, 47–63
    feelings and emotions, 67; 144–146
    needs, 146–149
    qualities of effective, 254–255
    responses to organization, 189–190
    summary of responsibilities, 263–268

Listening, basic principles of, 23–24
   directions for, 23–24; 216-220
   qualities of, 255–259
Logical proof, *See* Argument; Reasoning
Manuscript speaking, 243–244
Motivation, *See* Attention and interest;
   Audience; Emotional Proof
Organization, 20–21; 169–191
   conclusions, 164–166
   form and persuasiveness, 188–
      189
   introductions, 161–164
   listeners responses to, 189–190
   main ideas, 170–172
   patterns of, 179–187
   structure and clarity, 173–175
   testing ideas, 172–179
Persuasive Speaking, 86–93
Public Speaking, as communication,
   7–10
   basic principles of, 11–22
Purpose, 16–17; 81–99
   entertaining, 93–95
   informative, 84–86
   in listening, 254–255
   listeners' and speakers' com-
      pared, 99–100
   persuasive, 86–93
   realistic, 97–99

relationship to ideas, 170–172
   testing of, 97–99
Rationalizing, 135–140
Reasoning, 133–140; S *ee also* Argument
Repetition and restatement, 127
Research, 17–18; 103–113
Rhetorical situation, *See* Situation
Setting, 68–72; *See also* situation
Situation, 15–16; 68–72
   and ethos, 38–39
   and organization, 177–178
   and strategy, 77–80
   language appropriate to, 235–238
Source, 11–13; 29–40; *See also* Ethos;
   Image
Speaker, summary of responsibilities,
   269–266
Stage fright, 240–241; *See also* Delivery
Strategy, 75–82
Style, 21–22; 227–239
   and language, 227–239
   and listener response, 238–239
Summaries, internal, 187–188
Supporting material, 116–127; *See also*
   Evidence
Topic, selection, 30–34
Transitions, 187–188
Visual Aids, 128–132